RESPONSIBILITY, RIGHTS, AND WELFARE

RESPONSIBILITY, RIGHTS, AND WELFARE

The Theory of the Welfare State

EDITED BY

J. Donald Moon

Westview Press
BOULDER AND LONDON

Copyright © 1988 by Westview Press, Inc.

Published in 1988 in the United States of America by Westview Press, Inc.; Frederick A. Praeger, Publisher; 5500 Central Avenue, Boulder, Colorado 80301

Library of Congress Cataloging-in-Publication Data
Responsibility, rights, and welfare.
  Includes index.
  1. Social justice. 2. Human rights. 3. Welfare
state. 4. Liberalism. 5. Responsibility. I. Moon,
J. Donald.
JC578.R47 1988   320′.01′1   87-31587
ISBN 0-8133-0521-7
ISBN 0-8133-0522-5 (pbk)

Printed and bound in the United States of America

The paper used in this publication meets the requirements of the American National Standard for Permanence of Paper for Printed Library Materials Z39.48-1984.

10   9   8   7   6   5   4   3   2   1

CONTENTS

v

Part Three
The Welfare State:
Prospects and Problems

PREFACE

The chapters collected here were originally presented at a meeting of the Conference for the Study of Political Thought (CSPT) on "Poverty, Charity, and Welfare: The Theory and Practice of the Welfare State," which was held at Tulane University from February 14 to 16, 1986. This volume also represents something of a memorial tribute to Richard Krouse, who was involved in the conception and planning of the meeting. He brought to this project the keen intelligence and deep sensitivity that he brought to all of his work; tragically, he was killed in an automobile accident before this book could be published.

I am grateful to the Murphy Institute of Political Economy and Policy Analysis at Tulane for its generous funding of that conference, and to its director, Richard Teichgraeber III, who was cochairman of the meeting. Judith Schaefer did a superb job in making arrangements for the meeting. I would also like to acknowledge the assistance of Melvin Richter of the CSPT, without whom the meeting would not have taken place, and Spencer Carr of Westview, whose consistent interest in and attention to this project was vital to its success. Brian Fay read and offered valuable comments on an earlier version of the Introduction. My wife, Amy Bloom, gave me invaluable advice and support at every stage of this project.

J. Donald Moon

1

INTRODUCTION
Responsibility, Rights, and Welfare

The welfare state, once widely viewed as the crowning achievement of modern politics, has come to be seen as deeply problematic. Although reports of its crisis and imminent demise have been exaggerated, the hope it once offered of a just society, achieved without revolutionary violence, has not been realized. In the academy, its intellectual and moral underpinnings have come under increasing attack. In the polity, new movements have arisen that either reject important parts of the welfare state in the name of such traditional values as individual initiative and responsibility, or proclaim a vision of political life and address a set of issues for which the welfare state appears to be at best an irrelevance. Few today see the welfare state as an answer to the most pressing problems of society, as the "middle way" between the extremes of laissez-faire and collectivism, a way that promises to defuse the intense, ideological conflict that threatened democratic societies before World War II.

Yet, in spite of these doubts and in the face of these attacks, the welfare state endures. Even though conservative regimes may have reduced the rate of growth of public expenditures, they have not significantly changed the welfare state's major institutions and programs. On the other hand, as the French Socialists bitterly discovered, efforts to go beyond the welfare state have, so far at least, been unsuccessful. The chapters in this book explore the social, historical, and philosophical bases of the welfare state and so help us to understand why it has been durable while, at the same time, engendering so much criticism. The contributors examine the ways in which the welfare state gives expression to the deepest impulses and values of our way of life as it deals with the issues of poverty and social dislocation. Their discussions enable us to see the welfare state as an effort to resolve some of the deep tensions and conflicts among the most fundamental aims and conceptions that constitute our moral and political culture, and thereby

1

to understand why its success can never be or appear complete, why its very achievements call it into question, and yet why it is so enduring.

Michael Walzer has pointed out that "every political community is in principle a 'welfare state,'" for all "provide, or try to provide, or claim to provide, for the needs of its members as its members understood those needs" (1983, 68). But this very general definition does not adequately capture the moral or social reality of contemporary, liberal-democratic welfare states. These political communities try to satisfy only a certain range of the acknowledged needs of their members, relying upon other institutions and practices to meet the bulk of these needs. The most prominent of these institutions (apart from the family) is the "market." As Robert E. Goodin argues in his chapter, the welfare state is "a limited adjunct to the market economy." Paraphrasing his account, we can characterize it, first, as systematic intervention in a market economy to meet certain basic needs in a relatively "direct" way and, second, as "a system of compulsory, collective and largely non-discretionary welfare provision."

As Goodin points out, the welfare state is not intended to equalize the conditions of different classes or groups within the polity, nor to organize and direct economic activity as a whole, but to provide specific goods and services to individuals and families that meet certain criteria of need or entitlement. Moreover, the mechanisms through which it meets these needs are distinct. Paradigmatic welfare state programs, such as education, old-age pensions, medical care, disability, and family or child allowances, are universal in their scope of provision and are frequently organized in accordance with the "principle of social insurance." According to this principle, people are entitled to benefits as a result of having contributed to the scheme that provides them. Although poverty is a major concern of the welfare state, and although the alleviation of poverty was an important impetus to its development both in theory and in practice, what is characteristic of the welfare state today is the range of social contingencies it addresses and the universality of its programs.

How can we make sense of this particular combination of elements— the commitment to a market economy for the organization of most of economic life, together with redistributive mechanisms designed to meet only certain contingencies? Why do we try to meet some needs and not others? Why do we organize so much of our collective provision through universal programs and social insurance schemes, when more selective programs, directed at the poorest segments of the society, might do more to alleviate poverty and distress at much less cost?

It would be a mistake to expect that these questions can be answered in a simple, unequivocal way. Existing welfare states have not been built according to a common plan but, rather, are the work of many hands. Conservatives, liberals, and socialists have, at various times and places, played important roles in initiating and expanding different social policies; parties, interest groups, government administrators, and outside specialists have made essential contributions; and the construction of the welfare state has been shaped in important ways by changing attitudes and expectations of citizens.[1] Thus, there are today a variety of different and even inconsistent visions and accounts of the welfare state, each with its own answers to the kinds of questions posed above.[2]

One of the most important theories of the welfare state—or perhaps it would be better to say "family of theories"—are those that might broadly be called "liberal." This may not be surprising, given that welfare states are liberal-democratic regimes with market, capitalist economies. Thus, many of the chapters in this book begin from liberal assumptions or seek to explicate the relationship between liberalism and the welfare state historically and conceptually.

In some ways, it would appear that liberalism is antithetical to the welfare state. One of the distinctive commitments of liberalism is that "the state should not be the architect of social order"; rather, "most social functions should be performed through collective undertakings emerging spontaneously within the political community." What this means is that the "organization of production, religion, science, learning and the arts, of family and community life, should arise autonomously within a broad regime of freedom of expression, association and contract" (Anderson, 1984, 15).[3] The welfare state, however, represents a significant extension of the political sphere, replacing many voluntary, contractual relations with compulsory, political ones. Thus, important liberal theorists, such as Robert Nozick, Friedrich Hayek, and Milton Friedman, have attacked the welfare state, and their criticisms have been echoed in the retrenchment and "privatization" programs of Ronald Reagan and Margaret Thatcher.

But liberalism also provides powerful justifications for the welfare state, as several of the chapters in this book demonstrate. Goodin offers a persuasive argument for the welfare state by showing that an extensive system of welfare provision is required by, or in a certain sense is implicit in, the central institutions and values defining a liberal society. Goodin begins by arguing that the "internal logic" of the market requires that certain needs be met either through some form of welfare state provision or by other means that are utterly incompatible with the moral values of democracy. Given this choice, it is easy to see why all of the industrialized democracies are also welfare states. Goodin places great stress upon the role of the welfare state in "safeguarding the preconditions for the market," particularly a system of rights and duties that are necessary for the existence of market relationships in the first place. Critical to these rights and duties, Goodin argues, are (1) the moral duty we have, both individually and collectively, "to protect those who are particularly vulnerable to [our] actions or choices" and (2) the right of persons to be independent agents and therefore capable of participating in market exchange.

The notion of persons as "independent agents" is crucial for liberal political theory, particularly for liberal accounts of human rights. For many liberal thinkers, it is our capacity for choice, for self-determination and decision, that is essential to our identity as persons and that constitutes the basis for some of the most important obligations we owe others and the rights we can claim for ourselves. To treat others as agents or persons and not as mere "things," in this view, is to respond to them in terms of their choices, their reasons for actions, and so to refrain from coercing or manipulating them. When I am coerced or manipulated, I am used by others for their ends, in disregard of my own. My actions under these circumstances are controlled not by myself but by others, and so my essential capacities as a person are disregarded: I am treated as a mere object of nature, having no essential purposes of my own—that is, as something on which others are free to impose their ends, in much the same way as we impose our purposes on inanimate objects in shaping them into tools or consuming them to satisfy our needs.[4]

The obligation to respect others as agents and the right not to be coerced or manipulated are central to classical liberal conceptions of human rights and negative liberty. But, as Raymond Plant argues in his chapter, human agency requires more than the traditional rights to life, liberty, and property in one's person. To be an agent requires both certain capacities or powers and the satisfaction of certain needs, some of which can be realized effectively only through social provision. Against the claims of critics of the welfare state, who accept the idea of "negative" rights but reject welfare or "positive" rights, Plant shows that many of the distinctions held to separate these two kinds of rights cannot withstand close analysis. If we have any rights at all, he concludes, we have welfare rights; hence, a legitimate polity must be a welfare state.

But, we might add, it should only be a welfare state—at least so long as we reason from conceptions of human rights based on the idea of moral agency. For if we see our distinctive powers to be those of choice and self-determination, we are led to demand for ourselves, and to recognize in others, what have been called "option rights"—that is, "spheres of individual sovereignty . . . in which the individual is morally free to act on the basis of his own choices" (Golding, 1984, 122–123).

Even though agency also requires "welfare rights" (entitlements to certain goods or services necessary to exercise capacities for choice and self-determination), the scope of these entitlements is limited. In the first place, it is limited by the requirements of agency itself. It is true that certain needs must be met if one is to be able to exercise one's capacities as an agent: One must have a minimal level of income and economic security, one must have access to healthcare, and one must have educational opportunities that equip one to play a socially valued role in one's society. Further, because we are social beings whose capacities and aspirations are formed and exercised while living with others, the extent and forms of these welfare rights will vary with the circumstances of different societies. Inequalities must be limited, so that none is excluded from full membership in society; but the concept of agency does not support entitlements beyond that. Exactly what level of provision is required in order to exercise or even to develop one's capacities for agency is a matter of judgment, but it is surely fairly minimal.

In the second place, welfare rights are limited by the institutions required to realize our option rights. For if we are to have significant spheres in which we are free to act on the basis of our own choices, then important areas of social life will have to be organized outside the framework of the state—through markets, voluntary associations, and the like. That is why, in liberal theory, the welfare state is a limited adjunct to the market, serving to correct the outcomes it generates but not seeking to displace it.

Third, and in some ways most important, welfare rights are also limited by the idea of responsibility inherent in the concept of moral agency. As individuals who are the creators of our actions, we can properly be held responsible for what we do and for the foreseeable outcomes that our actions cause. Indeed, not to be held responsible in this way is to be treated not as a person but, at best, as a child or dependent whose capacity for autonomy is impaired or undeveloped. As Immanuel Kant argued, if "no-one can compel me to be happy in accordance with his conception of the welfare of others," then a paternalistic government, one "established on the principle of benevolence towards the people," is the "greatest conceivable *despotism*" (Kant, 1970, 74). If we are not to be treated as children, then we must be presumed capable of distinguishing "what is truly useful or harmful" to ourselves (Kant, 1970, 74), and so we cannot be "protected" from all of the consequences of our actions.

This injunction against paternalism poses well-known difficulties for the liberal theory of the welfare state, because it limits the ways in which welfare provision can be made. The commitments to the equality of persons as moral agents, and to the principle of individual responsibility, imply that the relations of adult citizens will be based on a norm of reciprocity. At least in the public sphere, asymmetrical relationships of dependence, in which one person is beholden to others without their being in a similar manner beholden to the first, violate this notion of reciprocity. This means that adult citizens are expected to be independent[5] in the sense of being self-supporting: They should provide for their own needs by exchanging their labor or other assets for the goods they require from others, and they should contribute to the provision of goods that are publicly provided through the state. Independence demands that the collective provision of social services be organized in a way that does not threaten the norm of reciprocity by rendering individuals dependent on the state in ways that undermine their autonomy as moral agents.

Prior to the modern welfare state, relief of distress—to the extent that it was provided—was conducted in a manner that violated these principles. It was, in the first place, often conceived of as public charity, and it was provided under conditions that effectively denied recipients the status of full citizenship. To receive support under the poor law in England or in the United States, for example, involved restrictions on one's freedom of movement and often required confinement to the "poorhouse," where one effectively became a ward of the state.[6]

A one-sided focus on the idea of independence might lead to the conclusion that the state should not provide welfare benefits at all, thereby undercutting the argument for welfare rights itself. This, of course, is the position advocated by some contemporary libertarians.[7] But such an interpretation of the idea of independence is deeply mistaken, for our lives are causally intertwined in any number of ways, such that many of the contingencies of social life involve factors beyond an individual's control. To deny assistance to children, to elderly people, to those who suffer from illness or disability, or to unemployed workers and their families is callously to disregard the fact that the conditions they face are not of their own making. Our sense of ourselves as autonomous, independent agents is essential to our identities as persons, but we also recognize numerous ways in which our autonomy and independence are circumscribed. The institutions and practices of our public life, then, must do justice to both aspects of our experience.

It is thus evident that a certain tension exists at the heart of the liberal theory of the welfare state. On the one hand, liberals wish to limit the sphere of political authority, creating as much space as possible for individuals to organize their social lives through voluntary interaction and exchange. Welfare provision is suspect because its compulsory character limits the scope of individual liberty, and because it poses the danger of paternalism. At the same time, liberals are driven to expand the scope of social provision in order to secure the welfare rights required by their commitment to moral agency, and out of the recognition that many of the contingencies individuals face are beyond their control.

From this perspective, we can see the welfare state as an effort to balance the opposing demands of agency and causal interdependence. The welfare state is firmly based on a conception of human agency that finds a central place for the morally responsible self; it does not project a vision of community in which there would be a strong coincidence of individual destiny and communal norms, in the manner of some socialist ideals; nor is it committed to egalitarianism. Rather, it presupposes that markets and individualized claims on social production will play central roles in social life. But it differs from the minimal or laissez-faire state in its recognition that genuine agency requires a certain minimal level of income, healthcare, and education. When individuals suffer contingencies in which these goods are denied them, the liberal state is required to provide them. Thus, the programs of the welfare state are intended to secure individuals from certain adverse outcomes precisely in order to preserve a wide scope for individual choice and differences.

The liberal welfare state attempts to manage this complex task by organizing the delivery of social services in accordance with two principles: universal provision and social insurance. It is a distinctive characteristic of the modern welfare state, as opposed to earlier forms of welfare, that all or virtually all citizens are eligible for benefits under its programs. This is particularly true of education and, in most welfare states, of healthcare and family allowances. These services are provided to everyone and financed out of general tax revenues to which everyone contributes, and so one's independence or autonomy is not violated in receiving them. Similarly, old age, disability, and unemployment benefits are provided universally on the basis of social insurance contributions. Those who receive these benefits have, at least in theory, contributed the resources that make them possible and have thereby "earned" a right to them. Thus, the distinctive programs of the modern welfare state, programs that account for the vast bulk of social expenditures, are provided in a manner consistent with the norm of reciprocity. There is no stigma attached to receiving these benefits, and they are enjoyed by (and are popular with) the overwhelming majority of the citizenry.

The evolution of the welfare state has been critically influenced by the prevailing understanding of the economic processes of industrial society. As our understanding of the ways in which personal situations depend on large-scale social processes has changed, and as our knowledge of how we can intervene to affect these processes has changed, the issues that appear to be appropriate for collective action and the ways in which such action can be taken have also changed. For example, the system of unemployment insurance was developed early in this century, partly in response to the growing awareness of the cyclical nature of economic activity in capitalism. This awareness undermined the view that unemployment could be attributed to a lack of effort or willingness to work on the part of the unemployed. There was a direct connection between the developing understanding of unemployment and the recognition that the principle of insurance was applicable to it. Similarly, the development of Keynesianism both enabled (by providing the policy means) and required (by changing our understanding of the ways in which individuals could properly be held responsible) significant changes in the scope of government activity.[8]

Unfortunately, social insurance and universal provision are not adequate to solve the problem of ensuring the satisfaction of everyone's welfare rights—or, at least, no welfare state has expanded such programs to that extent. Benefits that are tied to a particular contributory scheme, for example, are not available to people who are in need before they have been able to make contributions. And universally provided benefits (such as family allowance) are never so generously funded as to provide adequate support in the absence of other resources. Thus, every welfare state has more or less significant pockets of need that must be met through means-tested programs directed to the "poor," and that raise the problems of paternalism and responsibility discussed above. These are, as Claus Offe points out in his chapter, the programs that tend to be among the least popular, and that have attracted the most discussion and concern in recent years. Their persistence explains the continuing struggle involved in balancing our conflicting experiences of autonomy and contingency.[9]

Whereas the chapters in Part One by Goodin and Plant provide justifications for a more or less extensive welfare state based on essentially liberal premises, those in Part Two trace the historical relationships between liberalism and the welfare state. The arguments of these chapters confirm the commitments of liberalism to the welfare state, but at the same time they bring out the tensions and ambivalences the liberal welfare state attempts to resolve or at least contain. By setting out the actual development of these ideas, these chapters not only enrich our understanding of the liberal theory of the welfare state but also suggest new dimensions of it.

Chapter 4, "Liberal Guilt" by Stephen Holmes, explicitly addresses the argument, briefly discussed above, that liberalism is incompatible with the state's important, redistributive role in the economy. By carefully examining the views of theorists who have long been associated with the liberal tradition, Holmes demolishes the arguments of neoconservative critics of the welfare state who see it as a violation of liberal precepts. In the course of this investigation, Holmes adds a distinctive perspective to the one emphasizing autonomy, which we have been examining. He argues that central to liberal theory is a concern with security. This concern has dictated different responses as the sources and forms of insecurity have changed over time. In the early modern period, it justified the consolidation and strengthening of the central state in order to control the power of the nobility. Later, when the newly enhanced power of the king became a serious threat, it justified constitutional safeguards on political authority. And in contemporary times, when the whole population faces the insecurities of industrial society, it has given rise to the provision of a more or less extensive set of social services. After examining a number of supposed distinctions between liberal values and welfare state objectives, Holmes concludes that "the fundamental continuity between liberal rights and welfare rights" is very strong.

In Chapter 5, Thomas Horne adds a historical perspective to the argument that people ought to be guaranteed certain welfare rights. Horne explores what might initially seem to be an unpromising terrain to discover such rights—seventeenth- and eighteenth-century natural law accounts of property rights. But his historical investigations are broadly supportive of Plant's arguments for a right to welfare, or at least subsistence, as he finds a rich tradition of theorizing in which welfare rights are justified in the same terms, and on the same bases, as other basic rights. What is central both to Plant's arguments and to the accounts examined by Horne is the internal relationship between welfare rights and other rights. But whereas Plant's argument rests on a conception of the person as a moral agent, Horne's study offers a justification of (albeit very limited) welfare rights as an aspect of the right to property itself. Thus, according to these natural law theories, the right to subsistence does not involve a separate, contradictory right that must be balanced against, or used to override, property rights, as many contemporary libertarians would have it. Although eighteenth-century rights to subsistence do not require the distinctive institutions of the modern welfare state, institutions that provide benefits to all citizens facing certain contingencies such as old age or illness regardless of whether their subsistence is threatened, they demonstrate the deep historical roots of the concern with welfare in the liberal tradition.

The last three chapters in the book articulate a perspective rather different from that of the earlier chapters. Each in its own way is critical of the liberal welfare state, and each suggests a different understanding—and a different ideal—for contemporary societies. In Chapter 6, "The Logic of Liberal Equality," Richard Krouse and Michael S. McPherson read a serious critique of the welfare state into Mill. For John Stuart

Mill, the welfare state is deeply problematic—both because it deprives some citizens of their justly acquired property in order to support others, and because it encourages dependency and undermines the qualities of character that Mill admired. Further, it rests upon capitalist laws of property, which create unjust—because undeserved—inequalities of wealth and income. According to Krouse and McPherson, only some form of market socialism or property-owning democracy would be compatible with Mill's basic principles of justice. Mill's critique of the welfare state, like the defenses we examined above, is broadly liberal, based on the values of moral agency and individual autonomy. But Mill's alternatives to the welfare state, by either collectivizing property in the means of production or distributing it more widely, go far beyond the limits of the contemporary welfare state.

Of course, both of Mill's preferred systems would have to retain some of the characteristic institutions of the welfare state, as not all of the contingencies of modern life can be met through a family's private resources, even if property ownership were less concentrated than it is now. This is particularly true of education, which is increasingly becoming the most important asset of individuals in modern society. Nonetheless, the alternative systems Mill advocates would significantly reduce the inequalities of property ownership and access to education and skills that occur in capitalist societies and that create so much of the social distress that the welfare state is intended to relieve.

Whereas Mill's critique of the welfare state is based on liberal principles, David Miller's account points beyond liberalism to a more collectivist, or what might be called a social democratic, image of society.[10] The point of Miller's chapter is not so much to provide a justification of the welfare state as to offer a partial explanation of it. Unlike those "realists" who would explain the rise and persistence of the welfare state as a result of the successful manipulations of a particular class—whether the rich, the poor, or the new class of administrators and professionals employed by the state—to advance its own interests, Miller argues that altruistic motivations could and probably do play a significant role. He offers a careful analysis of the nature of these motivations, showing why they would lead people to prefer state provision rather than private charity. This is a surprising result inasmuch as one might expect that voluntary organization would be sufficient if people had altruistic motivations. But Miller's analysis reveals the enormous complexity of these issues and shows why compulsory, collective provision of social services is required. In concluding his argument, he brings out some important implications for the conditions under which the sentiments supporting the welfare state may be undermined—an issue taken up by Offe in the last chapter in this book.

Miller also suggests an alternative basis for the welfare state from those considered so far, which he calls the "social justice view." According to this view, the point of the welfare state is not to secure for everyone the minimum standard of living compatible with membership in the society, but to achieve an "overall distribution of goods of certain kinds" according to "criteria of need." Thus, the social justice view "dispenses with the idea of a welfare floor and looks at a society's general distributive practices." Clearly, this ideal is one that would require a much more thorough displacement of the market than the limited interventions of the liberal welfare state.

In Chapter 8, Offe, like Miller, is concerned with the reasons why citizens support the welfare state and, more especially, why this support has eroded in recent years—even within those groups in society that have been among its principal beneficiaries. Contrary to many students of this subject, Offe finds that there are important areas of tension between political democracy and the welfare state, for he argues that citizens will not always find it in their interests to support welfare state programs. In Offe's account, the preconditions for the development of the welfare state include certain normative and cultural conditions, particularly a sense on the part of most citizens of a common identity and mutual obligations. This sense of "sameness," of common membership and ties, supports the interventionist and redistributive measures of the welfare state, as it leads citizens to identify themselves not in terms of their particularistic, narrowly individual interests, but as members of a collectivity facing shared problems and concerns. From this perspective, the welfare state is a means through which *we* can provide ourselves with collective goods in the form of programs that protect us against the widely shared risks "inherent in the dynamics of the capitalist mode of production." These sentiments, in turn, are intelligible in the context of a society in which large numbers of people share a common life situation and are not deeply divided by ethnic, religious, or other cleavages. Concretely, this was to a significant extent the situation of the "propertyless male wage laborers" who, organized into trade unions and supporting social democratic parties, were the key force behind the formation of the "labor-centered collectivist statism" of the welfare state.

In more recent years, Offe argues, a process of "destructuration" occurred, as these "self-conscious interest communities" have become fragmented because of increasing internal differentiation among workers, the growing number of white collar and middle-class groups, and so on. As a result, people are less likely to see themselves as the "same" as others, less likely to share a common identity and sentiments of solidarity. Their more individualistic, self-interested orientations lead them to see welfare state programs not in terms of a common interest, not as collective goods, but in terms of the costs and benefits to them individually. More people find it in their interests, as they have come to conceive of these interests, to opt out of collective arrangements and to oppose programs that they increasingly come to see as benefiting others—a "them" with whom they do not identify. These structural and accompanying attitudinal changes in contemporary societies mean that neoconservative arguments will find a ready audience *and* make the long-term future of the welfare state problematic.

Offe's account of the welfare state departs significantly from the liberal assumptions examined above. The vision of the welfare state implicit in his remarks owes much to the social democratic view that Miller also suggests. But whatever one's ideal of the welfare state, Offe's analysis challenges us to examine its social preconditions and, perhaps, to develop a new, alternative vision of a just society.

The critiques of the welfare state presented or suggested in the last three chapters brings us back to the questions posed at the beginning of this "Introduction." In what ways do the chapters in this collection help us to understand the moral and political basis of the welfare state, its durability in the face of challenge, and the reasons why it is the target of so much criticism?

One reason the welfare state appears to be so vulnerable to criticism is that it embraces a set of conceptions and principles any one of which, if articulated in an extreme or pure form, would contradict the others. The welfare state embraces the market but, at the same time, seeks to limit and control it; it incorporates ideas of rights, especially rights to property and to the fruits of one's labor, but asserts a right to welfare, a right to have one's basic needs met; it is based on a conception of the person as a responsible agent but recognizes as well that many of the conditions of one's life are due to circumstances beyond one's control; it is premised upon sentiments of sociability and common interest, but its very success may undermine those sentiments; it seeks to provide security but embraces as well a commitment to liberty. The chapters in this book articulate these tensions, while exploring the ways in which they arise and the limits to their resolution. Because the welfare state must seek a balance among a number of opposed conceptions and principles, any resolution is vulnerable to criticism from many sides, for any particular balance will necessarily sacrifice some aspect, or some degree, of one value in order to realize another objective. And because the sacrificed value is one that the welfare state itself embraces, the criticism will appear to be telling. It will point to a failure that must be acknowledged even in terms of the justifying theories underlying the welfare state itself.

At the same time that its tensions are the source of its vulnerability, they are the source of its strength—of its durability in the face of criticism. Even Offe's argument, which suggests subtle ways in which the welfare state may be unstable, implies not so much that the welfare state will be radically transformed as that the scope for expansion of its activities is limited: As it satisfies the interests that called it into existence, it reduces the commitment to going beyond it. Conservative critics, advocating an expansion of the scope of market activities and a corresponding reduction in the extent of government, find that their very advocacy of autonomy or efficiency or individual responsibility can be turned against them and used to justify some part of the welfare state's far-flung activities.

This does not mean that the welfare state should be thought of as a system in dynamic equilibrium, in which opposing forces adjust to each other in such a way as to maintain the system over time. There can be no such guarantee in social and political life. But it does mean that the theoretical enterprise of criticizing the welfare state faces serious obstacles. For the arguments presented in these chapters suggest that the welfare state expresses, and is necessary to, some of the very deepest values and conceptions underlying our way of life. At the most fundamental level, it gives political expression to our understanding of ourselves as agents who can direct and control our own actions but who are caught up in systems of interdependence so that we face contingencies, and who must endure outcomes that we cannot fully control. The traditional terms of debate regarding the socioeconomic organization of society, which have dominated much of political theorizing for the past 150 years, appear to revolve around these issues. The alternatives of a pure form of either collectivism or individualism appear inadequate compared to some version of the welfare state. For to go to either extreme is to deny some essential part of our self-understanding, of who we are as persons and as a people. This does not mean that the welfare state is safe at least in theory. But it does mean that attacking it successfully will require a radical change in the terms of this debate.

NOTES

1. For a valuable account of the development of the welfare state that documents the variety of actors and the importance of social learning, see Heclo (1974); see also the essays in Flora and Heidenheimer (1981).

2. The welfare state has been interpreted from a variety of different theoretical and ideological perspectives. For representative treatments, see Pinker (1979), George and Wilding (1976), Taylor-Gooby and Dale (1981), and Weale (1983).

Offe (1984), Castles (1978), and Przeworski (1985) are particularly useful accounts of the "social democratic" understanding of the welfare state.

3. See Gray (1986) and Moon (1986) for accounts of the central concepts and values of liberalism.

4. The account in the text of the concept of rights and agency is highly schematic. It should be noted that the concepts developed here are intended to apply only to our public and political lives, and do not exhaust the moral considerations that are relevant even in these contexts. See Morris (1976) for an excellent discussion of the liberal concept of the moral agency and its relationship to rights, particularly option rights. See also O'Neill (1985) for some difficulties in applying these concepts to social practices.

5. Kant, notoriously, saw "independence" as a fundamental human right constituting and limiting the political order. But he interpreted this concept of independence as requiring that the citizen possess sufficient property to meet his needs and those of his family, and he denied full citizenship to others— notably women, domestic servants, and laborers. A more consistent position might be to deny the legitimacy of a social order in which some people have so few options that they are dependent in ways that compromise their moral personalities. In any event, contemporary liberal understandings of independence are rather more inclusive than Kant's.

6. For England, in addition to the chapter by Horne, see Himmelfarb (1983); for the United States, see Katz (1986).

7. It is advocated most notoriously by Nozick (1974).

8. See Heclo (1974) for an excellent discussion of these examples.

9. See Moon (1987) for further discussion of these dilemmas of the liberal welfare state.

10. The liberal democratic conception of the welfare state is developed in Castles (1978). See also Przeworski (1985).

REFERENCES

Anderson, Charles (1984). "Political Philosophy, Practical Reason, and Policy Analysis." Paper presented to the American Political Science Association. Annual Meeting, Washington, D.C.

Castles, Francis (1978). The Social Democratic Image of Society. London: Routledge and Kegan Paul.

Flora, Peter, and A. Heidenheimer, eds. (1981). The Development of Welfare States in Europe and America. New Brunswick, N.J.: Transaction Books.

Friedman, Milton (1962). Capitalism and Freedom. Chicago: University of Chicago Press.

George, Vic, and Paul Wilding (1976). Ideology and Social Welfare. London: Routledge and Kegan Paul.

Golding, Martin P. (1984). "The Primacy of Welfare Rights." Social Philosophy and Policy, 1.

Gray, John (1986). Liberalism. Minneapolis: University of Minnesota Press.

Hayek, Friedrich (1960). *The Constitution of Liberty.* Chicago: University of Chicago Press.

Heclo, Hugh (1974). *Modern Social Politics in Britain and Sweden.* New Haven, Conn.: Yale University Press.

Himmelfarb, Gertrude (1983). *The Idea of Poverty.* New York: Basic Books.

Kant, Immanuel (1970). *Kant's Political Writings,* edited by Hans Reiss, translated by H. R. Nisbet. Cambridge: Cambridge University Press.

Katz, Michael (1986). *In the Shadow of the Poorhouse.* New York: Basic Books.

Moon, J. Donald (1986). "Thin Selves/Rich Lives." Paper presented to the Foundations of Political Theory Group, American Political Science Association, Washington, D.C.

Moon, J. Donald (1987). "The Moral Basis of the Democratic Welfare State." In Amy Guttman, ed., *Democracy and the Welfare State.* Princeton, N.J.: Princeton University Press.

Morris, Herbert (1976). "Persons and Punishment." In Morris, *On Guilt and Innocence.* Berkeley: University of California Press.

Nozick, Robert (1974). *Anarchy, State and Utopia.* New York: Basic Books.

Offe, Claus (1984). *Contradictions of the Welfare State.* Cambridge, Mass: MIT Press.

O'Neil, Onora (1985). "Between Consenting Adults." *Philosophy and Public Affairs,* 14.

Pinker, Robert (1979). *The Idea of Welfare.* London: Heinemann.

Przeworski, Adam (1985). *Capitalism and Social Democracy.* Cambridge: Cambridge University Press.

Taylor-Gooby, Peter and J. Dale (1981). *Social Theory and Social Welfare.* London: Edward Arnold.

Walzer, Michael (1983). *Spheres of Justice.* New York: Basic Books.

Weale, Albert (1983). *Political Theory and Social Policy.* London: Macmillan.

Part One

JUSTIFICATIONS FOR WELFARE

2

REASONS FOR WELFARE

Economic, Sociological, and Political—
but Ultimately Moral

The focus of this chapter is normative rather than empirical. In it, I shall be considering various arguments that can serve to justify programs of public provision for social welfare. Throughout, I shall be concerned exclusively with determining whether those arguments are satisfactory for that justificatory purpose. Whether or how such arguments, however good they might be, ever get a motivational grip on people is another, empirical question that is best left for other occasions.[1]

Hence, I shall here be examining reasons—and, furthermore, reasons of a moral kind—for the welfare state, rather than its causes. Of course, such reasons can also serve as causes, if the agents adopt those reasons as their own. If that never happened, there would be no practical point in doing moral philosophy. If it always happened, there would be no practical point in doing social science in any other way. I take it that neither proposition is universally true. Under certain circumstances, at least, moral appeals can move people to action; but they are not the only things capable of so moving people, and some things can happen without people being "moved" at all. Normative and empirical questions about the welfare state are thus at least sometimes separable. When they do diverge, I shall here be following the former path.

The central themes of this chapter are that there is a good moral justification for the welfare state and that it is, at least to some extent, an independent moral justification. By that I mean merely to say that the moral justification for the welfare state cannot be found wholly in the interstices of the moral justifications for the other economic, social, and political institutions characteristically present in the sort of market society within which the welfare state is set. Not all of the moral arguments needed to justify the welfare state can, as it were, be read directly or indirectly off those moral arguments needed to justify the other more central institutions of market societies.

19

Although not quite all of the needed arguments are to be found there, a great many of them are. The strategy of this chapter is to make as much use of this fact as possible, to fight free-market opponents of welfare states on their own ground insofar as that can be done. After all, "internal logic" arguments are enormously powerful so far as they go. And in this case, it turns out that they go a long way, indeed, toward narrowing, both practically and morally, the choices available to us in market societies.

In the end, however, the internal logic of other (economic, political, sociological, and ultimately moral) arguments that lay the justificatory foundations for the rest of market society take us only part of the way toward a justification for the welfare state. They are not sufficient in and of themselves to dictate that outcome. Indeed, they prove distressingly indeterminate at what morally are some of the most crucial junctures: At one point, for example, their requirements could be met either by a fairly generous welfare state or by a viciously caste society. If the former is to be preferred over the latter, it must be for some independent moral reasons, rather than by reason of the internal logic of any of the standard (economic, political, sociological, or moral) arguments used to provide the moral supports for the rest of market society.

The crucial independent moral premise required to underwrite the case for the welfare state turns on the proposition that we, individually and collectively, have a strong moral responsibility for protecting those whose interests are especially vulnerable to our actions and choices. That proposition dictates making provision outside ordinary economic markets for certain kinds of people and certain kinds of interests. It also dictates, at least in broad outline, the institutional form that this extramarket provision must take.

This line of analysis holds the welfare state to be a distinctive, limited style of state intervention into the market economy. It is justified on distinctive moral premises; and, given that rationale, it has a distinctive and strictly limited (if, as argued in the fifth section below, ever-expanding) set of tasks to perform.

That is not to say that other, more interventionistic policies are not also justifiable. It is merely to say that, if they are to be justified, they must be justified *differently*. Appeal must be made to some reasons other than those that justify classically welfare state interventions.

DEFINING THE WELFARE STATE

In order to know what a defense of the welfare state has to justify, we must first know what the defining features of the welfare state are. It is my thesis that modest state interventions into the market economy can be justified on premises different from those required to justify more wide-ranging interventions. I shall, accordingly, be defining the welfare state in fairly narrow terms.

Of course, it is then open to critics to complain that I have justified not the welfare state but merely some pallid precursor or some enfeebled variant.[2] All definitions are stipulative, all terminological disputes inherently unproductive. I have no intention of arguing here that I have the "right" definition of the welfare state. All I want to argue is that there is a strong, persistent, and interestingly different ethical case to be made for the welfare state, thus defined. We may well want to move beyond the welfare state, so narrowly construed. But as we move beyond it, the reasons for moving as far as the minimal welfare state do not drop away or somehow get preempted. The morally distinctive reasons for making sure that those minimal tasks get accomplished always remain, even in a more robustly interventionist state. That, it seems to me, is what justifies us in confining our attention to the welfare state, minimally defined.

The welfare state ought to be distinguished from other sorts of state, on the one hand, and from other modes of welfare provision, on the other. That is the business of the following two sections.

Distinctive Features of the Welfare State

In distinguishing the welfare state from other forms of state, we must first and foremost stipulate that (1) the welfare state is set in the context of a market economy. The function of the welfare state is, as Briggs (1961, 228) says, to "modify the play of market forces" in various limited respects. Its function is not to supplant the market altogether.

Of course, planned economies ordinarily contain a social security or social service sector. But that is not the same as a "welfare state." The point of welfare state interventions is to remedy unplanned and unwelcome outcomes. The welfare state strives to produce a post-fisc distribution of certain goods and services that is preferable to the pre-fisc one. In a planned economy, by contrast, all outcomes are the outcomes of planning. Not all are necessarily intended or welcomed outcomes, to be sure. But correcting planning errors is surely qualitatively different from correcting the market's unplanned perversities.

It may well be that many of the same (e.g., demographic) factors that force growth in the social service sectors of market economies also force growth in the same sectors of planned economies. For certain purposes (crossnational public expenditure studies, perhaps), it might therefore make sense to lump together the social service activities of both types of economy. For the normative purposes considered here, however, the differences clearly matter. The justification for public interventions in private economies will surely be different in kind from the justifications for public interventions in public economies.[3] So here I shall treat the "welfare state" as a public intervention in a private, market economy—and that alone.

The welfare state must, furthermore, be distinguished from more thoroughgoing egalitarian regimes of either of two logically distinct sorts. The first strives to equalize everyone's share of consumption goods. The second strives to equalize everyone's share of productive resources. The welfare state makes no systematic attempt to do either.

Consider first the contrast with the sort of state that gives everyone exactly equal shares of all consumption goods and services. Such a state may well thereby promote the welfare of its citizens.[4] But we would hesitate to say that it is (merely) a welfare state, when it goes so far beyond the sort of minimal provision for basic social needs that we think ordinarily characterizes a welfare state.

The characteristic function of the welfare state is to "limit the domain of inequality" (Tobin, 1970), not to eliminate it altogether. It is to provide a social minimum, a floor, a safety net. Hence we can say that an important feature of the welfare state is that (2) it limits its provision to certain basic needs. The substance of these needs varies from society to society, of course. But what remains relatively constant across all societies is the recognition of a category of "needs" separate from that of "mere wants."

Consider next the contrast between a welfare state and one that strives to equalize productive resources. Imagine a state that gives everyone exactly equal shares of capital—perhaps through public ownership of the means of production, or through market-socialist redistributions of finance capital to equalize the shares of all citizens. That sort of a state, too, may well promote people's welfare, albeit less directly. But once again, we would be loath to say that a state that did that much was (merely) a welfare state.[5]

Welfare state interventions are characteristically much more modest. At the level of personal social service administration, the welfare state ordinarily opts for in-kind transfers or nonfungible vouchers for specific goods or services, rather than cash transfers. On the level of grand strategy, the welfare state ordinarily opts for readjusting final distributions, rather than altering the pattern of property rights in productive resources that gave rise to those undesirable distributions in the first place.[6] This feature of the welfare state can be summarized by saying that (3) the welfare state strives to meet people's welfare needs relatively directly, rather than indirectly.

All three of these features of the welfare state reflect what Tobin (1970) has called its "specific egalitarianism." The welfare state supplants ordinary economic markets only in limited ways. Its interventions are characterized by a relatively great concern to limit the inequality of certain specific needed resources (food, shelter, health, etc.), and by relative indifference to the distribution of assets in general (income, wealth, and the means of producing or acquiring them).

Pulling together features 1, 2, and 3, then, the first defining feature of the welfare state—that which distinguishes it from other sorts of states—can be rewritten as follows: The welfare state intervenes (1) in a market economy (2) to meet certain of people's basic needs (3) through relatively direct means.

Other Modes of Welfare Provision

The welfare state ought, secondly, to be distinguished from other modes of welfare provision. State welfare provision should be distinguished, most especially, from private, voluntary, charitable provision. The Salvation Army, United Fund, and Catholic Benevolent Fund are simply not parts of the welfare state, great though their contributions to social welfare might be.

The reason is not just that they are private organizations, not part of the state at all. In nations with established churches (e.g., England, Sweden, Norway), the church is part of the state, after all. Still, we would not want to say, on account of that fact, that the charitable activities of the Anglican or Lutheran churches there form part of the welfare state.

More important, such organizations are not part of the welfare state because their activities are voluntary—and doubly so. There is no compulsion, moral suasion apart, for donors to contribute to those charities. Nor is there any restriction determining who can or who must benefit from such charitable activities. Anyone can be included and anyone excluded from benefits, just as the benefactors please.

That latter feature was carried over even into pre–welfare state forms of poor relief. Under the Poor Laws (both Old and New), public assistance was conceptualized as a "gratuity," the dispensation of which was, therefore, entirely at the discretion of the official concerned. By virtue of such voluntariness, we can rightly call these schemes "public charity," distinguishing them in that way from the genuinely welfare state activities of the modern state.

To distinguish the welfare state from other modes of welfare provision (private philanthropy, or organized public or private charity) we must therefore stipulate that the welfare state is a system of compulsory, collective, and largely nondiscretionary welfare provision.

Of course, no system of rules can ever be wholly nondiscretionary. There must inevitably be legislative discretion in deciding which rules to adopt in the first place; and there must inevitably be a certain amount of administrative discretion in bringing particular cases under general rules. Although the welfare state cannot eliminate either sort of discretion entirely, it can and does minimize the impact of both. It is discretion being exercised at the point of service provision that is particularly objectionable, after all. Voluntary benefactors (and, to a large extent, even Poor Law guardians) can make up their own rules at the same time that they distribute their gratuities; in the welfare state, rule-making legislative discretion is exercised at a safe distance from the point of service provision. Furthermore, in the welfare state, the administrative discretion of those charged with providing services is substantially hedged by legislatively mandated rules, rights, and so on, in a way that the discretion of voluntary benefactors is not—and by its nature cannot be.

Thus, this second feature distinguishes state welfare provision from other modes of welfare provision. Combined with the first feature, which distinguishes the welfare state from other sorts of state, it uniquely identifies the welfare state form.

JUSTIFYING THE WELFARE STATE: MARKET FAILURE

The welfare state has been characterized above as a limited adjunct to the market economy. On that characterization, it is only natural that its justification should first be sought through an analysis of the various ways in which markets might fail.

After all, the market and the welfare state both officially aim at essentially the same end—promoting public welfare. Morally as well as economically, the fundamental justification of the market is simply that under certain, tightly specified conditions, the operations of the market will serve to maximize social welfare. That is the central tenet of modern economics, first formulated by Adam Smith and formalized in our own day by Arrow and Hahn (1971).

In cases of so-called market failure, maximizing social welfare is precisely what markets fail to do. Therein lies the neoclassical economist's rationale for state intervention—to remedy the many and varied forms of market failure.[7] The first and most natural hypothesis, then, is that the welfare state derives its justification from its role in correcting market failures of some distinctive sort.

Notice that justifying state welfare services in this fashion requires us to do more than merely show that those services serve some clear economic function. Much that the state does to promote health and education, for example, might be construed as "investing in human capital."[8] But demonstrating that certain gains flow to the national economy from undertaking such activities is not enough, in and of itself, to justify the state's assumption of that role. To do that, we must further show that the market will necessarily fail to provide such goods— or, at the very least, that the market is an inferior provider of them, in one way or another, as compared to the state. In most of those cases, that is not obviously true. A champion of the market might reply, with a fair bit of surface plausibility, that education, health, and housing all can be (indeed, all along have been) provided as private goods through ordinary market transactions; and there seems to be no compelling reason, economically, why they should not continue to be provided in that fashion.[9] There may, of course, be perfectly good political or sociological explanations (couched, for example, in terms of the political power of private capital) for how private enterprises manage to shift certain costs of their production onto the public at large. But the simple "economic functionality" of welfare services cannot, without much more argument, be said to justify those services being provided by the state rather than through some private agency.

Similarly, some commentators see the function of the welfare state as being one of coordinating people's charitable impulses. Andrew Shonfield (1965, 93), for example, writes that the welfare state "may be regarded as a means of eliminating those individual acts of charity which are designed to mitigate poverty, by centralizing them in the hands of the state." If each of us wants to give our charitable donations to those most in need, then some coordination of our donations clearly is required; otherwise, we may all end up giving to the same individual (because she appeared on last night's television news broadcast, for example). But, again, the need for coordination does not in and of itself argue for state intervention. Assuming that each of us genuinely wants his or her contribution to go to those most in need (and assuming that we are all operating with sufficiently similar standards of what constitutes an appropriate metric of "most in need"), coordination can easily be accomplished without the aid of the state's coercive sanctions. There being no conflict of interest among donors regarding how their contributions are to be spent, all of them would gladly acquiesce in the decisions of some central coordinating body without any threat of legal sanctions (Goodin, 1976, chs. 3 and 4). In practice, that is precisely what happens when the purely private United Fund coordinates charitable contributions in every major U.S. city.[10]

In seeking an economic justification for the welfare state, then, we must look not merely for ways in which state welfare services provide economic benefits. We must look for ways in which state welfare services provide benefits that private actors in private markets cannot. We must look for ways in which markets would necessarily fail.

Perhaps the most notorious case of market failure concerns the supply of "public goods." If, as Friedman (1962, 190–191) suggests, "charity" is a public good, then a substantial amount of welfare state intervention might be justified to provide an optimal supply of that public good. The basic argument would go like this. If people are altruistic, in the sense of internalizing the pains and pleasures of others (but, crucially, not in the sense of wanting to help relieve the distress themselves, necessarily), then their utility will increase whenever poor people's utility increases; and this would be true whether or not they were the ones who made donations to the poor in order to bring about that result. In that case, charity would indeed be a public good. Every altruist would have an incentive to free-ride on every other altruist's charitable donations; none of them would end up donating. All of them would regret that outcome. And all would welcome coercive public intervention to compel donations, instead of letting them remain voluntary.

Friedman's argument is plagued with many problems, however. One is that it is terribly sensitive to the question of how many altruists there are in the community. Ideally, we would like to tax only those who are truly altruists of this sort; only those who actually benefit from the provision of the public good should have to pay for it. In practice, of course, this is impossible, because we cannot discover who they are.[11] As a rough-and-ready second-best measure, we are therefore inclined to tax everyone. But that is justifiable only if we suppose that most of them really are "closet altruists" of this sort.[12] That may or may not be a plausible assumption, depending on the country and the period in question. Yet, morally, we are not inclined to believe that the rightness or the wrongness of the welfare state depends upon just how generously inclined people in some place or some period happen to be.

Besides, this model fundamentally misrepresents what it truly means to *care* about other people. Charity constitutes a public good susceptible to free-riding (and hence market failure) only if people's charitable inclinations focus totally on outcomes (i.e., that the poor be made better off) and ignore altogether questions of agency (i.e., that it does not matter who makes them better off). Most of us, perhaps, would agree that if more good can be done by others, then we ourselves should stand aside and let them do it rather than insisting upon our own agency. But the model in view goes well beyond any so sensible a proposition. It depicts as charitable paradigmatically someone who not only would *let* others help instead but, on balance, would *prefer* that others help instead. But that is just not what it is to *care* about someone else. That is just not the way that genuinely *charitable* impulses work.

Here our ordinary intuitions seem well supported by empirical evidence. On the model of charity considered here, the altruist would be expected to give less to the poor when other people are giving more. Empirically, the opposite seems to be true (Sugden, 1982b). That being so, however, charity does not seem to be a public good of the sort susceptible to free-riding, or hence requiring public intervention for its provision.

A more persuasive case for expecting market failures with respect to public welfare provision might be made in a somewhat more complicated fashion. The private analogue to the social insurance programs that constitute the bulk (if not the whole)[13] of welfare state activities would be private insurance programs.

There are various ways in which private insurance markets might fail in these contexts, however. One of the more important ways has to do with the problem of "adverse selection."[14] If participation in the insurance scheme were voluntary, and if individuals had better information concerning their own true risks than did underwriters, then those with better-than-average risks would opt out of the scheme (preferring to self-insure) and only bad risks would be left in it. Premiums would have to rise to cover the above-average level of claims from those now left in the pool. As they did so, more and more people would find it to their advantage to opt out. Eventually, only the very worst risks would remain in the pool, and the whole scheme would collapse.[15]

To remedy the problem of adverse selection, insurance must be made compulsory. Another problem with private insurance markets would still remain, however. The financial integrity of mutual insurance schemes in the private market presupposes that each person's risks are, to a very large extent, statistically independent of everyone else's. Only under that assumption will the law of large numbers guarantee that the actuarially expected pattern of outcomes will actually occur, and that premiums collected from "winners" (i.e., those who do not suffer the insured-against contingency) will suffice to meet claims from "losers."

Where risks are interdependent, no such guarantee can be given. Consider the example of unemployment insurance. The probability that any given individual will be unemployed is not just a function of trends within his or her own firm or industry. It is also a function of the state of the national economy in general. Under such circumstances, it would be impossible to guarantee the financial integrity of any mutual insurance scheme. The problem is not just that actuaries are unable to set the right rate for premiums. What is worse, with interdependent risks there can be no guarantee (as there can, through the law of large numbers, with independent risks) that premiums from "winners" (those still in work) will suffice to cover claims from "losers" (those out of work) *whatever* the rate that is set.[16]

That market failure is perhaps the most important argument for collective intervention in certain insurance markets. The government must act as underwriter of last resort, providing re-insurance out of general fund revenues as necessary. Social insurance must, in that way at least, supplant purely private insurance.[17]

Much welfare state activity can thus be justified as social insurance designed to remedy the failures of private insurance markets. Much of it cannot, however. (That is especially true of welfare state activity traveling under the heading of "social" or "public assistance.") The reason is that insurance is not fundamentally redistributive at all.

Superficially, of course, a fair amount of redistribution does take place within insurance schemes. There is redistribution between different periods of a person's life—from working to nonworking years in child-benefit and retirement insurance schemes, for example. There is redistribution between different people—from those who do not suffer certain contingencies to those who do, for example. And so on.

At root, however, insurance is "expectation-preserving," and non-redistributive for that reason. The function of insurance is merely to remove uncertainty. It works by transforming a statistical expectation into an equivalent certainty. People are charged premiums proportional to their risks. Those in desperate circumstances, whose every expectation is of probable disaster, can derive no comfort from such a solution.

Imagine someone with a 50 percent chance of getting either 5,000 calories or none. Actuarially fair insurance would (at best, ignoring administrative costs, profits, etc.) guarantee to provide that person 2,500 calories in bad times in exchange for a premium of 2,500 in good times. The upshot is that the person enjoys 2,500 calories no matter what happens. But if minimum subsistence requirements were 4,000 calories, insurance would have merely transformed a probable disaster into a certain one for that individual.

The most basic criticism of the insurance model of social welfare, then, is a moral one. Insurance norms simply cannot justify the welfare state's most characteristic function, which is to guarantee to meet the basic needs of those persons who are antecedently most likely not to meet them without assistance.[18]

There are various other ways in which *particular* welfare services might be justified as adjuncts to the market economy, designed to correct recognized market failures of one sort or another.[19] None, however, is adequate to justify the welfare state as a whole. Clearly, we should be seeking that justification elsewhere.

JUSTIFYING THE WELFARE STATE: SAFEGUARDING THE MARKET

The true justification of the welfare state is not, I submit, to be found in the strictly economistic logic of correcting market failures, narrowly conceived. Instead, it is to be found in the role of the welfare state in safeguarding the preconditions of the market. There are two such preconditions that merit special attention here.

First, allocating some things through the market presupposes that not everything will be so marketed. A variety of arguments (political, sociological, economic, and ultimately moral) converge on the conclusion that there are certain things that must not be marketed, if other things are to be. In order for there to be one sector that is governed by the laws of the market, there must be some other sector that is not.

Second, it is crucially presupposed that participants within the market sector are essentially independent agents. A variety of arguments (political, sociological, economic, and ultimately moral) converge on the conclusion that dependent agents ought to be beyond the play of market forces. In order for people to participate in the market as independent agents, there must be some nonmarket sector to meet the sorts of needs that would otherwise render those people dependent and hence unqualified for market relations.

The welfare state underwrites both these crucial presuppositions of market society. First, it provides for dependent agents outside the market. Second, it provides for dependent agents on terms that both allow and enable them to participate in subsequent market transactions as substantially independent agents.

Preserving Nonmarket Relations and Values

Notice, first, the various respects in which it is a condition of certain things being marketed that other things not be. To some extent, this is dictated even by narrowly economic considerations. One is that the market presupposes a system of enforceable property rights, guaranteeing that transfers will occur only voluntarily. If all things, including police and judges, were up for auction to the highest bidder in the market, however, the system of property rights upon which the market depends would itself be undermined (Arrow, 1972, 357). Another has to do with the need for "trust" in certain sorts of transactions. Where buyers cannot monitor directly the quality of the good or service being purchased, they have to trust the seller if they are to enter into the transaction at all; and where the seller is thus trying to show himself trustworthy, he "cannot act, or at least appear to act, as if he is maximizing his income at every moment of time" (Arrow, 1963, 965).

These narrowly economistic considerations relate to the internal—and almost strictly logical—presuppositions of the market. Something in the very nature of markets themselves make it impossible for them to operate unless those preconditions are met.

Focusing exclusively upon such internal, logical presuppositions of the market would badly understate the limits of the reach of the market, however. In addition to the logical preconditions of the market, there are sociological ones of a similar form. Sociologically, too, it seems to be a precondition of buying and selling some things that not everything go onto the auction block. Again, sociologically, it seems to be a precondition of some things being marketed that other things—some goods and some relationships—should be beyond the reach of the market.[20]

Details vary from society to society. But in virtually every society there is thought to be a broad class of people whom it would be wrong to deal with on a purely market basis, and there is thought to be a broad class of goods and services that would be wrong to buy and sell in ordinary economic markets.

In purely market terms, for example, someone in a very strong position would be able to drive a very hard bargain indeed with someone in a very weak position. (Reflect for a moment on Nozick's [1972, 115] example of someone "negotiating" with a millionaire drowning nearby for the supply of a life preserver.) The very factors that make it possible, in purely market terms, to drive a hard bargain with that person make it morally outrageous to do so. That would constitute the height of exploitation; it would amount to taking grossly unfair advantage.

What makes the taking of advantage (i.e., market behavior) unfair varies from situation to situation. It might be that you are playing for advantage where those playing "against" you have renounced playing for advantage themselves, as when you exploit friends or lovers. It might be that you are playing for advantage against people who are unfit for games of advantage (as in stealing from the blind) or who are not a fair match for you in games of advantage (owing, for example, to differential information [Arrow, 1963, 965] or power). Or it might be that your advantage is unfair because it derives from the other's grave misfortune. Each of these cases is discussed in greater detail elsewhere (Goodin, 1987). What unites all these cases of exploitation, however, is that by behaving according to ordinary market precepts in such cases you would in fact be violating your strong duty to protect those who are particularly vulnerable (for one reason or another, in one way or another) to your actions and choices.[21]

To some extent these sociological limits on the reach of the market may derive from the "internal logic"—here, the internal sociological logic—of market society. Some such neofeudal principle of protecting the vulnerable would surely have been required, in the transition from feudalism to capitalism, as a kind of "hold harmless" clause guaranteeing that no one would be made worse off by the switch-over. And perhaps some such guarantee to "protect the vulnerable" still serves an important role in reassurring those who intermittently threaten to disrupt social order in a big way today (Piven and Cloward, 1971).

But here again, "internal logic" arguments will take us only part of the way toward an adequate analysis of the phenomenon. The crucial point here is that those most in need of protection will characteristically be those least able to make trouble for society if they are denied it. Assuming it is for the protection of *these* individuals that we most especially desire the principle of "protecting the vulnerable," that principle must be understood as being primarily a moral appeal rather than a political or sociological imperative alone.[22]

Just as there are certain interpersonal relationships that should stay outside the market, so too are there certain goods and services that should be supplied outside the market. To some extent, this proposition derives from the last. In some cases, the reason that certain goods and services should be supplied outside the market is just that those are things that vulnerable others, with whom we should deal on nonmarket terms, require from us.

Beyond that, however, there is a further need to protect those things that we "take particularly seriously" from contamination by the "commercialization effect." As Hirsch (1976, ch. 6) wryly observes, "Bought sex is not the same." The market has a "corrosive effect" on values, debasing what was formerly precious and apart from the mundane world, by allowing everything to be exchanged for everything else. In the end, we are left with nothing but a "vending machine society" (Okun, 1975, ch. 1), where everything is available for a price (Goodin, 1982, ch. 6).

What sorts of goods and services we decide to take especially seriously, and toward which we therefore adopt this special sort of attitude, naturally vary from society to society. But conspicuous among them, in an individualistic market society at least, must be those things that are intimately connected to people's self-respect and dignity. Morally, that must be so: The only reason to respect people's choices (as the market ethos commands) is that we more fundamentally respect people, their dignity, and their self-images (Goodin, 1982, ch. 5). That, for example, is why we give people nonfungible rights of various sorts. As Okun (1975, 19) says, "If someone can buy your vote, or your favorable draft number, or a contract for your indentured service, he can buy part of your dignity."

Conspicuous among those things that are intimately connected with people's dignity, in turn, are those things that are required to meet material necessities. There are few things less dignified than rooting around someone else's garbage pail for one's evening's supper.

Securing Independence

Notice, next, the various ways in which participants in markets are presumed to be essentially independent agents. Let us start, once again, with economic theory. There, the case for the optimality of market allocations presupposes perfect competition. Operationally, that is taken to mean that there are so many buyers and sellers that none can independently alter the price of goods bought or sold.

Where buyers are dependent upon a single supplier, or sellers upon a single buyer, for some good or service (and where, furthermore, it is not a viable option for them to abstain altogether from buying or selling the good or service in question), competition is far from perfect. In the classic case, a profit-maximizing monopolist can produce less than the optimal amount and charge more for it. In the analogous case nearer our present concerns, those who enjoy a privileged position vis-à-vis some particular other agents who are dependent upon them for supplies of needed resources can practice "price discrimination" against their dependents, charging them more than they should (or would, if there had been a perfect market) for the needed goods and services.[23]

Much welfare state provision of needed resources is aimed at avoiding dependencies of just this kind. In the absence of state provision, people would be dependent upon a small set of particular others—family, friends, and neighbors—to provide needed resources. Those being purely voluntary transfers, the superordinates in the relationships would be at liberty to impose whatever conditions (or demand whatever "price") they liked for the needed assistance (Goodin 1985c,d). In light of such potential for the imposition of restrictions equivalent to "price discrimination" in markets, there is no reason to suppose that the results of "free" exchanges of this sort would be in any way Pareto-optimal.

Allied with this is the problem of "desperation bidding." It is a familiar phenomenon for someone dying of a disease that is curable, but only through a very expensive treatment, to be "willing to throw in all he owns" in exchange for such treatment (Calabresi and Bobbitt, 1978, 121).

Those who are "desperate" in this way might best be conceptualized as people who will not be able to go on to the next round of a game unless they secure some needed resource (medical care, food, shelter, etc.) in the present round.[24] They are therefore willing to bid everything they own in this round, even if that leaves them with nothing for the next, because unless they win this round of bidding they will not survive into the next. Simply by virtue of this temporal lumpiness, anyone in a position to practice "price discrimination" against them could extract an exorbitant "price" from desperate dependents.

Even from a narrowly economic point of view, there might be certain things wrong—inefficient—with such temporal lumpiness as this. These inefficiencies would have to do with the failure of proper future markets to emerge. At least one of the reasons that people often find themselves engaged in desperation bidding is that they have been denied full present access to resources that they could expect to enjoy over the course of their lives as a whole. And desperation bidding often consists essentially in an attempt to secure just such access to expected future resources now, when they are needed—access that would be provided automatically if there were a proper futures market in operation.[25]

The source of the blockages to such markets are multiple and their particular effects varied. As regards the causes of such market failures, most seem to have to do with something akin to the economist's "moral hazard" notion. Whether or not expected future resources do in fact materialize is largely a function of the future behavior of the persons currently raising monies on the strength of those future expectations. The more successful they are in that effort, the more heavily their future will have been mortgaged; and hence they have less incentive to invest the needed effort in realizing those expectations, which will now redound principally to the benefit of their creditors anyway.[26]

Whatever the source of such market failures, and however varied their particular effects, the misallocation of resources consequent upon them is nonetheless clear. People end up buying less now, or paying more for it, or both, than they would have done had such markets been in operation.[27] And what would have happened had markets been functioning effectively in all respects is, of course, the proper benchmark by which to judge the efficiency of allocations in market societies.

Talking in this way of the *inefficiency* of desperation bidding captures only half of our objection to it, however. The economic argument just sketched traces the inefficiency of desperation bidding to the failure of the market to allow people access to their expected future resources. That is all well and good for those who are suffering some temporary embarrassment, and whose future expectations are rosy. But what about those who can only expect a future as bleak as their present? Even with perfectly functioning futures markets, they would get no relief. We have no grounds, then, for saying that it is inefficient to leave them to suffer. Yet surely our objections to desperation bidding increase, rather than diminish, if we are talking about desperation bidding in perpetuity.

A large part of our objection to desperation bidding must, therefore, be moralistic rather than economistic. The fundamental objection must be to the *unfairness*, and not to the mere inefficiency, of such exchanges. Even economists can appreciate that "trades that are made as a last resort . . . could not be fair trades. . . . [They] would be distorted by vast differences in the bargaining power of the participants and by the desperation that spawns them" (Okun, 1975, 19–20). Neither American nor English law is now prepared to enforce such "unconscionable contracts" (Devlin, 1965, ch. 3; Kronman, 1983).

Just as dependency undercuts the presumption of formal economic markets, so too does it undercut the presumptions of other sectors of society organized along quasi-market lines. Among these, in the sort of liberal democracy normally associated with market societies, is the political arena. There, politics is conceptualized as just another kind of market, where the competitive struggle is for people's votes rather than for their money.

In the quasi-market of politics, just as in the formal market of economics, it is crucially presupposed that those in whom sovereignty is vested (consumers in the one case, electors in the other) are fundamentally independent agents. Those who are so dependent upon others that they might be obliged to bend their wills to those of their masters are deemed unfit subjects upon whom to confer sovereignty of either sort.[28] In economics, their dependency potentially skews their decisions as to how to allocate their economic resources; in politics, their dependency potentially skews their decisions as to how to allocate their votes.[29]

The "independence" qualification has, over the years, been used to justify disenfranchisement of diverse groups of potential electors.[30] Servants and apprentices were excluded, on grounds of their presumed dependence on their masters. Women were excluded, on grounds of their presumed dependence on their menfolk. And so on.[31]

A similar presumed lack of "independence" was traditionally used to justify the disenfranchisement of recipients of alms. The reason given—as in the cases of servants, apprentices, and women—was simply that "they depend upon the will of other men and should be afraid to displease" them (Petty, in Woodhouse, 1951, 82). Or, as others have put it, "Whose bread I eat, his song I sing" (ten Broek and Wilson, 1954, 265).[32]

That concern was quite a valid one, given the way in which Poor Law relief was traditionally administered. At best, it was regarded as a form of "gratuity."[33] As such, its dispensation was wholly under the discretionary control of Poor Law guardians. Recipients of such gratuities were, indeed, dependent upon the favor of the guardians for their continued support. So too were welfare recipients dependent upon the favor of state officials who, in the early years of this century, assumed responsibility for the administration of still largely discretionary programs of social assistance.

In the welfare state, in contrast, public assistance is placed as far beyond the discretionary control of those charged with its dispensation as it is possible to place it. To be sure, needy citizens will still have to depend upon such assistance for satisfaction of their needs. Critics of public relief programs—from Hegel (Moon, 1987) and Tocqueville (1835) to Anderson (1978, 56, 153) and Murray (1982, 9; 1984, 64–65)—have always made much of that fact and of the presumed psychological damage that such dependence inflicts. What those writers overlook, however, are important differences between different kinds of dependency.

In a welfare state, needy citizens no longer depend—as they did historically (and, if the New Right gets its way, once again would) under a regime of public or private charity—upon the arbitrary will of those dispensing the benefits. In a welfare state, the decisions of social service administrators are not left to their own arbitrary will. Instead, those decisions are tightly circumscribed by rules from above.[34] Recipients of welfare state relief are thereby freed to vote as they please, without having to fear that alms givers might withdraw their assistance in a fit of pique.

In short, the sort of dependency for which the welfare state is a cure is that which is akin to peonage. And the welfare state, characterized as it is by nondiscretionary benefits, addresses that particular problem quite successfully. It renders the poor politically independent of those who are directly responsible for providing them with needed resources.[35]

PREVENTING THE EXPLOITATION OF DEPENDENCY

The problem that the welfare state is designed to answer, then, is the problem of dependency.[36] And the problem of dependency is the problem of exploitation. Under the law of the market, those who are dependent could and would be mercilessly exploited. Economically, you can drive a very hard bargain indeed with someone who is desperately in need and dependent upon you for satisfaction of that need. Morally, however, you must not do so (Goodin, 1985b,d).

The point of extramarket provision for basic needs, according to this argument, is to prevent the exploitation of dependencies. Not all extramarket institutions necessarily attempt (much less succeed in) that task. Precursors to the welfare state conspicuously failed in it, treating public assistance as a gratuity to which any number of strings might be attached, thereby putting those dependent upon such assistance at the mercy of the largely arbitrary will of those administering such assistance. Everything from their morals to their family budgets were subject to administrative scrutiny.[37] In saying that extramarket provision for basic needs *can* render people independent in the ways that morally matter, then, I do not intend to imply that it necessarily *must*.

Let us assume, however, that that *is* our goal. There are various strategies available to us for pursuing it. One way to prevent the exploitation of dependencies is to eliminate dependencies. Although the elimination of certain dependencies is the business of macroeconomic policy or social policy more generally, there is much that the welfare state, even narrowly construed, can do. It can, for example, often prevent the infirm aged from having to enter nursing homes, simply by providing home help and meals-on-wheels (Kane and Kane, 1979; Gibson, 1985).

Some would argue that this strategy, especially as it is practiced by the welfare state, amounts merely to shifting dependencies, not to eliminating them at all. People who would otherwise be dependent upon a nursing home are dependent instead upon state-provided assistance to keep them out of a nursing home. The elderly are no less dependent than before. They are just dependent upon different people.

The general thesis underlying this challenge seems to be that there is always some constant quantity of dependency that can be shifted around but never eliminated. I am skeptical of that thesis. But as I am unsure how to individuate (and hence to enumerate, much less to weight) different distinct dependencies, I am unsure how such a position could ever be proven or disproven.

The better defense of the welfare state, in my view, ducks that question altogether. It rests instead on the second broad strategy for avoiding the exploitation of dependencies.[38] Whereas the first strategy aimed at the elimination of dependencies, the second aims merely at preventing their exploitation. Although this may be a less flamboyant solution to the problem of dependency, it is a more precisely focused one. The objections discussed above, recall, were directed not to the existence of dependency but merely to its exploitation. Eliminating dependencies, although more flashy, is a more roundabout strategy for solving that problem.[39] Eliminating dependencies is helpful insofar as that which does not exist cannot be exploited. But it is the exploitation of the dependency rather than its existence *per se* that, on the arguments developed above, really matters.

There are four conditions, all of which must be present if dependencies are to be exploitable.[40] First, the relationship must be *asymmetrical*. In any reasonably complex society, most people are dependent upon a great many other people for a great many things. Interdependence is the essence of all mutually profitable trades, of all political alliances, and of all friendships and loving relations (Baldwin, 1980; Wilson, 1978). No one thinks that there is anything wrong with such relationships merely by virtue of the fact that people within them depend upon one another. The reason is precisely that, as they are relationships of *inter*dependence, neither party can exploit the other through a credible threat to withdraw from the relationship. Each depends on the other in turn, and that mutual dependence guarantees the relationship against exploitation.

Second, even in an asymmetrical relationship, to be truly exploited the subordinate party must *need* the resource that the superordinate supplies.[41] There happens to be a single supplier of figs in our village. I depend upon him for my supply; he does not depend upon me for my custom (there being many fig-lovers in our village who will buy his figs even if I do not). Still, unilateral though my dependence upon him is, he cannot exploit me because, push come to shove, I can always protect myself by withdrawing from the relationship. Fond though I am of figs, I do not strictly need them. If the price becomes exploitative, I will simply do without them.[42]

Third, to be truly exploited, the subordinate party must depend upon some *particular* superordinate for the supply of needed resources. If there is a multitude of providers I can choose among, then no one of them (nor, absent some extraordinary feat of collective action on their part in forming a cartel, all of them taken together) can exploit me. Much though I depend on farmers as a group for my food, I am not exploited by them because there are so many I can choose among to satisfy my needs.

Fourth, the superordinate can truly exploit the subordinate only if he enjoys *discretionary* control over the resources that the subordinate needs from him. Consider my relationship with my bank manager. The relationship is clearly asymmetrical: He has something I need (my savings, deposited in his bank), while I have nothing he especially needs in return. Let us suppose that I need my savings desperately for some particular purpose—an operation, say—and that I have no other source of funds. Hence the situation meets all the criteria for the morally worrying dependency relationship thus far considered. Still, we need not be worried. The point is that my bank manager has, in the final analysis, no discretionary control over my savings. When I present him with a properly completed withdrawal form, he has no choice (legally) but to present me with my money. Hence, the dependency is simply not exploitable.[43]

Preventing the exploitation of dependencies by making assistance to needy, dependent people largely nondiscretionary is the hallmark of the welfare state. There, benefits are bestowed "as of right." Although I regard "welfare rights" as not quite right for the purpose (as I shall explain in the following section), that phrase does serve to emphasize what is crucial in the welfare state approach to dependency—that the supply of certain resources to those in need of them should, insofar as humanly possible, be put outside of the discretion of the officials responsible for dispensing them. By curtailing discretion, we will have curtailed the risk of people being exploited, however much they may still need the resources being dispensed or however few other sources of supply they may have.[44]

CONVENTIONAL UNDERSTANDINGS OF THE WELFARE STATE

Viewed from this angle, conventional understandings of the welfare state can be shown to be morally near the mark, but also slightly off the mark. Ordinarily, for example, it is said that the welfare state provides needed resources "as of right," and the notion of a welfare "right" is ordinarily meant to be taken quite literally.

As I have shown elsewhere (Goodin, 1986), however, the notion of a "right" is not quite what is needed for the purposes that the welfare state serves. The notion of a "right," strictly speaking, implies a restrictive notion of who has "standing," legally, to claim and to complain. In the context of the welfare state, and given what we know about the propensity (not to mention capacity) of poor people to pursue legal claims for themselves, that restriction is wholly inappropriate (Goodin, 1986).

It *is* essential that we should think in terms of firm legal rules that, insofar as possible, bind officials to providing welfare benefits to all those who are qualified to receive them. But what is crucial about those rules is that they should allow minimal scope for official discretion, rather than that they should take the particular form of rules embodying welfare rights. We should instead be thinking in terms of imposing obligations, duties, and responsibilities upon officials dispensing welfare benefits. It is important—for their self-respect, if nothing else—that recipients should be given standing to claim such benefits, and to complain if they are not given them when they are due them. But it is also important that such standing to complain about nonfeasance or misfeasance of official duties not be limited merely to would-be beneficiaries, who would be understandably reluctant to antagonize officials with whom they must continue to deal.

Or, again, we often talk in terms of the welfare state's meeting people's "basic needs." Up to this point, I have conformed with that standard usage. But I am frankly skeptical that any neat account of "needs" can be given that would effectively distinguish them from "mere wants" in a way that would justify the priority we ordinarily think should be accorded to needs over mere wants. Certainly needs do correlate in a rough-and-ready way with factors that *do* deserve such priority. The correlation is only an imperfect one, however, and does not translate into a blanket priority for needs over wants as such (Goodin, 1985a).

My discussion of preventing exploitation of dependencies once again helps to cast this old problem in a slightly new light. Needs give rise to exploitable dependencies because people in need have "no reasonable choice" but to pay any price, and comply with any conditions, that those upon whom they are dependent for satisfaction of their needs might care to lay down. It is simply "not reasonable" to expect them to do without the needed resources instead of complying.

The "no reasonable choice" standard is much weaker than the "no choice" standard that is ordinarily—and rightly—taken to define "needs." Those things that we need are commonly said to be those things that physically (or, perhaps, psychologically) we simply cannot do without. There are certain purposes for which that stronger standard is clearly more appropriate. Central among them is the matter of removing moral responsibilities for actions committed under duress of one sort or another. Exculpation clearly does require that it was impossible, and not just awfully costly, to do the right thing (Frankfurt, 1973, 77).

For purposes of identifying which dependencies might prove exploitable, however, the weaker standard is quite sufficient. Very strong desires can be exploitable in much the same way as physical requirements or psychological compulsions. You can drive a very hard bargain with someone who is dependent upon you for something he desires very badly, and who sees himself as having "no reasonable choice" but to accede to whatever demands you might make. In practice, it may (and often will) be every bit as hard a bargain as you would be able to drive with someone who is dependent upon you for something that he strictly needs, and who objectively has "no choice" but to accede to your demands. If preventing the *exploitation* of dependencies is our aim, then we should be equally concerned with the protection of those who have "no choice" and of those who have "no reasonable choice." Each is potentially as exploitable as the other.

Thus, it is the business of the welfare state to prevent the exploitation of dependencies, and that is a matter of providing support to people who would otherwise be left with "no reasonable choices." That, in turn, might explain why the "needs" to which the welfare state responds are defined by relative and shifting standards, rather than being absolute and invariable across all societies.

There are some things that it would be inconceivable to do without (and unreasonable to expect anyone to do without) in American society today, but which are (or were) usually done without in Sudanese society (or in the United States in the past). Americans would ordinarily be willing to engage in something very much like desperation bidding to avoid doing without things that a Sudanese (or our own grandparents) would not think twice of doing without. To avoid the exploitation that that willingness to engage in desperation bidding makes possible, the modern welfare state must therefore provide many things that the welfare state of other places or in earlier eras did not need to provide.[45] Because our needs have grown, there has been an escalation of the welfare state's claims over time, both in terms of the range and the level of services it takes upon itself to provide and in terms of the cost to the public treasury of its doing so.

JUSTIFYING THE WELFARE STATE: ULTIMATELY MORAL

The welfare state thus succeeds in removing certain things from the market and distributing them through another mechanism altogether. In that way, it helps satisfy the first precondition of market societies. Furthermore, this extramarket allocation is arranged in such a way as to guarantee that the dependencies for which it caters cannot be exploited. In that way, the welfare state underwrites the independence of people, which is the second precondition of market societies.

The latter, however, goes well beyond what the "logic of the market" strictly requires. All that this logic demands is that dependents not be allowed to participate in markets. That is consistent with either of two possible approaches to the problem of dependency. One is to make extramarket provision for dependents' needs in such a way as to leave them still exploitably dependent and for that reason precluded from participating in markets and quasi-market politics. The other is to make extramarket provision for dependents' needs in such a way as to render them independent and hence qualified to participate in markets and quasi-market politics. If the latter solution is preferable to the former, it must be so for *moral* reasons. So far as the "internal logic" of arguments for markets is concerned, which solution we select is a matter of indifference.

Historically, the former was the option customarily pursued. Those in need of extramarket assistance were branded "paupers," stripped of their rights of citizenship, and confined to the workhouse to earn their keep. The dependent poor were thus kept from contaminating market society in its many forms. Politically, recipients of Poor Law relief were formally disenfranchised. Economically, they were just as effectively precluded from participation in the market economy by rules governing the conditions, forms, and levels of relief granted.[46] Having thus guaranteed that recipients of Poor Law relief would not be participating in the market or quasi-market institutions of society, their extreme and continuing dependence upon the largely arbitrary will of Poor Law officials posed no threat to those other institutions.

Within the narrow logic of the market, there can be no objection to such arrangements. All that it requires is that participants in markets be independent agents. There is no objection, internal to that logic, to the existence of dependent agents elsewhere in society, just so long as those agents are kept out of the market. By all accounts, the Poor Law was remarkably successful in accomplishing that task.

While such arrangements violate none of the narrow tenets of the logic of markets, there is still much to object to in them. The first objection is narrowly pragmatic: Too many people would have to be excluded, on these principles, for the market or the polity to function effectively. Duncan (1984, 4), reporting the results of a University of Michigan panel study spanning a decade straddling the late 1960s and early 1970s, observes that "nearly one-quarter of the population [of the United States] received income from welfare sources at least once in the decade." Barring a quarter of the population from the marketplace or the pollbooth would, just speaking in narrowly pragmatic terms, wreak untold economic and political havoc on the country.

Beyond narrow pragmatism, however, we would find that sort of caste society morally repugnant. Communitarians are right in this respect, at least: We think our society truly ought to be a single-status moral community. And if full participation in our societies is indeed to be conditional upon a person's being a minimally independent agent, then morally we feel ourselves obliged not only to serve the needs of those who are dependent upon us but also to do what we can to render those persons independent (at least so far as they want to be).

There are various arguments against holding people in an unnecessarily dependent status against their will. These are couched in terms of self-respect, autonomy, and the like (Goodin, 1982, ch. 5; 1985b, chs. 7 and 8; 1985d; see also Postow, 1978-9, and Weale, 1982, ch. 3). The point about these arguments, however, is that they move outside the narrow bounds of the argument for the market itself. They have nothing to do with what is required to make market societies work, either pragmatically or morally. The "imperatives" that they represent are thus distinctively moral and morally distinctive.

These distinctive moral goals, so badly flouted by the caste society of the Old Poor Law, are successfully accomplished by the modern welfare state. Providing as it does needed assistance in a substantially nondiscretionary manner, the welfare state safeguards those dependent upon its services from exploitation of several forms. It thereby secures for them the sort of minimal independence that is required for them to participate in the other market and quasi-market sectors of their society.[47]

CONCLUSION

The argument offered here in defense of the welfare state is admittedly circuitous. Those who depend upon particular others for satisfaction of their basic needs are thereby rendered susceptible to exploitation by those upon whom they so depend; and it is the risk of exploitation of such dependencies that, in my argument, justifies public provision, of a welfare state form, for those basic needs.

A more direct—and more familiar—defense of the welfare state moves straight from the proposition that basic needs are not being met to the proposition that we, individually and collectively (and the state, as the proper repository of our collective duties), should see to it that they are met. The problem, from this standpoint, is not that starving people can be exploited. Rather, it is that they are starving. That, on the standard analysis, is the problem to which the welfare state provides a solution.

Posed that way, however, the problem is one arising *outside* the market, outside its operative laws and its underlying justificatory logic. The welfare state, on the standard analysis, derives its justification from a *wholly* distinct set of principles standing over or alongside—but entirely outside—the principles at work in the market itself.

It may well be true that there are some such principles at work in this area. Indeed, it is the theme of this chapter that there are *some* such principles. But how much justificatory weight they can reasonably be expected to carry is, perhaps, disputable.

The strategy of this chapter has been to indicate that they do not have to carry *all* the weight. The aim has been to show advocates of the market that their own principles go a long way toward committing them to at least a minimalist welfare state. Not quite all the way, to be sure: Some further independent moral premise is required, time and again, to make the last move. But market principles pare down the choices so dramatically that marketeers wishing to resist the argument for the welfare state will be left with utterly unpalatable choices at every turn.

NOTES

Earlier versions of this chapter were read at the University of Edinburgh and the CSPT conference at Tulane University. I am particularly grateful for the comments, then and later, of Michael Adler, Allen Buchanan, John Chapman, Vinit Haksar, Desmond King, Martin Krygier, Eric Mack, David Miller, Donald Moon, John Pocock, Richard Rose, Timothy Tilton, and Jeremy Waldron.

1. For my own views on these empirical matters, see Dryzek and Goodin (1986) and Goodin and Le Grand et al. (1987).

2. Briggs (1961, 222), for example, might call it merely a "social service state" rather than a proper "welfare state."

3. Rimlinger (1961) launches his comparative U.S./USSR study of social security expenditures with an argument that the two are analogous, each being "a system of secondary income distribution . . . different in its distributive principles and primary objectives from the economy's functional income dis-tribution." By the end of the article, however, it is clear that the differences between the two social security systems, their rationales, and their operative premises utterly swamp any such similarities. Likewise, see de Jouvenel, 1960; Lowenthal, 1960; and Nove, 1960.

4. I say "may" because in a desperately poor country an equal division may leave everyone starving.

5. We would be similarly loath to call even the social security sector of such a state a "welfare state." To do so would have this paradoxical consequence: The more successful the state is in promoting people's welfare by producing the right pre-fisc distribution, the less there is for the social security sector to do by way of patching up a better post-fisc distribution. But it is absurd to say that a state that does more toward (and succeeds better in) promoting people's welfare has a smaller "welfare state." Still, that is what we would be committed to saying, were we to regard the social security sector alone as the welfare state component of such a state.

6. Or, as Cohen (1981, 14) more pejoratively puts it, supporters of the welfare state ("social democrats") contrast with more radical "revolutionaries," who "find confiscation a more appropriate response to severe inequality of ownership than perpetual rearguard action against the effects of that inequality. . . . Social democrats are sensitive to the effects of exploitation on people, but not to the fact of exploitation itself. They want to succor the exploited while minimizing confrontation with those who exploit them."

7. For a taxonomy, see Bator (1958). There are many classes of market failure other than those to which the welfare state can possibly constitute a plausible response. Conspicuous among them are such things as natural monopolies and the provision of public goods (e.g., roads, sewers, clean air, and national defense) used by rich and poor alike.

8. Not all welfare services can be thus construed, however; consider, for example, care for the mentally or physically handicapped, or for the infirm aged.

9. Unless, of course, there is some compelling "public good" aspect to those goods. Often there is. A trite example is the public health measure against epidemic disease. More important examples have to do with "group-oriented" or "social" desires that are concerned fundamentally with "the state of the social environment" rather than with private consumption. Public education or health care is indeed necessarily a public good, insofar as its goal is to bolster community fellow-feeling (Margolis, 1955; Steiner, 1970, 31; Miller, 1981, 326–327).

10. Buchanan (1984, 71) offers a variation on Shonfield's theme, modeling charity as an Assurance Game: "I am willing to contribute . . . , but only if I have assurance that enough others will contribute to achieve the threshold of investment necessary for success." But the same objection may be lodged against this model as against Shonfield's: If charity is just an Assurance Game, why should the coercive intervention of the state be required to provide the requisite assurance? After all, in Assurance Games, people are as keen to give as they are to receive assurances that they will contribute, provided others do likewise; and each is as good as his word, just so long as others are likewise. Coercion being superfluous in these cases, so too is the state.

11. We cannot just ask them to identify themselves on their tax returns. For the same reason altruists of this sort would free-ride on the charitable donations of other altruists in the absence of government intervention, so too would they deny their altruistic preferences on their tax returns. That, after all, is just a way of free-riding on the public transfer payment funded by taxes collected from those who admit they are altruists on their tax return. With all altruists in hiding, however, no taxes will actually be collected for this purpose.

12. Furthermore, in order to explain the "specific egalitarianism" of the welfare state, we have to suppose that most people are altruistic with respect to some goods and services (i.e., those relating to "basic needs") but not others. And, furthermore, in order for those preferences to best be satisfied through in-kind transfers or nonfungible vouchers of the sort that the welfare state ordinarily employs, rather than through cash transfers, we must also assume certain things about the distribution of income and the variability of tastes across the population (Browning, 1975; Weitzman, 1977).

13. What is left out is noncontributory social assistance benefits, such as those paid to the congenitally handicapped and those who have never been in employment. I return to this omission at the end of the section.

14. The other widely discussed market failure in the insurance realm relates to "moral hazard"—the tendency of people, once insured, to run far worse risks than before, because they have less incentive to try to avoid the insured-against contingencies now that they will be compensated should they occur. Moral hazard, however, is a problem that confronts both public and private insurance schemes alike.

15. In defending the original 1911 National Insurance Bill in parliamentary debates in Britain, Winston Churchill referred explicitly to this problem of adverse

selection to justify a compulsory rather than a voluntary scheme (Churchill, 1911, 495).

16. Epstein (1985, 649–650) offers a parallel example: "A life insurance program that covers all the workers in a firm may find that all are subject to a common risk of death. . . . So long as the insured risks may be interdependent, the insurance company is no longer in the enviable position of a bookie who stands to win no matter what state of the world emerges. Instead, if the common risk materializes, the insurance company stands to suffer very heavy losses. If all other factors were held constant, insurance companies would drop out of a market" where risks were interdependent in this way.

17. That, in any case, is the role it must logically play, and the defense to which it must ultimately appeal. In introducing social insurance programs, of course, politicians are always anxious to reassure one and all that this will never happen; sometimes they go so far as to suggest that administrative arrangements are such that it cannot happen. But that is just rhetoric.

18. For a discussion of how "social" insurance differs from "true" (i.e., private) insurance, see Hayek (1960, ch. 19) and Titmuss (1968, 173–187). On the nonredistributive nature of insurance, see Goodin (1982, ch. 8) and Dryzek and Goodin (1986).

19. For a survey, see Le Grand and Robinson (1976). Welfare economics aside, there are also various macrosociological arguments to the effect that welfare state redistributions are politically necessary to "legitimate" market society and thus quiet social unrest. The focus of those arguments, however, is on the question of why legitimation is sought: an explanatory task. The focus of the present chapter is on the question of how legitimation is achieved morally: a justificatory task.

20. Indeed, according to Macpherson (1985, 1), "The idea of economic justice arose only when market-determined systems of production and distribution encroached on politically determined ones. . . . It arose then as a defensive action against the encroachment of the market on traditional political society."

21. As I show elsewhere (Goodin, 1985b; 1987), this is a duty (a) not yourself to harm and (b) to prevent others from harming those who are vulnerable to your own actions and choices or dependent upon you for protection from third parties' actions and choices. Thus, those who attach great significance to the distinction between positive and negative duties can construe much positive assistance to people as actually just discharging our negative duties to prevent harm from coming to them.

22. Elsewhere (Goodin, 1985b,d) I have argued at length that there is such a moral principle, providing evidence for it from the way that our particularly strong "special duties" are treated in ordinary moral discourse and, especially, in the formal embodiment of that, the common law.

23. On price discrimination in general, see Pigou (1932, pt. 2, ch. 17) and Robinson (1933, bk. 5). Sraffa (1926, 549), although explaining the attachment between particular consumers and particular suppliers differently, similarly shows that even with "a very slight degree" of attachment there is a general tendency for "the general price of the product . . . to reach the same level as that which

would be fixed by a single monopolistic association in accordance with the ordinary principles of monopoly."

24. That is why we give priority, at least of a "temporal" sort, to satisfying needs (Goodin, 1985a).

25. Thus, Atkinson and Stiglitz (1980, 349) write, "A second illustration of the consequences of market failure is provided by the case of an intertemporal economy where only spot markets exist—no future contracts can be entered into. (One important reason for the non-existence of futures markets is that the agents potentially involved may not be alive.) In this situation it is possible that the competitive economy may follow a path that is Pareto-inferior."

26. Similar risks of self-induced defaulting are presumably what led to the prohibition of "post-obits"—that is, the practice of borrowing money against an expected future bequest. The more money an heir-presumptive raises in this way, the greater the incentive for the benefactor to write him out of his will (Trollope, 1883).

27. Often it is said that, on the contrary, desperation bidding leads people to end up buying too much of the good in question and paying too much for it (Zeckhauser, 1973, 162; Calabresi and Bobbitt, 1978, 115–122). That is true, however, only if we take people's *ex ante* judgments (as reflected in insurance decisions they have made) as authoritative over their *ex post* judgments (of how much they now want to spend to cure this disease, for example). There is no reason to do so. We know that people systematically underinsure, for all sorts of perfectly understandable (if utterly irrational) psychological reasons. See Goodin, 1982, chs. 3 and 8; Kahneman, Slovic, and Tversky, 1982; and Sugden, 1982a, 213–214.

28. As Schumpeter (1950, 254) says, "volitions and inferences that are imposed upon the electorate obviously do not qualify for ultimate data of the democratic process." Just as those who are dependent upon others are at risk of having their wills *bent* by them, so too might those under the influence of others sometimes be at risk of having their wills *subverted* by them. It is the latter sort of interference—via the effects of propaganda, advertising, and pressure-group activity in particular—that most worried Schumpeter himself. And it was that which led him to recommend that the competitive struggle for people's votes be confined to the choice of leaders, rather than to the choice of policies themselves.

29. This is a central theme in the civic humanist tradition traced by Pocock (1975; 1985). It runs through the Putney debates (Woodhouse, 1951, 82–83), Jefferson's *Notes on Virginia* (1785, query 19), and Blackstone's *Commentaries on the Laws of England* (1783, bk. 1, ch. 2, sec. 2). As Blackstone writes, "If it were probable that every man would give his vote freely and without influence of any kind, then every member of the community, however poor, should have a vote in electing . . . delegates. . . . But, since that can hardly be expected in persons of indigent fortunes, or such as are under the immediate dominion of others, all popular states have been obliged to establish certain qualifications, whereby some who are suspected to have no will of their own are excluded from voting, in order to set other individuals, whose wills may be supposed

independent, more thoroughly upon a level with each other" (cf. Macpherson, 1962, ch. 3; 1973, ch. 12; 1985, 102). Similar themes were sounded in Norwegian and German suffrage debates (Bendix and Rokkan, 1964, 97). This theme, although submerged in later discussions (Miller, 1978), arguably remains always central to the deeper liberal theory of citizenship (van Gunsteren, 1978).

30. At least it served as the excuse; Kousser (1983) argues that the real reasons were often otherwise.

31. The other members of this conventional catalog—Catholics and Jews— were presumably excluded less on grounds of dependence upon anyone else than on grounds of voluntary subservience to someone (their submission to a higher spiritual authority counting as the functional equivalent of allegiance to a foreign crown). Interestingly, ways were found to argue for extending the suffrage to wage-earners even within this larger logic: "Wage earners outside the immediate household of the employer" were, in some sense perhaps, "dependent" upon their employers; "but it was not evident that they would inevitably follow their employers politically" in the way that servants in their own households would ordinarily have done (Bendix and Rokkan, 1964, 98). Notice, in this connection, Tocqueville's (1840, vol. 2, ch. 5) report: "In democracies, . . . the servant always thinks of himself as a temporary inmate in his master's house. He has not known his ancestors and will not see his descendants [as masters would have done in aristocracies]; he has nothing lasting to expect from them. Why, then, should he identify his life with his master's, and what reason could there be for such a strange sacrifice of himself [merging his sense of his own self and interests with those of his master]?"

32. "Dependence begets subservience and venality, suffocates the germ of virtue, and prepares fit tools for the designs of ambition," inveighs Jefferson in his *Notes on Virginia* (1785, query 19). Jefferson's own advice to his fellow Virginians was that, "while we have land to labor, . . . let us never wish to see our citizens occupied at a workbench, or twirling a distaff"; he admonished them to engage in husbandry rather than in manufacture or commerce. Others writing at about the same time, however, saw commerce as an alternative solution to the same problem of personal dependence, pointing to "the mobility of the individual in an increasingly commercial society" (Pocock, 1985, 107).

33. Worse, when many U.S. state courts found that public assistance constituted a "payment of gratuities to individuals from the public treasury" of the sort normally prohibited by state constitutions, it was justified instead by appeal to the state's "police power" (Smith, 1949, 269). Looking upon public assistance payments as a mode of social control, in this way, not only allows but encourages administrators of the programs to set terms and conditions upon payment of benefits, in ways that compromise the independence of recipients.

34. It is never possible to eliminate discretion entirely, for reasons discussed in Goodin (1986). The ideal is to push those discretions that cannot be eliminated as far back from the point of service delivery as possible. Thus, welfare recipients are still dependent upon legislators to enact and to fund social welfare programs; but that dependence is less worrisome, since there is so much less scope for recipients to be exploited at such a distance from the point of service provision.

But it is not always feasible to push inevitable discretions back away from the point of service delivery in this way. Street-level bureaucrats will, in practice, continue to exercise some discretionary powers—some of it within the rules, and much of it outside them (van Gunsteren 1978, 29–32; Lipsky 1980)—whatever we do. The goal of the welfare state must be to minimize that, even if it cannot completely eliminate it.

35. Some would suggest that we disenfranchise those with an interest in the outcome, preventing welfare recipients from voting up welfare payments just as we prevent members of the U.S. Congress from voting up their own salaries during a session of Congress. Then, however, all owners of private property would have to be disenfranchised, since they too clearly benefit from certain of the state's activities (e.g., the exercise of its police power). See Kousser, 1983, fn. 30.

36. Notice the emphasis upon "dependency" in the early and influential opinion of Justice Daniel Brewer (1875, 74–75): "Something more than poverty . . . is essential to charge the state with the duty of support [of indigents]. It is, strictly speaking, the pauper, and not the poor man, who has claims on public charity. It is not one who is in want merely, but one who, being in want, is unable to prevent or remove such want. There is the idea of helplessness as well as of destitution. We speak of those whom society must aid as the dependent classes, not simply because they do depend on society, but because they cannot do otherwise than thus depend."

37. For examples, see ten Broek and Wilson, 1954, 264–265; Reich, 1965, 1247–1251; and UK SBC, 1977, para. 1.43.

38. Goodin (1987) shows that all exploitation is the exploitation of dependencies or vulnerabilities—terms that I here use interchangeably. Not all forms of unfair dealing necessarily involve the exploitation of such vulnerabilities or dependencies, of course. Being tricked into paying vastly over the market price for an item through fraudulent misrepresentation of the goods is David Miller's example (personal correspondence, 1986). But neither do all forms of unfair dealing necessarily involve exploitation. It would, to persist with Miller's example, be odd to say that everyone who has been disadvantaged by a breach of the Trades Description Act has been *exploited*, as opposed to having been cheated, tricked, or duped. (Certain things *about* them—for example, their ignorance or gullibility—have been exploited, to be sure; but then, that is merely to say that the buyer was indeed vulnerable to and dependent upon the seller for an honest description of the goods.) Insofar as a form of unfair dealing does not involve the exploitation of vulnerabilities or dependencies, it seems better not to describe it as a case of exploitation at all but, rather, as a case of one of those other sorts of abuse.

39. If the goal were "eliminating dependencies," interventions in the labor market (e.g., full-employment policies) or in the capital market (e.g., "demogrants") might be more appropriate. But since the problem is instead the exploitation rather than the mere existence of dependency, the welfare state's interventions in the market for goods constitutes a more direct solution.

40. These are discussed in more detail in Goodin (1985b, ch. 7).

41. I say "truly exploited," because the monopoly supplier of desirable but not strictly necessary luxury goods can take advantage of his market power to charge more for figs in our village than the market price in the nearest big city, where there are many suppliers. That might, at first brush, appear exploitative. But my inclination is to say that it is not "truly" so: There is nothing particularly unfair about seizing such advantages, and it is the "taking of unfair advantage" that constitutes exploitation, as analyzed in Goodin (1987).

Arguably, this condition should be phrased "the subordinate party must *believe* he needs the resource"—for people will be as desperate to satisfy (mis)perceived needs as genuine ones. I prefer the present formulation on the grounds that, although any given perceptions may be in error, all people's perceptions are unlikely to be (or remain, even if all briefly are) in error; and so far as the public policy question of what resources should be publicly provided is concerned, it is the "standard" perception rather than anyone's idiosyncratic perception of need that matters.

42. See, for example, Sraffa, 1926, 545–546; Hayek, 1960, ch. 9; and Plant, 1985, 305.

43. As Rousseau (1762, bk. 2) points out, "If there is any cure for this social evil [of dependence of men on men], it is to be found in the substitution of law for the individual, in arming the general will with a real strength beyond the power of any individual will. If the laws of nations, like the laws of nature, could never be broken by any human power, dependence on men would become dependence on things; all the advantages of a state of nature would be combined with all the advantages of social life in the commonwealth."

44. See, for example, Smith, 1946, 1949, 1955; Marshall, 1949; Keith-Lucas, 1953; Reich, 1964, 1965; Goodin, 1985b, ch. 7, 1985c. It is of course possible that people's "welfare rights" might conflict with one another. My argument here does not deny this fact, but merely implies (a) that that should be avoided insofar as possible, through, for instance, generous funding and proper structuring of the assistance programs designed to meet people's basic needs; and (b) that where such conflicts are unavoidable, there should insofar as possible be some central, legislative determination of which right wins out over which other, so as to avoid a conflict of laws or of rights giving rise to discretion in those administrators who are directly responsible for dispensing the benefits. Neither does my argument here deny the fact that the political behavior of would-be welfare beneficiaries might be skewed by the availability (or possibility) of social welfare programs. But saying that people are dependent upon programs, and that their dependence upon these programs skews their votes, is importantly different from saying that people are dependent upon particular other individuals who can thereby control their votes. In the welfare state, the poor are not dependent upon the arbitrary will of any other person. They are no less free to vote independently than is the oil tycoon who depends upon the government's policy of oil depletion tax allowances for his profits.

45. The point is not that people's tastes change but, rather, that their circumstances do. Suppose people have a tendency to get desperate (and hence exploitable) whenever there is a threat of their present standard of living being

reduced by, say, 50 percent or more. Then the higher the present standard of living, the higher their "desperation point," and hence the higher the "social minimum" that the welfare state in their society will have to guarantee. Although this explanation of the relativity of the "needs" to which the welfare state responds is not predicated on changes in people's tastes, it *is* predicated on other facts about people's tastes, and in that way provides an essentially subjectivist account of the phenomenon. There may also be objective grounds for taking account of relativities, as shown in Sen (1983).

46. Perhaps the most dramatic examples are the late nineteenth-century American "seed and feed" cases, holding that farmers fallen on hard times could under the Poor Law be given grain to eat but not grain to plant or to feed to their livestock. The result was to guarantee that the farmers would be dependent upon Poor Law relief in perpetuity, rather than reestablishing an independent economic existence for themselves after a bad harvest in one year (Brewer, 1875).

47. In van Gunsteren's (1978, 29) phrasing, "Effective citizenship does not only require a political say and a legally protected status, but also a certain level of socio-economic security. Older theories of citizenship did not ignore this requirement. They solved the problem it posed by denying citizenship to those who did not have independent and secure socio-economic positions already. The welfare state accepts all its subjects as citizens and aims to guarantee to all and each of them the minimal socio-economic security that the free exercise of citizenship requires."

REFERENCES

Anderson, M. 1978. *Welfare.* Stanford, Calif.: Hoover Institution Press.

Arrow, K.J. 1963. Uncertainty and the welfare economics of medical care. *American Economic Review* 53: 941–73.

————. 1972. Gifts and exchanges. *Philosophy & Public Affairs* 1: 343–62.

Arrow, K.J., and Hahn, F.H. 1971. *General competitive analysis.* San Francisco: Holden-Day.

Atkinson, A.B., and Stiglitz, J.E. 1980. *Lectures on public economics.* Maidenhead, Berkshire: McGraw-Hill.

Baldwin, D.A. 1980. Interdependence and power: a conceptual analysis. *International Organization* 34: 351–79.

Bator, F.M. 1958. The anatomy of market failure. *Quarterly Journal of Economics* 72: 351–79.

Bendix, R., and Rokkan, S. 1964. The extension of citizenship to the lower classes. In R. Bendix, *Nation-building and citizenship,* pp. 74–104. New York: Wiley.

Blackstone, W. 1783. *Commentaries on the laws of England.* London: Strahan.

Brewer, D.J. 1875. Opinion of the Kansas Supreme Court. *Griffith v. Osawkee Township.* 14 Kansas 418. Reprinted in E. Abbott, ed., *Public assistance,* pp. 73–80. Chicago: University of Chicago Press, 1940.

Briggs, A. 1961. The welfare state in historical perspective. *Archives Européennes de Sociologie* 2: 221–58.

Browning, E.K. 1975. The externality argument for in-kind transfers: Some critical remarks. *Kyklos* 28: 526–44.

Buchanan, A.E. 1984. The right to a decent minimum of health care. *Philosophy and Public Affairs* 13: 55–78.

Calabresi, G., and Bobbitt, P. 1978. *Tragic choices.* New York: Norton.

Churchill, W. 1911. Speech on the National Insurance Bill. *Hansard's parliamentary debates (Commons),* 5th series, 26: 493–510.

Cohen, G.A. 1981. Freedom, justice and capitalism. *New Left Review* 126: 3–16.

Devlin, P. 1965. *The enforcement of morals.* London: Oxford University Press.

Dryzek, J., and Goodin, R.E. 1986. Risk-sharing and social justice: The motivational foundations of the post-war welfare state. *British Journal of Political Science* 16: 1–34.

Duncan, G.J. 1984. *Years of poverty, years of plenty.* Ann Arbor, Mich.: Institute for Social Research, University of Michigan.

Epstein, R.A. 1985. Products liability as an insurance market. *Journal of Legal Studies* 14: 645–69.

Frankfurt, H. 1973. Coercion and moral responsibility. In T. Honderich, ed., *Essays on freedom of action.* London: Routledge & Kegan Paul. Pp. 63–86.

Friedman, M. 1962. *Capitalism and freedom.* Chicago: University of Chicago Press.

Gibson, D.M. 1985. The dormouse syndrome: Restructuring the dependency of the elderly. *Australian and New Zealand Journal of Sociology* 21: 44–63.

Goodin, R.E. 1976. *The politics of rational man.* London: Wiley.

————. 1982. *Political theory and public policy.* Chicago: University of Chicago Press.

————. 1985a. The priority of needs. *Philosophy & Phenomenological Research* 45: 615–25.

————. 1985b. *Protecting the vulnerable.* Chicago: University of Chicago Press.

————. 1985c. Self-reliance versus the welfare state. *Journal of Social Policy* 14: 25–47.

————. 1985d. Vulnerabilities and responsibilities: An ethical defense of the welfare state. *American Political Science Review* 79: 775–87.

————. 1986. Welfare, rights and discretion. *Oxford Journal of Legal Studies* 6: 232–61.

————. Exploiting a situation and exploiting a person. In A. Reeve, ed., *Modern theories of exploitation.* London: Sage.

Goodin, R.E., and Le Grand, J., et al. 1987. *Not only the poor: The middle classes and the welfare state.* London: Allen & Unwin.

Hayek, F.A. 1960. *The constitution of liberty.* London: Routledge & Kegan Paul.

Hirsch, F. 1976. *Social limits to growth.* Cambridge, Mass.: Harvard University Press.

Jefferson, T. 1785. *Notes on Virginia.* New York: Harper & Row, 1964.

de Jouvenel, B. 1960. Toward a "communist welfare state": The logic of economics. *Problems of Communism* 9: 13–16.

Kahneman, D.; Slovic, P.; and Tversky, A., eds. 1982. *Judgement under uncertainty.* Cambridge: Cambridge University Press.

Kane, R.L., and Kane, R.A. 1979. Alternatives to institutional care of the elderly. RAND Paper P-6256. Santa Monica, Calif.: RAND Corporation.

Keith-Lucas, A. 1953. Political theory implicit in social case-work theory. *American Political Science Review* 47: 1076–91.

Kousser, J.M. 1983. Suffrage and political participation. Social Science Working Paper no. 471, California Institute of Technology, Pasadena, Calif. Forthcoming in J.P. Greene, ed., *Encyclopedia of American history.*

Kronman, A.T. 1983. Paternalism and the law of contracts. *Yale Law Journal* 92: 763–98.

Le Grand, J., and Robinson, R. 1976. *The economics of social problems.* London: Macmillan.

Lipsky, M. 1980. *Street-level bureaucracy.* New York: Russell Sage Foundation.

Lowenthal, R. 1960. Toward a "communist welfare state": Ideology, power and welfare. *Problems of Communism* 9: 18–21.

Macpherson, C.B. 1962. *The political theory of possessive individualism.* Oxford: Clarendon Press.

––––––. 1973. *Democratic theory.* Oxford: Clarendon Press.

––––––. 1985. *The rise and fall of economic justice.* Oxford: Oxford University Press.

Margolis, J. 1955. A comment on the pure theory of public expenditure. *Review of Economics and Statistics* 37: 347–9.

Marshall, T.H. 1949. *Citizenship and social class.* The Marshall Lectures, Cambridge University, 1949. Reprinted in T.H. Marshall, *Class, citizenship and social development,* pp. 70–134. Chicago: University of Chicago Press, 1977.

Miller, D. 1978. Democracy and social justice. *British Journal of Political Science* 8: 1–19.

––––––. 1981. Market neutrality and the failure of cooperatives. *British Journal of Political Science* 11: 309–29.

Moon, J. Donald (1986). Thin selves/rich lives. Paper presented to the Foundations of Political Theory Group, American Political Science Association, Washington, D.C.

Murray, C.A. 1982. The two wars against poverty: Economic growth and the Great Society. *Public Interest* 69: 3–16.

––––––. 1984. *Losing ground.* New York: Basic Books.

Nove, A. 1960. Toward a "communist welfare state": Social welfare in the USSR. *Problems of Communism* 9: 1–10.

Nozick, R. 1972. Coercion. In P. Laslett, W.G. Runciman, and Q. Skinner, eds. *Philosophy, politics and society,* 4th series, pp. 101–35. Oxford: Blackwell.

Okun, A. 1975. *Equality and efficiency.* Washington, D.C.: Brookings Institution.

Pigou, A.C. 1932. *The economics of welfare,* 4th ed. London: Macmillan.

Piven, F.F., and Cloward, R. 1971. *Regulating the poor.* New York: Random House.

Plant, R. 1985. Welfare and the value of liberty. *Government & Opposition* 20: 297–314.

Pocock, J.G.A. 1975. *The Machiavellian moment.* Princeton, N.J.: Princeton University Press.

———. 1985. *Virtue, commerce and history.* Cambridge: Cambridge University Press.

Postow, B.C. 1978–9. Economic dependence and self-respect. *Philosophical Forum* 10: 181–205.

Reich, C.A. 1964. The new property. *Yale Law Journal* 73: 733–87.

———. 1965. Individual rights and social welfare: The emerging legal issues. *Yale Law Journal* 74: 1245–57.

Rimlinger, G.V. 1961. Social security, incentives and controls in the U.S. and U.S.S.R. *Comparative Studies in Society and History* 4: 104–24.

Robinson, J. 1933. *The economics of imperfect competition.* London: Macmillan.

Rousseau, J.-J. 1762. *Emile,* trans. B. Foxley. London: Dent, 1971.

Schumpeter, J.A. 1950. *Capitalism, socialism and democracy.* 3rd ed. New York: Harper.

Sen, A.K. 1983. Poor, relatively speaking. *Oxford Economic Papers* 35: 153–69.

Shonfield, A. 1965. *Modern capitalism.* London: Oxford University Press.

Smith, A.D. 1946. Community prerogative and the legal rights and freedom of the individual. *Social Security Bulletin* 9 (pt.8): 6–10.

———. 1949. Public assistance as a social obligation. *Harvard Law Review* 63: 266–88.

———. 1955. *The right to life.* Chapel Hill: University of North Carolina Press.

Sraffa, P. 1926. The laws of returns under competitive conditions. *Economic Journal* 36: 535–50.

Steiner, P.O. 1970. The public sector and the public interest. In R.H. Haveman and J. Margolis, eds., *Public expenditure and policy analysis,* pp. 21–58. Chicago: Markham.

Sugden, R. 1982a. Hard luck stories: The problem of the uninsured in a laissez-faire society. *Journal of Social Policy* 11: 201–16.

———. 1982b. On the economics of philanthropy. *Economic Journal* 92: 341–50.

ten Broek, J., and Wilson, R.B. 1954. Public assistance and social insurance—a normative evaluation. *UCLA Law Review* 1: 237–302.

Titmuss, R.M. 1968. *Commitment to welfare.* London: Allen & Unwin.

Tobin, J. 1970. On limiting the domain of inequality. *Journal of Law & Economics* 13: 363–78.

Tocqueville, A. de. 1835. Memoir on pauperism. *Public Interest* 70 (1983): 102–20.

———. 1840. *Democracy in America,* trans. G. Lawrence, ed. J.P. Mayer and M. Lerner. New York: Harper and Row, 1966.

Trollope, A. 1883. *Mr. Scarborough's family.* London: Oxford University Press, 1973.

UK SBC (United Kingdom, Supplementary Benefits Commission). 1977. *Annual report 1976.* Cmnd. 6910. London: HMSO.

van Gunsteren, H. 1978. Notes on a theory of citizenship. In P. Birnbaum, J. Lively, and G. Parry, eds., *Democracy, consensus and social contract,* pp. 9–35. London: Sage.

Weale, A. 1982. *Political theory and social policy.* London: Macmillan.

Weitzman, M.L. 1977. Is the price system or rationing more effective in getting a commodity to those who need it most? *Bell Journal of Economics* 8: 517–24.

Wilson, J.R.S. 1978. In one another's power. *Ethics* 88: 299–315.

Woodhouse, A.S.P., ed. 1951. *Puritanism and liberty.* London: Dent.

Zeckhauser, R.J. 1973. Coverage for catastrophic illness. *Public Policy* 21: 149–72.

3

NEEDS, AGENCY,
AND WELFARE RIGHTS

A fully developed theory of rights has to provide an account of at least four things:

1. The agent to whom the rights are ascribed.
2. The features of the agent that justify the ascription of such rights.
3. The nature of the objects, resources, states of affairs, processes, or forbearances to which the rights are rights.
4. The range of individuals or institutions who have the duties or obligations that correspond to the rights of other agents: that is, who or what has the duty to respect, implement, or satisfy the rights that individuals have.

Following Gewirth (1982, 3) we might put these features into the following formula: **A** has a right to **X** against **B** in virtue of **Y**.

So we have to give an account of the agent, **A**; what it is about the nature of **A** that grants the right, **Y**; the nature of the right asserted, **X**; and against whom it is asserted, **B**. Can a theory of welfare as a basic right satisfy the various elements of this formula in a cogent and coherent manner? I shall argue that it can, basing the justification of the right on an account of the needs of a rational agent. However, as we shall see, such a view also challenges some generally accepted assumptions about the scope of the responsibilities and obligations that accompany rights. My strategy in this chapter will be to consider ways in which arguments in relation to the four features mentioned in Gewirth's formula are deployed in relation to rights such as life or liberty, and then to try to show that there are corresponding and equally cogent arguments in the case of the rights to welfare.

Two elements (at least) of Gewirth's formula are interdependent— the account of the agent to whom rights are ascribed and the characteristics in virtue of which they are ascribed (i.e., features **A** and **Y** in the formula). Clearly these cannot be wholly separated because the features in terms of which rights are justified will have a clear bearing upon the identity of the agents to whom they are ascribed.

What might such features be? In answering this question it is, I believe, possible to apply two formal constraints upon any potential answer. First, if certain features of existence are potential grounds for basic rights, then these features must be universal. That is to say, if they are to underpin a theory of universal rights, then those features of life in virtue of which such rights are held must themselves be universal. By "universal" here I mean not specific to culture, religion, or ethnic origin.

The second constraint is moral relevance. Because the attribution of rights specifies a range of claims and duties that rights bearers can hold against one another, these rights presuppose some moral sensibility, an ability to claim rights and to recognize duties as binding in the light of rights. As rights specify a sphere of moral relationships, those features of life that are held to ground rights must be morally relevant. Hence, although it might be a distinctive feature of human beings that they possess ear lobes, this could not be a ground for the ascription of rights because, however biologically distinctive this feature is, it is not morally relevant! Given these two constraints, we can say that any account in virtue of what X's rights are will have to be both universal and morally relevant.

The criterion of moral relevance here can be taken in two ways. It could mean that a proposed criterion is part of a particular substantive morality, or it could mean that it is a presupposition of any possible morality. It is fairly clear that a theory of universal rights could be compatible with the former view only if this particular substantive morality could objectively and rationally be grounded so that other individuals accepting other moral outlooks would have to accept *it* as rational and fundamental. However, the history of moral thought since Plato does not give us any grounds for optimism for believing that such a foundational and acceptable moral theory could be arrived at. The diversity of values is so great that if the ground for ascribing rights to individuals could be derived only from a particular substantive moral code, then, although such a view of rights might be cogent and authoritative *within* that morality, its authority would extend only as far as the general authority of that morality. Thus, to provide the grounds for a general or universal theory of rights we must look at the other possibility. Instead of looking to a *particular* moral code or outlook, we should rather look at the question of whether, given the facts of moral diversity, there are still any universal features of human life that appear to be necessary presuppositions or conditions for morality, whatever such moralities may turn out to be. If there are any such features, then they would be universal and, as presuppositions of morality, necessarily morally relevant.

This basically Kantian way of posing the problem seeks a transcendental deduction of the grounds of rights by reflecting upon the necessary preconditions of morality. Kant, of course, argued that such preconditions were to be understood in terms of rational, autonomous agency and the ability to formulate rules of universal scope (Kant, 1974). These features of existence would be very difficult to deny in terms of moral relevance in the sense that any moral code is presumably going to invoke ideas of ought and ought not, right and wrong, good and bad— all notions that presuppose a capacity for choice between alternatives, at least as they are envisaged *within* that morality. We might argue with Kant that rational agency could be seen to be a necessary condition of any moral code inasmuch as any such a code will prescribe ends to be followed and alternatives to be avoided, and these presuppose a capacity for agency. This does not mean that agency would of itself have to be rated highly or at all within the moral code in question; only that, recognized or not, it is implicitly assumed in the very notion of moral conduct.

On this view the capacity for rational agency might be regarded as both a universal and necessary condition for morality and therefore a possible foundation for a theory of rights. What sense of rights could the idea of rational agency or autonomy ground? One answer is: rights to forbearances of various sorts. If we emphasize autonomy as the basis of rights, then it seems an easy thing to move to the Nozickian position that the central way of protecting human inviolability is through a set of rights that impose constraints upon the possible range of interferences by others (Nozick, 1974). In other words, rights are to be understood negatively as requiring the absence of interference, coercion, assault, killing, and so on.

This view would, of course, exclude the idea that agency could act as a ground for welfare rights understood as the positive right to resources rather than as the negative view of liberty. If agency and autonomy are universal, necessary features of a morality that could act as a basis for rights, then on a negative view of liberty, freedom and autonomy are diminished only by intentional coercion. My freedom to choose and to act is constrained only if there is an identifiable individual who is intentionally coercing me. A negative account of rights could then cope with these sorts of infringements of autonomy because such rights demand forbearance from coercion and interference of all sorts. However, on this view, freedom and autonomy require not resources and opportunities but merely the absence of coercion. This kind of autonomy can ground a negative view of rights; that is, it is in virtue of their possession of autonomy that individuals should be protected by a set of rights against coercion and interference. However, it cannot ground a more positive view of rights as rights to resources, just because on the negative view of liberty the absence of resources is not a restriction of freedom. The only restrictions on freedom arise from the intentional coercive actions of other agents.

This negative view of the requirements of autonomy is based upon the following considerations. It is argued that there must be a clear distinction drawn between freedom and ability in the sense that there is a wide range of things I am unable to do that it would be absurd to regard as infringements of my liberty. These inabilities may be of all sorts:

1. Logical inabilities: I cannot draw a picture of a mountain without a valley.
2. Physical impossibilities: I cannot as a male bear a child.
3. Inabilities arising from my own nature and character: I am unable to become a creative mathematician.
4. Episodic inabilities: I cannot ride my bicycle uphill today—the wind is too strong.
5. Inabilities arising from my own earlier choices, which have affected my present circumstances: I am now unable to become a Roman Catholic priest; I am unable to run in a marathon.
6. Inabilities arising from circumstances that are not alterable by human action: An irreparable lesion in the spinal cord may limit physical activity.

There are, no doubt, many other forms of inability that could be categorized in different ways, but in each of these cases the limitations on my power are not caused by intentional coercion; and although in each case my abilities may be limited, my freedom is not. I am free to do these things; I am unable to do them. This point is made very clearly by Hayek in *The Constitution of Liberty:* "We presuppose a human agent if we say that we have been coerced. . . . Coercion implies both the threat of inflicting harm and the intention thereby to bring about certain conduct" (1960, 9).

Given this definition of coercion, autonomy does not require resources; on the contrary it requires the absence of intentional restraint and coercion. Autonomy is thus to be protected by negative rights and not by guaranteed rights to resources.

There is a subsidiary argument here, turning upon the intentional nature of coercion. Economic markets in particular are not to be seen as coercive in their outcomes for the worst-off members of society. The poverty that an individual may experience as the result of the operation of a free market is not, on this view, to be construed as a limitation of liberty and autonomy. The reason for this is a conjunction of the points made above. First, the possession of resources, powers, and opportunities is distinct from liberty, which is freedom from coercion; second, the outcomes of markets are an unintended and unforeseen result of individual decisions to buy and sell, taken on all sorts of different grounds. Hence, poverty is not caused by intentional action and is not a restriction of liberty. Sir Keith Joseph and Jonathan Sumption, in their book entitled *Equality* (1979), have clearly seen the point at stake here. In a chapter devoted to arguing that poverty is not unfreedom, they argue that the contrary view—that it is a limitation on liberty— would require coercive action on the part of the state to remove poverty in order to secure liberty as a basic right. Accepting the arguments stated above, they reject this approach.

Hence, on this view, although agency, autonomy, and liberty are universal and necessary preconditions for any moral code, they do not imply any welfare rights. The demand for autonomy is the demand to be left alone, requiring a right to forebearance rather than rights to welfare. However, there are arguments that can weaken the force of this position.

The first is the idea, which John Rawls has developed, of the worth or value of liberty. For if freedom is the absence of intentional coercion, we must surely be able to explain what the worth of liberty is to an individual. Why do we want to be free from coercion? The answer must surely be that if we are free from coercion we shall be able to do more of what we want to do. In this sense the idea of ability, of being enabled to do more things, enters into the justification of liberty because it contributes to the worth of liberty. So if we are interested in the worth and value of liberty to an individual person, we must also be concerned with what the individual is able to do. This would be the basis for saying that the value of liberty, as an effective power to act, requires resources. Thus, the value of liberty requires not just rights against intentional coercion but also rights to those resources, which would secure the same value of liberty for each individual considered as a moral equal. If the power to do something is central to why we find liberty valuable, and if we believe in an equal right to liberty, there is no clear reason why this should be defined only as an equal basic liberty to be free from coercion, as opposed to an equal right to those basic resources that are necessary for individual agency and that will secure an equal basic value of liberty between individuals.

These points about the interrelationship between liberty and ability or power are also reflected in our ordinary language distinctions. For example, if one is freed from a clear, direct intentional coercion, (e.g., the removal of handcuffs), we could say that this removal enabled one to do certain things (if one chooses) that one was not able to do before. On the other hand, to place such coercion on someone is to render one unable to do what one was able to do before. There are therefore great dangers in arguing that to be free is to be protected by rights against coercion, but that one's ability and power need not be protected at all by rights.

However, not all inabilities should be seen as a restriction of freedom. If they are, then it would absurdly follow that the state could protect my liberty only if it could secure my omnipotence, because any restriction on my ability or power would be a limitation on my freedom. If we wish to provide a defense of positive freedom and the positive welfare rights that would flow from this, we will have to try to define a class of basic goods that are necessary conditions of agency, as such, and should therefore be protected in terms of rights, and distinguish between these goods and all the other goods that a particular agent might desire.

The attempt to define a class of basic goods of agency is important in another way, too. Many critics of positive liberty have objected to it because it moralizes the concept. I am free only if I am able to do certain things and these things are sanctioned by a specific moral code. This definition is held to be illiberal and potentially totalitarian. If we can identify in a morally neutral way a set of basic goods of agency, then both objections to positive freedom, at least in this restricted form, would fail.

This strategy has two advantages. First, it would meet the Hayekian objection that the positive libertarian cannot distinguish between freedom and omnipotence; it would also be more logically coherent with a theory of rights because it would be concerned with whether there are any basic goods of agency, autonomy, and liberty, irrespective of the particular culture within which an individual might live and the individual conceptions of the good life that individuals might be enabled to attain within that culture. In this sense, attempting to identify the basic goods that would be required by agency would meet the universalistic requirement implicit in a theory of rights.

One way of putting the point, and one that might make it sound less abstract, would be to argue in terms of needs, or basic needs. The issue can be put thus: Are there any needs basic to agency that can be defined independently of the specific needs that an individual may have in a particular culture or morality? If there are such needs, they would then define the set of basic rights that would reflect such needs.

The needs of agency will plausibly include, first of all, physical survival in the platitudinous sense that an agent is unable to exercise agency without physical integrity and survival. But there is more to the physical needs of agency than mere survival; agency must also include some element of a worthwhile life or physical well-being, because it is very difficult to imagine how a life of rational agency could ever be pursued if the whole effort of a person's life is devoted to securing the bare minimum to survive. In this sense, to secure the capacity for agency for individuals will require not just restrictions on coercion defined by negative rights but also positive rights to those resources that will contribute to both survival and well-being. Hence, food, shelter, and health care of a sort relevant to and effective in a particular society would constitute basic goods of agency. However, the capacity of agency will also require other kinds of basic goods such as education, which, in the terms relevant to a particular society, will be needed to sustain a capacity for agency, choice, and effective functioning.

The rights to freedom secured by rights to these sorts of resources is not a freedom to do any specific thing but, rather, a general set of conditions that will enable the individual to go on to the sorts of things she or he wants to do. Basic needs have to be satisfied in order to do anything at all; nonbasic needs are for those goods an individual needs to fulfill one's particular plan of life in *one person's* particular circumstances. Rights have to do with the first type of need but not with the latter. The first are universally and morally relevant; the latter are morally relevant but not universal.

So, if the ideas of agency, autonomy, and freedom are basic to morality, then they could underpin a set of rights that would be both negative rights to freedom from coercion, but also to those positive resources that are necessary conditions of acting in a purposeful way at all. These conditions would ground a positive theory of rights. At the same time it would answer the Hayekian objection that there would be no difference between freedom and omnipotence. The difference would be in terms of defining a set of necessary basic goods for liberty, rather than the optimal set of goods required for a particular free action.

This kind of argument can, I believe, provide a basis for thinking about the coherence of positive rights, and it answers the first point of the formula with which I began. It will also give us a way of characterizing those who are bearers of rights—namely, those who are capable of rational agency, or at least have the capacity for such agency.

However, when we move to other parts of the formula, the idea of positive rights to welfare runs up against a number of severe difficulties that will have to be countered before a conception of welfare rights can be regarded as morally defensible. If we concentrate attention first of all on what individuals have a right to (the X in Gewirth's formula quoted at the beginning of this chapter), then it is clear that problems arise. On a negative view of rights, what the individual has a right to is a form of forebearance on the part of others—a right to their abstaining from action. So the right to life is the right *not* to be killed, and the right to freedom of speech is the right *not* to be interfered with (unless, in exercising my right, I am interfering with another's right). Because these rights are therefore rights that certain things *not* be done, they are, so it is argued, costless and not subject to scarcity. Welfare rights, however, as rights to resources, always imply costs and scarcity. This, it is sometimes argued, entails a theoretical difference between negative and positive rights. More important, these considerations give rise to issues of practicability. Because negative rights are asserted to fore-bearances, they are costless and always practicable, whereas welfare rights always involve costs and may not be practicable. How can a theory of human rights consistently endorse a set of rights that may not be practicable, because the resources to meet them in particular society may be too great? Charles Fried poses the problem as follows:

> A positive right is a claim to something—a share in a material good, or some particular good such as the attentions of a lawyer or doctor, or perhaps a claim to a result like health or enlightenment—while a negative right is a right that something not be done to one, that some particular imposition be withheld. Positive rights are inevitably assigned to scarce goods and consequently scarcity implies a limit to the claim. Negative rights, however, the rights not to be interfered with in forbidden ways, do not appear to have such natural, such inevitable limitations. If I am left alone, the commodity I obtain does not appear of its nature to be a scarce or limited one. How can we run out of people not harming each other, not lying to each other, leaving each other alone? (1978, 110)

On this view, there is a major difference between the kinds of things to which rights are asserted as between negative rights and positive or welfare rights. The critic of welfare rights will also argue that these considerations actually strike at the heart of the rationale of rights. If positive rights are always rights to scarce resources, then, by definition, such rights cannot be realized at the same level simultaneously by all right holders. If scarcity prevents an equal realization of this right, then there will have to be a rationing procedure to determine whose rights are to be realized to which resources in a set of given circumstances. The critic will argue that these decisions will typically be made on consequentialist or utilitarian grounds (Glover, 1977), whereas the whole thrust and rationale of rights-based theories is against consequentialist and utilitarian considerations—that there are ways of dealing with people that are wrong irrespective of the calculation of consequences. However, the very fact of scarcity plunges us into consequentialist considerations. Take, for example, the right to life as construed as a right to resources rather than as the negative right not to be killed. If circumstances arose in which there is only one life-saving resource with two persons having a right to it, then assuming there are no overriding clinical reasons for giving that resource to one rather than to the other, the distribution of the resource will be based upon consequentialist arguments such as a cost-benefit analysis or whatever. In that sense, the positive right to life cannot be assigned or respected without getting into utilitarian calculation. However, if the right to life is the negative one of not killing, then, so it is argued, the failure to give a life-saving resource to **A** does not, on **A**'s death, mean that **A** has been killed. Rather, it will be said that he or she died of, for example, kidney failure, not as the intentional result of the failure to provide dialysis. Hence, negative rights to the nonperformance of actions imply no scarcity, and so enable us to steer clear of utilitarian calculation.

These are very cogent points, and any theory of positive rights has to confront them. There are two basic issues here: the extent to which negative rights can be regarded as costless and the problems of acts and omissions in relation to forbearance. The first of these is easier to deal with than the second.

There is a common initial objection to the point that Charles Fried makes—namely, that negative rights are not costless because the appropriate amount of forbearance may not be present. Thus, protecting negative rights will require legislation, sanctions, police, law courts, and prisons, and these are not costless. In this sense, in the world as it is, the decision of how far to go in the legal protection and enforcement of negative rights may well involve utilitarian calculation. However, the critic of welfare rights could still argue that there is a logical or conceptual difference in the sense that we could imagine a world—for example, a community of saints—in which there was always the degree of forbearance required to secure negative rights in a costless and unconstrained way, whereas even in such a world positive rights are rights to resources and will still involve utilitarian calculation. In such a possible world, therefore, we can see the logical difference between positive and negative rights, even though in the world in which we live the differences are less obvious in practice.

However, this is a difficult thesis to sustain, not just because of its counterfactual basis but also because a very similar counterfactual is open to the defender of welfare rights. One can envisage a possible world without material scarcity, and in such a world securing the rights to welfare goods would be costless. In other words, both counterfactuals are about scarcity. The first imagines a world in which there is no scarcity in those forms of human motivation that underpin forbearance; the latter imagines a world in which there is no material scarcity. Both are equally logically possible, but neither throws much light on the nature of rights. Indeed, one would be inclined to say that in a community of saints, as in a world without material scarcity, rights would be irrelevant. What would be the point of insisting upon rights in such a world? Thus, rights have a place in a world where there is scarcity both of motivation and resources; moreover, if a theory of rights is of any point and purpose in life, it has to be capable of making sense in the world as we know it, marked as that world is by scarcity.

That said, it still remains the case that, as both negative and positive rights are asserted against a background of scarcity of both motivation and material goods, there may have to be procedures for dealing with priorities to claims to rights. If these are not to be dealt with on a consequentialist/utilitarian basis, which might undermine ideas of rights, then a rights-based theory must be able to produce a decision procedure and a way of prioritizing rights claims that will avoid utilitarian calculation. This is a very difficult theoretical issue, but it is one that affects negative as much as positive rights, if my arguments in the previous paragraph are accepted as cogent. If the rights in question are supposed to be absolute, then one cannot choose one right over another on consequentialist or utilitarian grounds. However, the assumption that these rights are absolute seems unrealistic. If all rights involve costs, there may have to be choices made among them. But if they are thought of as only prima facie rights that can be overridden by consequentialist calculations, then in what sense are they rights at all? Jonathan Glover in *Causing Death and Saving Lives* has argued this point: "A doctrine of absolute rights goes further than this and excludes the possibility of ever justifying killing by its consequences. But the claim that we have only a prima facie right to life does not exclude this possibility" (1977, 83).

So, is there a decision procedure within rights theory that could avoid the collapse of absolute rights into prima facie rights and these into utilitarianism? I certainly cannot construct such a procedure here, but in any event it would have to satisfy two criteria. It would first have to be developed out of a further elaboration of the grounds in virtue of which rights are ascribed in the first place. In terms of the theory offered here, this would be a development of the theory of needs and agency. If these needs can be ascribed in greater detail than I have attempted in this chapter, then they could perhaps be put in order of priority in terms of the urgency of their satisfaction. Thus, for example, the need for survival would come before that of well-being and autonomy. However, there are difficult issues beyond this; but without confronting these, both negative and positive rights run the risk of collapsing into utilitarianism.

The other strategy is to claim that rights can only be overridden by other rights:

> A theory of *prima facie* human rights could be to the effect that only rights, and never other values or consequences, can override rights. Such a *prima facie* rights theory would have no affinities at all with utilitarianism other than having a maximising calculus. However, it would be a calculus about maximising satisfactions of rights and only that. Such a theory could be one in terms of a hierarchy of rights, such that, solely by reference to the rights involved and their place in the hierarchy, we could determine what rights were absolute. (McCloskey, 1984, 132)

Clearly such a hierarchical theory would have to develop its hierarchical structure from reflection upon, for example, the theory of needs on which rights are based, perhaps combining such reflection on needs with a contractual model of justice. In this sense, a theory of rights can only be a *part* of a theory of justice. It is necessary to elaborate the decision procedure for prioritizing rights claims in a way that seeks to avoid a collapse into utilitarianism.

There is a further difference between the nature of the rights in negative and positive rights claims—a difference that is often used by critics of welfare rights to assert that there is a categorical difference between the two sorts of rights. It is argued that the sorts of resources to which positive rights are asserted are vague and indefinite so that it is difficult to specify the corresponding duty with any precision. In the case of negative rights, the duty is clear and precise—it is abstinence from action, interference, killing, and so on. In the case of welfare rights, these rights are asserted to physical well-being, education, and so forth. If there is a corresponding duty to satisfy these rights, based as they are upon an account of the needs of a rational agent, then it is very unclear how extensive this duty is. Any attempt to define the duty with more precision will be arbitrary. For example, if we take the right to life on the negative view, it is the right not to be killed and this duty is plain and categorical; whereas if the right to life is taken to imply a right to the means to life, then it is much less clear how far this duty extends. Do I have a right to all those medical interventions and technologies that will keep me alive? If not, then the cutoff point will be arbitrary, probably based upon utilitarian calculation; it will also be inconsistent with the general theory of rights in question. This point is often made with reference to the idea of needs, which, as I have argued, provides us with the basic criteria in terms of which rights are ascribed.

The argument here is twofold. First of all, there is a claim that needs are insatiable and that they are essentially culturally relative, so that in the light of these two considerations it is impossible for a theory of needs to provide a basis for a clear duty corresponding to the rights claimed on the basis of such supposed needs. These features of needs, which yield such unclear duties, mean that institutions and authorities seeking to satisfy such needs will be forced to act in an arbitrary and discretionary way just because a theory of needs cannot provide us with a watertight account of corresponding duties (Gray, 1984). Such arbitrariness and unpredictability in relation to rights makes a nonsense of the whole idea of rights. Insofar as needs are culturally relative and relative to subcultures within a society, similar problems of corresponding duties will arise. Gray argues this thesis as follows:

> The objectivity of basic needs is equally delusive. Needs can be given no plausible cross cultural content but instead are seen to vary across different moral traditions. . . . One of the chief functions of the contemporary ideology of social justice may be, as Hayek intimates, to generate an illusion of moral agreement whereas there are in fact profound divergencies of values. (Gray, 1983, 182)

This latter point can perhaps be answered first. The argument is that there is some objectivity of basic needs as a ground for rights. This objective content will be generated by arguing not about what are the necessary conditions for pursuing a view of the good as seen within this, that, or the other moral code but, rather, by arguing that there are certain basic needs that will have to be fulfilled if *any* conception of the good is to be pursued. These needs will be both negative and positive; that is, freedoms from intentional coercion and interference are necessary for agency, but so also are certain resources such as physical well-being and education. Now it may well be that what is thought to be appropriate in the way of resources to provide well-being and education may vary from society to society, but nevertheless the right to some standard in these cases provides a benchmark against which to assess the social responsibilities of government. It has to be accepted, however, that the exact content of these responsibilities in terms of the possession of goods and services cannot be settled in advance by reflection on the conceptual structure of the rights involved. However, although this is a concession to the critic, how serious is it? Does it mark a difference between positive rights to resources and negative rights?

If we accept the argument deployed earlier, that in the world as we know it, negative rights cannot just be based upon noncoerced forbearance but will have to involve positive protection by government in the way of police, courts, prisons, and so on, then it becomes very unclear that the concession does mark a difference. The degree of protection that may be required to secure negative rights cannot be excogitated from the nature of the rights in question any more than it can in the case of welfare rights. These are matters for policy and politics; but, nevertheless, a right such as the right to privacy does not lose its force as a benchmark against which to assess governments any more than does a right to welfare. But the extent of the institutional provision to protect a right of privacy is a contingent matter, not a conceptual one, and, furthermore, one that, like medical needs, will change with technological advances. Computers and information technology pose a range of threats to privacy that could not have been foreseen two or three decades ago, and the degree of protection needed to secure such rights will therefore vary with technological advance. Very similar kinds of arguments can be made about the nature of political and legal rights, assuming, as I argued earlier, that such rights do require institutional forms of provision. Such forms will then be a matter of political negotiation and cannot just be "read off" the nature of the rights in question.

This point can be resisted only if we were to take a purist view of negative rights, that they do not in fact require, as I have suggested they do, a positive form of protection by government. This point is argued in the following way by Charles Fried:

> My right to freedom of speech is not a right to be heard, much less a
> right to have my views broadcast and applauded. If my right implied
> these things, then certainly it would be equivalent to a positive right, and
> would run up against the limits of scarcity. . . . But what if others would
> deprive me of my freedom of speech—a hostile mob for instance? Surely
> it is the case that in asking for protection against the mob I make an
> affirmative claim upon the scarce resources of the community. But this
> objection misses the point too, for the fact that I have a right to freedom
> of speech against the government does not mean that I have a right that
> the government protect any exercise of that right. (Fried, 1978, 120–122)

Fried goes on to argue that this type of argument, which he is here criticizing, neglects the distinction between what is done to a person and what is allowed to happen. This point is crucial and, as we shall see, has salience not only for the object of the right in Gewirth's formula but also for forming a coherent idea of against whom a right is asserted.

The point at stake in Fried's argument is that a negative right can be wholly satisfied by forbearance. The right to life is satisfied by my not being killed, the right to privacy by not having my mail tampered with, the right to freedom of speech by not interfering with my exercise. The forbearance in question is a duty that is always capable of being discharged. Thus Trammel argues as follows:

> It is an empirical fact that in most cases it is possible for a person not to inflict serious physical injury on another person. It is also an empirical fact that in no case is it possible to aid everyone who needs help. The positive duty to love one's neighbour or help those in need sets a maximum ethic which would never let us rest except to gather strength to resume the battle. But it is a rare case when we must really exert ourselves to keep away from killing a person. (1980, 168)

To extend rights to resources and aid extends our responsibilities in an irrational way and makes the duties connected with rights difficult to characterize and thus to discharge.

Clearly part of the answer to these claims rests upon what has gone before—namely, that a theory of rights based upon needs is bound to imply that even so-called negative rights are going to imply the commitment of resources; and therefore the sharp distinction made by Fried and Trammel cannot be maintained. However, the more serious criticism of this view is about the definiteness of the duties of negative rights based upon the idea that we have a very clear idea of forbearance and omission and the responsibilities connected with these. Yet, particularly in the case of not killing, this can be doubted, and in doubting this we shall be forced to look briefly at the ethical issues of killing and letting die. The assumption of the argument is that there is a categorical moral distinction between the two, that the former involves the infringement of rights whereas the latter does not, and that responsibility in the former case is clear and unequivocal, and in the latter case vague and extensive. However, there are a number of reasons for coming to doubt the view that there is a simple moral distinction at stake here. The issues are very complex, but there is no clear distinction and the assumption about acts and omissions upon which it rests are not sufficient to account for a difference in the rights at stake in each case. If killing and allowing to die are, in certain circumstances, morally equivalent, then these acts and omissions cannot be correlated with rights in terms of forbearance and the provision of resources, because the failure to provide resources for life could then be regarded as morally equivalent to killing and thus an infringement of the right to life.

A more general way of putting the point is this: If the fundamental duty implied by a negative right is the duty not to harm, then this may well imply positive duties because the failure to act (to forbear) can itself produce harm and, indeed, a degree of harm that is morally equivalent to the intentional infliction of harm. Certainly John Stuart Mill held this view when he argued in the *Essay on Liberty* that "a person may cause evil to others not only by his actions but by his inaction and that in either case he is justly accountable to them for the injury" (1910, 74). If this argument is accepted, then it is difficult to maintain the idea that infringing a right is always an intentional action and that the right can always be respected by the appropriate form of forbearance.

One way in which critics of positive rights attack this idea is by arguing that harm can be caused only by omission, if there is an antecedent duty toward the person or if the omission is performed by an agent who has some special responsibility toward the individual in question. Consider, for example, a contractual relationship between X and Y such that if X omits an action, she or he may say that Y has been harmed. Thus if a doctor has assumed responsibility for the care of a patient and then fails to fulfill that obligation, we can say that his or her inaction has caused harm. Similarly, if a parent neglects a child, this inaction causes harm because there is an antecedent obligation to aid and care for one's children. In an example used by Gewirth, in *Reason and Morality,* he discusses the case of a signalman whose failure to pull a lever causes the train to crash and thus harms those involved (1978, 222). However, although it may be true in these cases that inaction causes harm and so violates the rights of the people concerned, this is only because there is an antecedent duty based upon contract (in the case of the doctor), a conventionally accepted set of expectations (in the case of the parent), or a rule book (in the case of the signalman). In these cases the individual who fails to act stands in a special relationship of duty with the person harmed, and it is in this case that we can say that the inaction or the forbearance causes harm. Unless there is an antecedent basis for a duty that creates a corresponding right to benefit from the performance of such a duty, there can be no basis for accepting the rights in question.

This argument turns upon two considerations. The first is whether omissions can cause harm only if there is a specific contractual or quasi-contractual relationship between individuals; the second is whether the theorist of positive rights has a cogent argument for saying that there is an antecedent duty to meet the needs of people more generally. If so, which people and how generally?

The first question raises a deep problem not only in political theory but also in the philosophy of science because the issue is about negative causal responsibility—namely, that a failure to act causes harm. This way of putting the point should alert us to the potential weakness in the critic's position. If X, in failing to act, is negatively causally responsible for the harm that befalls Y, then presumably, as with all cases of causation, this will depend upon the state of the world. Yet how can X's *moral* relationship with Y, which for the critic is crucial, make a difference to the sequence of causation? The critic is prepared to say that in certain circumstances in which X and Y stand in a moral relationship, X's inaction may cause harm to Y; however, assuming that X does not stand in such a moral relationship to Z, the same failure to act does not cause harm. If this is so, then we have to be prepared to argue that a conventional relationship, of the sort that a contractual relationship is, may make a categorical difference to whether X causes harm to Y.

Take the following example. In the first instance the parent, at no possible personal risk, fails to rescue his or her child from drowning in shallow water. In this case, we would have to say that the failure to act caused harm and that the parent infringed the rights of the child because, given the moral relationship in question, the child had a right to expect protection in both the positive and the negative sense from its parent. In the second case, imagine that a total stranger failed to save a child in similar circumstances knowing that he or she is the only person in a position to save the child. This failure to save the child would not be said to have caused it harm because there is no antecedent relationship between the child and the potential rescuer. Saving the child would be a meritorious act, but failing to save the child would not mean that one is responsible for the harm that befalls it. In each case the child ends up dead as the result of two forms of inaction. But what is not clear, and what is vital to the critic's case, is how the issue of the moral relationship or the lack of it between the parties concerned makes any difference to the causal circumstances. These are obviously very large issues, but I doubt whether a theory of antecedent moral obligation can enable us to draw the distinctions required in the categorical way assumed by distinction between negative and positive rights in the way the critic takes to be central. If, as Jan Narveson argues (criticizing Gewirth), the signalman's "inaction is a cause because there is an antecedent basis for the positive duty" (1973, 99), *we need to have a theory about how obligations can make a difference to causation.*

The second crucial question is whether the positive rights theorist can in fact provide a basis for the obligation to aid. The negative rights theorist will argue that we have a positive duty to aid only when we stand in a specific moral, contractual, or professional relationship with another individual and that we cannot generalize from these to other cases. So if the positive rights argument is to go through, we need antecedent grounds for the obligation to aid others even when we do not stand in such a self-assumed relationship with them. Part of the argument to be deployed by the positive rights theorist here will be in terms of needs and the resource preconditions of rational agency. However, the critic of positive rights can still argue that this argument is insufficient. We still need arguments on which my supposed obligation to meet needs of others as a right can be based. It may be true that rational agency requires these needs to be satisfied, but that does not of itself yield a right to the resources of others. Why should I pay attention to the needs of others even though I recognize them? What moral force, if any, do needs have, and how do they relate to the claim that they can serve as the basis of rights?

This argument is central, but complex. I have tried to deal with it elsewhere (Plant et al., 1981) in relation to Kant's views on the subject, but let me make an attempt of my own in this context. Any rights-based theory, whether positive or negative, is going to have at its center some basic idea of human dignity and worth, and this idea has to be defended by argument before it can provide a secure basis for a philosophical theory of rights. The most obvious defense of it is to be found in the Kantian idea of moral capacity noted earlier—the capacity to form a view of the good and to follow it. If moral capacity is the basis of human respect and the dignity of persons, then we have to ask what such respect requires from us. On Nozick's view it requires negative rights because anything more would itself interfere with the autonomy of persons. But I have defended the view that morally illegitimate harm can be caused by inaction as well as by interference, and that argument alone should weaken Nozick's case. However, there are additional points to make. The first is that respect for persons requires us to respect not their particular view of the good but, rather, the capacity of a person to pursue such a good—namely, the capacity for agency. As I have already argued, this capacity requires resources as well as forebearance. We cannot both respect a person's moral capacity and be indifferent to whether he or she has the means on which the realization of that capacity depends. This means that respect requires that the person be provided not with the specific means to meet specific goals but, rather, with the basic goods of agency that are required for the pursuit of any good at all.

We have to turn now to the final aspect of Gewirth's formula—namely, the person, persons, or institutions against whom or which the right is claimed. On the face of it, if human rights are generally universal, then they should be held equally as claims against every other person. In the case of the negative interpretation of rights, it is argued, sense can be made of this requirement. The reasoning here is parallel to the cases discussed earlier—that forbearance and abstaining from action is sufficient to satisfy negative rights. So, insofar as I am not actively killing, assaulting, and interfering with the rights of others, I am respecting their rights. If we take the case of an individual who is destitute, insofar as I did not intentionally cause her or his poverty I can respect her or his right merely by abstaining from action, and this is as true for a destitute member of my own society as it is for any other society. Hence, the idea of each having a duty to respect the rights of all other right holders individually is capable of fulfillment on this basis. However, it is not at all clear against whom social and economic rights are claimed. It would seem clear that although I have a strict duty to respect the negative rights of all other individuals simultaneously, and given the nature of those rights, this can be done in a costless way; nevertheless, no single person can have a duty to fulfill the economic and social rights of other persons. As Narveson says: "One could work twenty-four hours a day at the relief of suffering and could impoverish oneself contributing to charity, but it is felt that to require one to do this would be going rather too far" (1973, 235).

Although I have a general moral duty not to harm and interfere with the lives of others, and although others have a right to claim such forbearance from me, I cannot have a general and strict moral obligation to provide resources to relieve the suffering of all who suffer, and they in turn have no right to my resources for such relief.

If this is so, then it would seem that welfare could not be a right just because the right could not be claimed against any particular person; no particular individual could be blamed for the nonfulfillment of the right, and no specific individual would be responsible for any claim to compensation falling due as the result of the failure to implement that right. It would seem that, again, it would be best to see welfare as a matter of humanity, generosity, altruism, and therefore an imperfect duty, to which there would be no corresponding right.

It might be thought that the answer to this argument would be that the right to welfare is a right to be claimed not against individuals but, rather, against society as a whole, or more specifically the government, and this is in part the answer that Narveson gives in his interesting utilitarian discussion of this question. However, this still does not go quite as far as the welfare right theorist wants to go. As Narveson himself says (1973, 275), this move would still make the right in question an imperfect one. If we go back to Mill's distinction—that an imperfect duty is one that is directed against no particular person—the case we are now considering is closely parallel (1910, 305). The right to welfare would become a right against no one in particular and thus, by parity of reasoning, would be an imperfect right. In the same way as no specific right corresponds to an imperfect duty, so an imperfect right could not imply a specific duty on the part of anyone. To be forced into this position would be just about the same as having to recognize that there is no right to welfare.

However, it is possible, following the lead of Narveson, to take matters further than this. Consider what Narveson says:

> But a duty has to be someone's duty. It can't just be no one's in particular. Consequently the thing to do is to make it everyone's duty to do something, even if that "something" is a matter of seeing that someone else does it. Those who are put on the business end, such as the police, medical people, firemen, etc., should, of course, be compensated for going to the trouble of performing these activities. The simplest solution is simply to make these professions supportable by the public. (1973, 235–236)

If this is accepted, and I think that there are good reasons for accepting it, then the strict or perfect duty of individuals would be not the personal provision of resources to deprived individuals but, rather, the support of institutions, welfare agencies, social workers, and so on, that attempt to meet social needs. As a strict duty such support could then be required by government through taxation to support the meeting of social needs. In this way we could still see the welfare state in terms of rights and duties rather than in terms of institutionalized altruism. To see the human right to welfare as implying a duty to support government welfare measures would be equivalent to seeing due process of law as a human right. A specific individual has the duty not to provide such due process but, rather, to see that the procedures of due process are in fact carried out. The perfect duties corresponding to the rights of welfare are not, then, the personal provision of resources and services to individuals but the duty to support governments and institutions that are organized to meet such needs. Hence my argument has been that if there are rights at all, then there are positive as well as negative rights, and that a positive theory of rights can be developed in such a way as to satisfy the cogent demands of Alan Gewirth's formula. Clearly the moral basis on which rights of any sort are grounded needs further elaboration. Nevertheless, it is a consequence of the argument deployed in this chapter that the case for negative and positive rights stands or falls together.

REFERENCES

Fried, Charles (1978). *Right and Wrong.* Cambridge, Mass.: Harvard University Press.

Gewirth, Alan (1978). *Reason and Morality.* Chicago: University of Chicago Press.

———— (1982). *Human Rights.* Chicago: University of Chicago Press.

Glover, Jonathan (1977). *Causing Death and Saving Lives.* Harmondsworth, England: Penguin.

Gray, John (1983). "Classical Liberalism, Positional Goods and the Politicization of Poverty." In Adrian Ellis and Krishan Kumar, eds., *Dilemmas of Liberal Democracies.* London: Tavistock.

———— (1984). *Hayek on Liberty.* Oxford: Basil Blackwell.

Hayek, Friedrich A. (1960). *The Constitution of Liberty.* London: Routledge and Kegan Paul.

Joseph, Keith, and J. Sumption (1979). *Equality.* London: J. Murray.

Kant, Immanuel (1974). *Groundwork to the Metaphysics of Morals.* H.J. Paton, trans. London: Hutchinson.

McCloskey, H.J. (1984). "Respect for Moral Rights Versus Maximising Good." In R. Frey, ed., *Utility and Rights.* Oxford: Basil Blackwell.

Mill, John Stuart (1910). *Essays on Liberty.* London: J.M. Dent.

Narveson, J. (1973). *Morality and Utility.* Baltimore: Johns Hopkins University Press.

Nozick, Robert (1974). *Anarchy, State, and Utopia.* Oxford: Basil Blackwell.

Plant, Raymond, H. Lesser, and P. Taylor-Gooby (1981). *Political Philosophy and Social Welfare.* London: Routledge and Kegan Paul.

Trammel, R. (1980). "Saving Life and Taking Life." In B. Steinbeck, ed., *Killing and Letting Die.* New York: Prentice-Hall.

Part Two

LIBERALISM AND THE WELFARE STATE

Historical Perspectives

4

LIBERAL GUILT

Some Theoretical Origins of the Welfare State

Is Milton Friedman the legitimate heir of Adam Smith? Did Locke's antagonism to political tyranny imply a repudiation of public provision for the needs of the poor? Does Marshall's famous sequence of legal rights, political rights, and social rights map the smooth unfolding of an initial promise or a step-by-step disavowal of the past? What is the relation between the old *Rechtsstaat* and the new *Sozialstaat*, between constitutional rights and welfare rights?

These questions are neither uninteresting nor unanswerable. But the point of asking them is not immediately clear. Even if we could announce that public assistance represented a betrayal or a consummation of classical liberal principles, no political consequences would follow, one way or the other. The perpetuation of traditional values may be a sign of heroic tenacity; but it may also be a symptom of moral sclerosis. Some adversaries of the welfare state try to make us feel derelict for having abandoned our noble libertarian heritage. Contrariwise, friends of the welfare state commend us for having thrown off the shameful inheritance of Social Darwinism. Depending on one's perspective, in other words, historical continuity can deserve praise or blame.

I stress this admittedly obvious consideration to avoid a misconstrual of my objectives in these remarks. While aiming to highlight the similarities and interconnections between eighteenth-century liberal rights and twentieth-century welfare rights, I remain conscious that such an exercise has limited value. Policy debates, for one thing, cannot be sensibly conducted as legacy disputes. The liberal movement, moreover, was complex and diffuse. It evolved over the course of centuries and assumed different forms in different national contexts. Even when studying a single country during one and the same period, we can only use "liberalism" (which before the nineteenth century is always an anachronism) as an umbrella term covering a variety of political tendencies and outlooks. As a result, diverse historical perspectives on liberal thought remain possible; and they will inevitably yield divergent answers to the continuity question. Furthermore, a similarity or correspondence of beliefs, which is all I shall attempt to document, does not constitute proof of historical continuity. Evidence of transmission and reception would be required to support any kind of stronger claim.

Normative continuity, moreover, the bequeathing and inheriting of a system of moral values, even if it could be established, would not provide a *causal explanation* of the emergence and stabilization of contemporary welfare regimes. General affluence, a dramatic increase in state revenues during wartime, the need to secure political stability in the face of boom-and-slump cycles in the economy, the growing bargaining power of previously disenfranchised groups—these and many other factors played a decisive role in the emergence of contemporary economic rights. Public relief programs have sometimes been embraced by political élites for purely self-interested reasons: because, for example, "Rebellions of the Belly are the worst" (Bacon, 1985, 45–46) or because "poverty in the midst of a generally wealthy society is likely to increase the incidence of crime" (Posner, 1986, 439). Similar considerations were no doubt relevant to the enactment of modern redistributionist legislation. If normative continuity outweighed normative discontinuity, as I think it did, it was only one element among the many that contributed to the rise of the welfare state. The erroneous assumption that classical liberals would have been utterly hostile to transfer programs is such a commonplace, however, that a succinct refutation can still be useful.

FOUR RIVAL VIEWS

Although quaint and pseudo-scientific, a two-by-two table is the most economical way to survey possible responses to the continuity question. We can distinguish, along a *descriptive* dimension, between those who assert a sharp rupture between liberal rights and welfare rights and those who discern an unbroken continuity linking the two. Along an *evaluative* dimension, we can then contrast those who approve with those who disapprove of these first two alternatives (see Figure 4.1).

1. In the first cell, we can locate the standard Hayekian view that liberalism was a basically "negative" or antistatist philosophy, concerned with limiting abusive government—that is, with preventing tyranny and restricting political power. Liberalism, from this perspective, is wholly incompatible with positive programs of public provision, all of which require confiscatory taxation, a "taking" from A in order to give to B, and other acts of governmental invasion into a sphere of otherwise voluntary relations. Liberal citizens can be prevented from harming

FIGURE 4.1
Possible Responses to the Continuity Question

	disapprove	approve
discontinuity	1	2
continuity	3	4

each other but never forced to make each other prosper or even relieve each other's distress.

2. The second possibility is equally well known. To build the welfare state, it is said, modern citizens had to leave behind the anticommunal, privatistic, beggar-thy-neighbor, and devil-take-the-hindmost attitudes purportedly typical of classical liberalism. Before they could endorse the welfare state, they had to be weaned from *sauve qui peut* liberalism and converted to warm-spirited, communal, samaritan-like, organic values and traditions.

3. Third, and quite distinctly, many theorists and publicists have perceived a continuity between liberalism and the welfare state but have gone on to argue that this continuity is morally deplorable—indeed, that it discloses either the original sin of liberalism or the phoniness of welfare rights. This third category is interesting largely because it encourages us to ponder the disconcerting bedfellowship of far-left and far-right critics of economic rights. Remember that both Marxists and Reaganites (the latter inhabiting Cell One) denounce welfare benefits for weakening the moral fiber of recipients, infantilizing them into dependency—defusing their revolutionary potential in the one case, destroying their frontiersmanlike self-reliance in the other. A different coincidence of opposites is underscored by our two-by-two table. Both radicals and ultraconservatives[1] passionately assail the individualistic and bourgeois materialism of liberal society—as the extinction of deference and hierarchy on the one hand and as the obstacle to a classless society on the other. Neither sees anything in welfare states that fundamentally changes the picture, anything transcending the limits that, in their view, hideously deform the liberal tradition.

However it is judged politically, the first position is both historically inaccurate and conceptually confused. Similarly, even those who sympathize with some of the policy implications of the second view may find it more than a little dissatisfying as a historical account. The third alternative should evoke a response converse to the second: Even those who find it morally and politically unpalatable may concede that it is historically on the right track.

Having signaled the existence of these three alternatives, I turn now to the fourth and, I am convinced, superior claim that there is a demonstrable historical continuity, or at least compatibility, between liberalism and the values embodied in the welfare state, and that this common ground is, by and large, a moral and political advantage. If we wished to attach a name to this final position, we would probably be justified in citing John Rawls, a defender of welfarist redistribution as well as a self-proclaimed theoretical descendant of Locke and Kant.

In fact, evidence suggesting historical continuity is bountiful. Consider, as one randomly chosen example, Montesquieu's (1951, 712; translation: 1949, vol. 2, 25) unambiguous affirmation of the state's duty to relieve poverty: "Quelques aumônes que l'on fait à un homme nu dans les rues, ne remplissent point les obligations de l'Etat, qui doit à tous les citoyens une subsistance assurée, la nourriture, un vêtement convenable, et un genre de vie qui ne soit point contraire à la santé" (The alms given to a naked man in the street do not fulfill the obligations of the state, which owes to every citizen a certain subsistence, a proper nourishment, convenient clothing, and a kind of life not incompatible with health). No series of such quotations, of course, would demonstrate the compatibility of welfare measures with the principles of liberalism, much less the logical derivation or historical emergence of the former from the latter. Montesquieu may well have been an inconsistent or incomplete liberal, unable to free himself from vestigial strains of aristocratic paternalism or Christian almsgiving. Perhaps, if he had thought through the implications of the "rule of law," he would have written more like Dicey. I think not, however. To make my position credible, I must now show how redistributionist conclusions are not merely consistent with but, in some sense, follow directly from liberal principles themselves.

THE PRIMACY OF JUSTICE

To skirt the problem of defining *liberalism*, I am going to adopt a nominalist strategy and take as my benchmark the cluster of views advanced and defended by the following theorists: Locke, Montesquieu, Hume, Adam Smith, Madison, Kant, and John Stuart Mill.[2] This list allows us to register skepticism, at the very outset, about the assumption that classical liberals were fiercely hostile to social planning. One of the theorists mentioned actually wrote a constitution; most recognized the potential benefits of clever constitutional design; and constitutions, of course, *are* social plans. According to Milton Friedman, welfare measures are profoundly illiberal: "The central defect of these measures is that they seek through government to force people to act against their own immediate interests in order to promote a supposedly general interest" (1962, 200). But there is nothing particularly illiberal about the realization that, in the absence of coercion, self-love will induce individuals to exempt themselves from generally useful rules. Liberal constitutions, in fact, are designed to do precisely what Friedman apparently deplores: to *force* office-holders to act against their own immediate interests in order to promote the general interest.

Our list of representative liberal theorists also suggests that liberalism should not be considered principally an antistatist philosophy of limited government.[3] Liberals were as wary of anarchy as of tyranny. They advocated not merely freedom from government but also order through government (Hume, 1963, 453). Security is impossible without a state monopoly on the legitimate use of violence. To the extent that he defined freedom as security,[4] a definition to which I shall return, even Montesquieu conceived sovereign power, organized along liberal lines, as an indispensable instrument of freedom.[5]

The order that liberals admired, moreover, was not any kind of order, not simply the repression of random violence and civil war. Instead, it was a certain kind of order, an order qualified in a specific way: a *just* order. The primacy of justice in liberal thought is sometimes underestimated. According to Friedman, again, "The egalitarian . . . will defend taking from some to give to others . . . on grounds of 'justice.' At this point equality comes sharply into conflict with freedom; one must choose. One cannot be both an egalitarian, in this sense, and a liberal" (Friedman, 1962, 195). Classical liberals, however, seldom placed *justice* in disdainful quotation marks; they never sacrificed or subordinated justice to freedom in the way this passage implies. On the contrary, as Hume wrote: "We are . . . to look at the vast apparatus of government, as having ultimately no other object or purpose but the distribution of justice" (1963, 35). In a similar spirit, Montesquieu (1951, 233; translation: 1949, vol. 1, 2) asserted that "Il faut donc avouer des rapports d'équité antérieurs à la loi positive qui les établit" (We must therefore acknowledge relations of justice antecedent to the positive law by which they are established). According to Adam Smith, too, justice was the "main pillar" of society (1976, 86). Smith was committed not simply to the natural system of liberty but to "the natural system of perfect liberty *and justice*" (1937, 572; my emphasis). Every man should be free to follow his own interests in his own way, he argued, but only "as long as he does not violate the laws of justice" (Smith, 1937, 651). Interest-governed behavior can only enhance social stability and security if the interests propelling action are just.[6] Madison agreed: "Justice is the end of government. It is the end of civil society" (*Federalist Papers*, 1961, 324).

Justice, to be sure, is a slippery and polysignificant concept, difficult to define in a univocal way. Perhaps the theorists cited above were thinking about *just retribution* and not *just distribution*. Perhaps they meant to affirm "the limits of justice," confining the term *just* to the giving and receiving of what individuals had voluntarily contracted to give and receive. According to Hobbes, for example, "The definition of INJUSTICE, is no other than *the not Performance of Covenant*" and "the nature of Justice, consisteth in keeping of valid Covenants" (1965, 110–111). Even this restrictive definition of justice, of course, includes an explicit entitlement to affirmative state action to protect individuals from harm by third parties.

We can say with some confidence, moreover, that liberals did *not* uniformly conceive justice in this narrow fashion, as a simple matter of enforcing contracts. For one thing, they universally associated justice with a more substantive idea of impartiality: *All* individuals must be protected *equally* from third-party injury. In other words, they all explicitly advocated *equal access to the law*, a norm incompatible with many ostensibly "contractual" relations (e.g., those involving indentured servitude). Access to the courts must not be distributed according to merit, contribution, inherited social status, or even prior consent. A jury trial must be made available to *all* similar offenders. A just distribution of the community's legal resources was, in principle, an equal or universal distribution—not conditional, for example, on the quantity of taxes paid. One might even argue that a just distribution of, say, trial by jury was conceived as a distribution according to need.

THE REDISTRIBUTION OF SECURITY

The semantic trajectory of the word *security* is obviously germane to any study of the transition from classical liberal rights, such as habeas corpus or protection from arbitrary search and seizure, to modern welfare rights, such as legal aid to the poor or public housing and rent subsidies. As the resources of states grew, one might argue, the concept of security was naturally stretched to include more and more basic guarantees. Originally designating protection from private and public violence, "security" eventually came to include universal public schooling and various economic rights—that is, protection from the caprice of family upbringing and from violent fluctuations in the market. But what is the relationship between the "security" protected by liberal constitutions and the homonymous value guaranteed, for example in the U.S. system of "social security"? Is there a conceptual continuity here or merely a verbal one?

Theorists may have neglected the possibility of a substantive continuity between classical liberalism and the moral foundations of the welfare state because of their commitment to a misleading contrast between *two kinds of rights*, between rights as liberties from government interference and rights as entitlements to government support.[7] This is particularly unfortunate because, as I mentioned, the original right to protection from unjustified and unpredictable physical violence was a right that *entitled* all citizens to affirmative state action.[8] By focusing directly on this right, as a result, theorists should have been encouraged to abandon the seductive but unhelpful contrast between latitudes and entitlements.

In his fanciful re-descriptions of liberal thought, Friedman routinely slights the importance of state power not only for the establishment of security but also for the enforcement of the norms of fairness and impartiality:

> The intellectual movement that went under the name of liberalism emphasized freedom as the ultimate goal and the individual as the ultimate entity in the society. It supported laissez faire at home as a means of reducing the role of the state in economic affairs and thereby enlarging the role of the individual. (1962, 5)

Reading such a passage, one is forced to ask: Who precisely is "the" individual? Is there more than one? Do some ever suffer while, or even because, others prosper? By discussing *the* individual, in fact, Friedman manages to repress any worries about impartiality *among* individuals or about the illegitimate use of *private power*. Focused on the norm of justice, classical liberals did not share this blindness.

True, Smith sometimes made statements that seem to rule out a "taking" from the rich to give to the poor: "To hurt in any degree the interest of any one order of citizens, for no other purpose but to promote that of some others, is evidently contrary to that justice and equality which the sovereign owes to all the different orders of his subjects" (1937, 618). But it is unwise to infer any blanket hostility to redistribution from this claim alone. For one thing, Smith enthusiastically favored the use of state power to break up growth-stifling private monopolies. Privileged groups certainly could not be expected to relinquish their monopolies voluntarily. "Interests," as Locke had already made clear, can be legitimate or illegitimate, proper or improper, just or unjust.[9] The interests of monopolists were invariably unjust. Despite his disclaimers, in other words, Smith emphatically believed that natural justice *required* the state to hurt the (sinister) interests of one order of citizens for no other purpose than to promote the (innocent) interests of others.

In simpler language, he thought that the interests of the few must be forcibly sacrificed to the interests of the great majority of the people.

Private power poses just as great a threat to security as does public power.[10] Strict noninterference in social life by the state would produce not wholesome competition but an outcropping of brutal monopolies. Far from being simply antistatist, as a consequence, liberals ascribed important trust-busting functions to sovereign, centralized, and bureaucratic authority. State intervention was essential for a just distribution of security, for protecting the vulnerable from the mighty. Smith, for one, laid great stress not only on freedom from government but also on the affirmative duties of the state in restricting private power: "The second duty of the sovereign," after national defense, is "that of protecting, as far as possible, every member of society from the injustice or oppression of every other member of it" (1937, 669). Even the nightwatchman state, concerned exclusively with preventing mutual harm, was profoundly *redistributionist*, charged explicitly with an equitable allocation of security. But what did "security" mean to classical liberals?

The most ardent enemies of an ideological stance are often its keenest analysts. Both Marx and Nietzsche, in attacking liberalism, poured particular scorn on the norm of security (Marx & Engels, 1972, 365–366).[11] This was a shrewd strategy because, in many ways, security was the *idée maîtrisse* of the liberal tradition. According to Mill, for example, the interest in security is "the most vital of all interests" (1969, 251).[12] When considering Friedman's claim that classical liberals preferred liberty to equality, in fact, we should recall that many liberals actually *defined* freedom as security; that is, they identified liberty with a good that cried out for some sort of just or justifiable distribution. Paraphrasing, not to say plagiarizing, Montesquieu, Jaucourt wrote in the *Encyclopédie* (1765, vol. 9, 472; cf. Montesquieu, 1951, 712): "La *liberté politique* du citoyen est cette tranquillité d'esprit qui procede de l'opinion que chacun a de sa sûreté; & pour qu'on ait cette sûreté, il faut que le gouvernement soit tel, qu'un citoyen ne puisse pas craindre un citoyen" (The political liberty of the citizen is the tranquility of spirit deriving from the sense each has of his own security; for one to have security, the government must be such that no citizen need fear another.) Bentham, too, followed Montesquieu: "A clear idea of liberty will lead us to regard it as a branch of security" (Bentham, 1979, 59; see also pp. 67–68).

The importance of security for all liberal thinkers suggests that liberal justice, far from being limited to the protection of property and contract, had a marked redistributionist dimension. The idea that security might be allocated more justly was originally popularized by the ideologues of absolutism. Giving advice to Louis XIII, for example, Cardinal Richelieu wrote: "It is also necessary to see that [the nobles] do not exploit those beneath them." And he continued:

> It is a common enough fault of those born to this order [the nobility] to use violence in dealing with the common people whom God seems to have endowed with arms designed more for gaining a livelihood than for providing self-defense. It is most essential to stop any disorders of such a nature with inflexible severity so that even the weakest of your subjects, although unarmed, find as much *security* in the protection of your laws as those who are fully armed. (Richelieu, 1961, 20–21; my emphasis)

Contemplated here was a rudimentary "transfer plan." Having hitherto engrossed security by means of private armies, the nobility had to be, to some extent, disarmed. The security of the baron had to be diminished, his fortresses torn down, to increase the security of the *roturier*. The modern French monarchy was legitimated not solely by its capacity to keep the peace but also by its trust-busting program aimed at protecting the weak from the strong, destroying the old baronial monopoly on security, and enforcing the norm of impartiality.

In other words, although it eventually became the premier rationale for constitutional restrictions on government power, the need for security had originally been invoked to justify a sharp increase in state power. Mill, among others, was acutely aware of this paradox. Reflecting on the general insecurity plaguing early modern Europe, he explained why sovereigns had to be granted such inordinate power: "The passions of those who were strong by station or by personal endowment were in a state of habitual rebellion against laws and ordinances, and required to be rigorously chained up to enable the persons within their reach to enjoy any particle of *security*" (Mill, 1977, 264; my emphasis). Originally, private power had been the most conspicuous threat to individual liberty. To guarantee the security (and therefore freedom) of the weak, restrictions had to be placed on the freedom (and therefore security) of the strong.[13] Security could not be completely *equalized* in this manner; but some redistribution could guarantee a *bottom floor* or minimum of security to all.[14]

For basic security to be universally available, the state had to retain its monopoly on the legitimate use of violence; but public officials also had to be made accountable and subject to punishment. Mill describes the transition from the absolute to the liberal state in exactly this way:

> To prevent the weaker members of the community from being preyed upon by innumerable vultures, it was needful that there should be an animal of prey stronger than all the rest, commissioned to keep them

down. But as the king of the vultures would be no less bent upon preying on the flock than any of the minor harpies, it was indispensable to be in a perpetual attitude of defense against his beak and claws. (1977, 217)

Constitutionalism took the original redistribution of security from nobles to commoners a step beyond where absolutism had left it: The security of rulers themselves had to be diminished in order to increase the security of the ruled.

JUSTICE AND CHARITY

According to Locke, a person's exclusive property rights are only valid "where there is enough and as good left in common for others" (1965, 329). Our duty "to preserve mankind" (1965, 311) requires that we abstain from invading our "neighbor's share," reveling in superfluities while others lack necessities (1965, 337). Property, too, is closely associated with security, or at least with dampening a fundamental human insecurity: the uncertainty of where one will find tomorrow's meal. To possess property, in an orderly and predictable political environment, means—in Locke's language—to quell a basic human uneasiness or restlessness, to be somewhat more secure. Thus, it is not unreasonable to read Locke's argument for redistribution of property in case of extreme want as an argument for a partial transfer of security in case of extreme danger. Although quite well known, the fundamental passage is worth citing at length:

> We know God hath not left one Man so to the Mercy of another, that he may starve him if he please: God the Lord and Father of all, has given no one of his Children such a Property, in his peculiar portion of the things of the world, but that he has given his needy Brother a Right to the Surplusage of his Goods; so that it cannot justly be denied him, when his pressing Wants call for it. And therefore no man could ever have a just Power over the Life of another, by Right of property in Land or Possessions; since 'twould always be a Sin in any Man of Estate, to let his brother perish for want of affording him Relief out of his Plenty. As *Justice* gives every Man a Title to the product of his honest Industry, and the fair Acquisitions of his Ancestors descended to him; so *Charity* gives every man a Title to so much out of another's Plenty, as will keep him from extream want, where he has no means to subsist otherwise. (Locke, 1965, 205–206)

That this passage enunciates a universal *entitlement to welfare* cannot be denied. Less obvious is the basis for such an entitlement. Some commentators have argued that, in a Lockean world, our obligation to help the needy is divinely ordained (Tully, 1980, 131–132). To justify any sort of redistribution, it is claimed, Locke had to appeal to some nonliberal principle, such as God's will. This approach has much to be said in its favor. Ultimately, however, it underestimates the close parallel between Locke's argument and the claims advanced by more obviously secular theorists including Hobbes, Hume, Smith, Kant, and Mill.

Hobbes, for instance, is quite explicit about the need for public assistance to the incapacitated:

> And whereas many men, by accident unevitable, become unable to maintain themselves by their labour; they ought not to be left to the Charity of private persons; but to be provided for, (as far-forth as the necessities of Nature require), by the Lawes of the Common-wealth. For as it is Uncharitablenesse in any man, to neglect the impotent; so it is in the Soveraign of a Common-wealth, to expose them to the hazard of such uncertain Charity. (1965, 267)

In this passage, of course, Hobbes explicitly invokes charity, and for the disabled alone. Remarkable about his general argument, however, and more relevant for our purposes, is his claim that *justice requires redistribution*—that is, a taking from the strong and a giving to the weak. Possessive individualism, the desire for superfluities needed by others, must be dealt with severely. By nature, people wish to profit from the self-restraint of others while also profiting from their own lack of self-restraint. While the tenth law of nature commands an acknowledgment of human equality, arrogant men continue to assert their own superiority: "The Greeks call the violation of this law *pleonexia*; that is, a desire of more than their share" (Hobbes, 1965, 118). Whenever individuals make exceptions of themselves, act partially, and take more than their share, they must be compelled to accommodate themselves to others. But despite Hobbes's explicit claim that "equal distribution is of the Law of Nature" (1965, 119), the redistributionist dimension of his contractarian argument has not been fully appreciated.

Consider, again, the tenth law of nature: that "no man require to reserve to himself any Right, which he is not willing should be reserved to any one of the rest" (Hobbes, 1965, 118). This is a perfect illustration of the self-exemption taboo, a universalistic principle crucial to all liberal theorists.[15] The egalitarianism of the claim is striking. Security must be distributed equally to the "poor and obscure" and to the "rich and mighty." Indeed, Hobbes advocates a quite ruthless approach to redistribution, including the redistribution of property: "a man that by asperity of Nature, will strive to retain those things which to himselfe are superfluous, and to others necessary; and for the stubbornness of his Passions, cannot be corrected, is to be left, or cast out of Society, as combersome thereunto" (1965, 116). Not pity but justice demands an unwavering commitment to fair shares.

For further evidence that redistribution can be justified on purely secular and contractarian grounds, consider an argument advanced more than a century later by Immanuel Kant: "Indirectly, inasmuch as he takes over the duty of the people, the supreme commander possesses the right to levy taxes on them for their own conservation, in particular, for the relief of the poor" (1965, 92–93). Kant grounded the obligation to provide relief for those who cannot provide for themselves on the nature of the original contract, making no reference at all to God's will, but only to the will of the people:

> The general Will of the people has united itself into a society in order to maintain itself continually, and for this purpose it has subjected itself to the internal authority of the state in order to support those members of the society who are not able to support themselves. Therefore, it follows from the nature of the state that the government is authorized to require the wealthy to provide the means of sustenance to those who are unable to provide the most necessary needs of nature for themselves. Because their existence depends on the act of subjecting themselves to the commonwealth for the protection and care required in order to stay alive, they have bound themselves to contribute to the support of their fellow citizens, and this is the ground for the state's right to require them to do so (1965, 93).[16]

My duty to help the impoverished is not inborn or God-commanded but, rather, a result of the social contract. Individuals renounced their primitive right to use violence and possess all things in order to acquire legal and economic security. For the social contract to be a just bargain, *all* signers must actually receive some degree of legal and economic security within civil society. Those who have gained such security have done so only because of the social contract. They are therefore morally obliged to exchange equivalents for equivalents, to ensure that all parties to the bargain get what they bargained for. In other words—and this is an aspect of contractarianism omitted from Robert Nozick's version— redistribution to relieve distress is a form of just exchange. Such an argument is explicit in Kant. It may also be implicit in Locke.

That Locke's conventional distinction between justice and charity, derived from classical sources, may be less significant than it first seems is also suggested by a parallel passage in Hume where a title to the product of one's industry is subtly fused with a title to relief of want through redistribution: "Every person, if possible, ought to enjoy the fruits of his labour, in a full possession of all the necessaries, and many of the conveniencies of life. No one can doubt, but such an equality is most suitable to human nature, and diminishes much less from the *happiness* of the rich than it adds to that of the poor" (Hume, 1963, 271). Hume is obviously recommending redistribution in this passage. To guarantee citizens all the necessities and some of the "conveniencies" of life, we must *diminish* the happiness of the rich to some extent. Indeed, Hume even seems to go further than Locke, justifying redistribution of happiness not merely of those resources necessary for survival.

Unwilling to invoke natural rights, Hume regularly appealed to the welfare of the majority. The self-exception taboo required that, in policy decisions, the happiness of one person count no more or less than the happiness of another. This principle also governed the discussion of justice in the *Wealth of Nations*. Smith advocated free trade because he believed it would increase the welfare of "the lowest ranks of the people" (1937, 11) and would work "for the benefit of the poor and the indigent" (1937, 609). Istvan Hont and Michael Ignatieff have usefully demonstrated that, for Smith, "the moral legitimacy of distribution in commercial society lay in the fact that those who were 'left out in the partition' of property, i.e., the wage-earning poor, received adequate subsistence" (1983, 13). Writing in the tradition of natural law theorists such as Pufendorf, Smith rejected attempts to impose a just distribution of property itself and instead embraced a system which, although radically inegalitarian, was immensely productive and could therefore guarantee "equal . . . access to the means to satisfy basic need" (Hont & Ignatieff, 1983, 44).

A utilitarian concern for the greatest happiness of the greatest number, in Smith's view, made it obligatory to improve the circumstances of the lower ranks of people: "Servants, labourers and workmen of different kinds, make up the far greater part of every great political society. But what improves the circumstances of the greater part can never be regarded as an inconveniency to the whole. No society can be flourishing and happy, of which the far greater part of the members are poor and miserable" (1937, 78–79). In these sentences, Smith refers only to the utility of majority happiness. But he then turns a corner and includes justice: "It is but equity, besides, that they who feed, clothe and lodge the whole body of the people, should have such a share of the produce of their own labour as to be themselves tolerably well fed, clothed and lodged" (1937, 79). This is a fruits-of-one's-labor argument combined with some kind of Rawlsian assumption that society is a cooperative venture from which all participants deserve to derive some benefit. If we distinguished roughly between contribution-based and needs-based justifications for redistribution, we would certainly classify Smith's second argument here as falling into the first category.[17] To those who feed and clothe us, we owe, as a quid pro quo, as a just exchange, tolerable food and clothing.

Far from being scrupulously impartial regarding the relations between workers and employers, Smith wrote shockingly that when a regulation is "in the favour of the workmen, it is always just and equitable" (1937, 142). In other words, he displayed less wholesale hostility to redistributive policies than his commentators sometimes suggest (Hont & Ignatieff, 1983, 24–25). For example, he opposed taxes on necessities and favored taxes on luxuries because, in this manner, "the indolence and vanity of the rich is made to contribute in a very easy manner to the relief of the poor" (Smith, 1937, 683). Such *redistribution* is justified not by a theory that the rich got rich at the expense of the poor, but on the basis of a more general commitment to universal welfare.

A more consistently needs-based justification for welfare transfers was advanced later by J. S. Mill:

> Apart from any metaphysical considerations respecting the foundation of morals or of the social union, it will be admitted to be right that human beings should help one another; and the more so, in proportion to the urgency of the need: and none needs help so urgently as one who is starving. The claim to help, therefore, created by destitution, is one of the strongest which can exist; and there is *prima facie* the amplest reason for making the relief of so extreme an exigency as certain to those who require it, as by any arrangements of society it can be made. (1899, 468)[18]

Mill explicitly refused to qualify this needs-based argument for redistribution with any reference to merit: "The state must act by general rules. It cannot undertake to discriminate between the deserving and the undeserving indigent. It owes no more than subsistence to the first, and can give no less to the last" (1899, 470). Equality of needs overrides inequality of virtue, making it politically irrelevant to blame poverty on the improvidence or delinquency of the poor. His commitment to impartiality and fairness, moreover, prompted Mill to reject any suggestion that the task of relieving poverty should be left to "voluntary charity." The state must use tax-derived revenues to provide public assistance because "charity almost always does too much or too little: it lavishes its bounty in one place, and leaves people to starve in another" (Mill, 1899, 470).[19]

Mill justified "a legal provision for the destitute" on other grounds as well. For one thing, "since the state must necessarily provide subsistence for the criminal poor while undergoing punishment, not to do the same for the poor who have not offended is to give a premium on crime" (Mill, 1899, 470). In the course of his argument, moreover, he explicitly questioned the conventional wisdom that poverty was a spur to effort. Correcting the one-sided argument that public assistance creates a crippling disincentive to work, he wrote: "Energy and self-dependence are . . . liable to be impaired by the absence of help as well as by its excess" (Mill, 1899, 468). Like other liberals, he valued security of ownership not solely for negative but also for positive reasons, not only as a means of repressing fear but also as a stimulant to creativity and innovation.[20] Economic security provided by government "help" functioned in the same way.

Smith had been even more adamant in asserting that public provision could actually foster private initiative. His bold argument in favor of high wages was explicitly based on a denial of the poverty-as-a-spur-to-effort thesis: "That men in general should work better when they are ill fed than when they are well fed, when they are disheartened than when they are in good spirits, when they are frequently sick than when they are generally in good health, seems not very probable" (Smith, 1937, 82–83). Smith's ultimate justification for high wages was the well-being of the majority. But he chose the *majority*'s welfare as the criterion to guide public policy because of a prior commitment to distributive justice. His concern for fairness is made explicit in the following often-cited passage:

> Our merchants and master-manufacturers complain much of the bad effects of high wages in raising the price, and thereby lessening the sale of their goods both at home and abroad. They say nothing concerning the bad effects of high profits. They are silent with regard to the pernicious effects of their own gains. They complain only of those of other people. (1937, 98)

The merchants under attack here had violated the norm of impartiality, the self-exemption taboo. They subjected others to a principle to which they had refused to subject themselves. Impartiality demanded the abandonment of the mercantile system, which was nothing other than an expression of the unjust and unjustifiable partiality of merchants.

THE INVIOLABILITY OF PRIVATE PROPERTY

Those who discern an unbridgeable gap separating legal rights and welfare rights commonly focus on liberalism's commitment to the "sanctity" of private property (an institution associated alternately with vampirish greed and with hardy self-reliance). But liberals were well aware that concentrations of property spelled potentially dangerous concentrations of power. In Hume's words, "Where the riches are in few hands, these must enjoy all the power" (1963, 271). Because concentrations of property, even in a free enterprise system, can produce concentrations of power, private property must be a source of distress as well as of solace to the heirs of the liberal tradition. Distrust of power alone, an irreproachably liberal sentiment, can clearly justify some degree of state regulation of private property.

If the government did not use its coercive powers to enforce contract and trespass laws, of course, private property would be worthless. What would be the distribution of income in a stateless society? Could such a "spontaneous" distribution of wealth possibly serve as an ideal standard of freedom and justice? For liberals the answer was obvious: "The rich would be far better able to protect themselves, in the absence of government, than the poor, and indeed, would probably be successful in converting the poor into their slaves" (Mill, 1969, 255). In a stateless society the mafia, or equivalent wielders of private power, would, among other things, engross all available wealth. The whole purpose of the social contract was to correct the unbearable maldistributions of power routine in the state of nature. Ownership was no exception. Private property can be enjoyed only in security because (and this is the way liberals such as Hume and Montesquieu conceived it) it is a monopoly granted and guaranteed by the government for the sake of the public interest. In other words, the pattern of "ownership"—if we can call it that—characterizing sovereignless societies was an unrelieved nightmare. It could provide neither a benchmark of freedom nor a justification for limiting the power of the state.

In the seventeenth and eighteenth centuries, of course, to affirm private property was to attack the politics of confiscation.[21] To advocate the rights of property owners was to question the state's authority to billet soldiers in one's home—a practice threatening to the integrity of the family and not merely to the profits of acquisitive individualists.[22] The political meaning of property rights was also underlined by the slogan "No taxation without representation." That is to say, the campaign to protect private property was difficult to disentangle from the campaign to establish representative institutions.[23] This connection between private property and self-government is corroborated by *Federalist Papers*, no. 10. There, Madison put forward a wholly democratic—that is, neither an individualistic nor an economic—defense of private property. Unless property-owners are protected from fellow citizens as well as from government employees, they will be too frightened to cooperate in the fragile system of collective self-rule (*Federalist Papers*, 1961, 83–84). In this period, moreover, to oppose monopolies and advocate the circulation of legally unencumbered private property was to attack primogeniture and entail—that is, to assault the foundation stone of Europe's landed aristocracy. Indeed, liberals valued the market itself as the most efficient vehicle for redistributing social wealth and, thus, for redistributing security. Despite Hayek's jibes about "teleocracy," liberals were never reticent to engage in *purposive* behavior: Their end-in-view was a collapse of inherited privilege and a general diffusion of private wealth.

The liberal concept of property contained a strong universalist element: It offered hope to at least some commoners and less advantaged groups. Questions of distribution, of course, were never separated from questions of production in liberal thought. The unequal allocation of property rights characteristic of commercial society would, it was thought, stimulate productivity and thereby guarantee subsistence to all. Equal opportunity to satisfy basic needs could be achieved indirectly through unequal rights to control the means of production. With a minimum of violence and pain, growing affluence would, for the first time, provide economic security for the majority.

Finally, the institutionalization of modern property rights did not "loose acquisitive instincts onto the world," as Straussians love to regret. For one thing, medieval peasants and barons were no strangers to greed. For another, modern property law required short-term self-restraint: Do not covet thy neighbor's goods! More important, as I have been stressing, the liberal embrace of private property initiated a partial *transfer* of security from the old monopolists of land to other less well-established groups. What was "loosed" onto the world, in fact, was not acquisitiveness but disrespect for inherited status.

The question now arises: How did liberals react when private property and the free market began to generate unprecedented forms of insecurity and to allocate security in a blatantly unfair way? As is well known, the sovereign enforcement of contracts was unable, in the wake of massive industrial development, to provide security for workers, to guarantee any sort of just allocation of security. When industrial change overwhelmed modern Western societies, certain doctrinaire heirs of the liberal tradition rigidly opposed curtailments of property rights despite the insecurities and maldistributions that these rights, because unqualified, tended to generate in new circumstances.[24] Others, more true (I believe) to the spirit of liberalism, agreed to infringe some property rights for the sake of greater and more justly distributed security. This welfarist turn was explicitly conceived as an *alternative* to socialism and collective ownership of the means of production. It was also, it seems to me, fully consonant with the original intention behind the liberal celebration of private property.

SHIFTING SOURCES OF INSECURITY

Intriguingly, the nineteenth- and twentieth-century shift in attitudes toward private property paralleled the seventeenth-century shift in attitudes toward state power. In both cases, initial reverence changed into partial doubt. Absolute monarchy gained legitimacy by campaigning to eliminate civil wars and highway murder gangs. State power was relatively immune from devastating criticism so long as the insecurity it was trying to conquer was socially pervasive and universally feared. After they succeeded in destroying these sources of insecurity, however, the state's peace-keeping agencies began to look somewhat like a solution without a problem.[25] Once centralized authority had overcome the anarchical conditions in response to which it had arisen, its enormous powers were themselves suddenly thrown into question. As one source of insecurity (say, baronial squabbling) faded from consciousness, another (the state itself) became more conspicuous and annoying.[26] A similar story can be told about the fate of the ideology of private property.

Proponents of both absolutism and liberalism shared a common commitment to security. Where they parted company was in the identification of the most urgent threats to secure living and social cooperation—the former worrying most about private armies and the second about the agents of the state. The same can be said about classical liberals and proponents of the welfare state: The former focused on state-induced insecurity, whereas the latter emphasized market-induced insecurity. The *source* of insecurity changed in both cases. But the value of security itself remained more or less the same.

Why did James Madison cling to the rights of private property with what now seems like monomaniacal zeal? For one thing, private property was a symbol of security against the whims of political authority and the violence of rowdy neighbors, not to mention more impersonal forces. It was one of the few things an individual could count on in a sea of uncertainty. As other sources of security, such as a more reliable legal system, became established, private property had to bear less of this burden and thus absorbed fewer of life's uncertainties. Hence, it lost its former immunity to criticism. It even became visible as a source of insecurity itself.

As documented above, classical liberals, from Locke to Mill, routinely assumed that the state should infringe the property rights of the rich to satisfy the subsistence needs of the poor. According to Montesquieu, to choose another example, the security of individuals can be threatened not only by tyrannical rulers and by religious and baronial civil wars, but also by unpredictable fluctuations in the market. Security dictates government intervention to help workers whenever an industry suddenly fails. All citizens profit from a flourishing economy. As a just recompense, the state must compensate those workers who, for the common benefit, expose themselves to the periodic incompetence of the market. Indeed, unemployment compensation provides a necessary incentive for people to enter socially useful but individually risky occupations. As Montesquieu (1951, 713) argued,

> Les richesses d'un Etat supposent beaucoup d'industrie. Il n'est pas possible que dans un si grand nombre de branches de commerce, il n'y en ait toujours quelqu'une qui souffre, et dont par conséquent les ouvriers ne soient dans une nécessité momentanée.
>
> C'est pour lors que l'Etat a besoin d'apporter un prompt secours, soit pour empêcher le peuple de souffrir, soit pour éviter qu'il ne se révolte: c'est dans ce cas qu'il faut des hôpitaux, ou quelque réglement équivalent, qui puisse prévenir cette misère.
>
> (The riches of the state suppose great industry. Amidst the numerous branches of trade it is impossible but that some must suffer, and consequently the mechanics must be in a momentary necessity.
>
> When this happens, the state is obliged to lend them a ready assistance, whether it be to prevent the sufferings of the people, or to avoid a rebellion. In this case hospitals, or some equivalent regulations, are necessary to prevent this misery. [Montesquieu, 1949, vol. 2, 26])

Just as legal rights protect citizens from the tyranny of magistrates, so economic rights protect them from the tyranny of the market.

This passage is additionally interesting for the casualness with which Montesquieu juxtaposes several distinct justifications for redistributive relief measures. To the compensatory justice of helping those who contribute to the common advantage, he adds the wisdom of avoiding a potential revolt as well as a more general humanitarian concern to prevent unnecessary suffering.[27]

A few subsidiary points deserve mention here. First of all, competition serves consumers. But it does not serve *all* consumers. For-profit hospitals may well tend to concentrate on profitable illnesses, leaving difficult and costly cases to public institutions, just as private schools tend to exclude children with disciplinary and learning problems. This is a liberal reason for refusing to allocate health care and education by pure market mechanisms. Markets promote freedom by allowing individuals, without the intervention of authority, to purchase what they want. But what happens to individuals with no money? How does a market system enhance their freedom? That even libertarians sometimes feel compelled to propose voucher schemes suggests a latent guilt about the mysterious partiality of the market toward those who have money to spend.

Liberal hostility to inherited authority hardly needs be mentioned. But if property is, or can be, power, by what right can liberals defend hereditary wealth? Liberals argue against confiscatory inheritance taxes, when they do, on practical grounds, not because of any hidden doubts about the meritocratic ethic. To undermine a family's capacity to educate and shape its children would do incalculable damage to individual liberty. Nevertheless, liberals remain justly worried about individuals who are left without any resources at birth, who (by a natural lottery) are deprived of a realistic opportunity to participate in the market system. For this reason, too, welfare systems can be conceived as expressions of liberal guilt about the anti-individualistic implications of the inheritance of wealth.

MUTUAL OBLIGATION WITHOUT A COMMON PURPOSE

Romantically inclined theorists typically argue that no welfare program can be justified without appeal to a very strong concept of *community*. I will be willing to pay taxes for support of the poor only if I identify, morally and emotionally, with the collectivity to which we all, tax-payers and welfare recipients alike, belong. Identification with a larger unit leads me to a selfless concern for my fellow citizens, and so forth. Man is a social animal; *ergo*, the welfare state!

This analysis is not completely convincing. Indeed, the opposite case seems more plausible. To erode primordial loyalties of caste, clan, sect, race, ethnic or regional group, and so on, it was necessary to convince people to conceive of themselves primarily as individuals. Only after traditional groupings had been disaggregated was it possible to reintegrate individuals into a larger national community. When you begin to conceive yourself as an individual, rather than as a Capulet or a Montague, you can also conceive yourself as a citizen.

Individualism is essential to the welfare state in this respect. If inhabitants of Scarsdale were primarily driven by loyalty to their ethnic community, they might be unwilling to pay taxes destined for Harlem.[28] Though acknowledging a social or inborn grouping instinct, liberals simply argued that it sometimes had barbaric consequences. Consider Hume's view of factions, quintessential expressions of human sociality: "Factions subvert government, render laws impotent, and beget the fiercest animosities among men of the same nation, who ought to give *mutual assistance* and protection to each other" (1963, 55; my emphasis). Though entirely selfless, faction-members may destroy all possibility of community-wide mutual support.[29] Small-group selflessness, the underside of xenophobia, must be overcome to achieve the rarer selflessness exhibited in national systems of poor relief.

Of course, critics might admit that primordial affiliations must be dissolved before individuals conceive themselves as members of a national community. But they could still argue that a new emotional attachment to the *national* community must step in and replace old loyalties before people will willingly help their neediest fellows. But here again, doubts are possible. Nationalism, a quasi-erotic attachment to one's fellow citizens and a corresponding coolness toward foreigners, is indeed illiberal. But need it play a role in the moral justification of the welfare state? Tending to be universalistic or cosmopolitan rather than nationalistic in outlook, liberals are more willing to support wars, such as World War II, in which cosmopolitan values are at stake than wars for national aggrandizement or national interest. In the same spirit, liberals would support, by inclination, an international transfer play whereby wealthy individuals helped support the poor wherever they lived.

In fact, liberals support national transfer plans. This fact does not imply any betrayal of cosmopolitan values or a covert communitarian ideology, however. Instead, it can easily be interpreted as another concession to the practical. Without sovereign power, notoriously absent in the international arena, mutual assistance on a large scale is almost impossible to implement effectively. Payments across borders will tend to fill the pockets of the rich and may well exacerbate urbanization, making poor countries increasingly dependent for food supply on rich countries. Practical problems and stumbling blocks, not nationalist "bonds," explain the liberal commitment to *national* transfer programs.

War, it is true, cements citizens into a tightly knit community ready to make individual sacrifices for a common purpose (avoiding defeat). That warfare contributes to welfare by accustoming citizens to higher tax burdens seems beyond dispute. Welfare, however, is not quite like military victory, not exactly a common goal. Sparta was not a welfare state. Welfare, in fact, may be less like a goal and more like a condition for the pursuit of a variety of goals. In any case, it seems possible to justify redistributionist policies by appealing solely to equality or impartiality. This, in essence, is Ronald Dworkin's argument. Being unwilling to admit that poor citizens are less worthy of respect than rich ones, or that their ideals deserve less chance of realization, liberals are committed to providing the poor with at least some resources for working out and trying to fulfill their own goals. Redistribution can be justified even in the absence of fraternal sentiments. Welfare rights express liberal neutrality, not illiberal community. Or again: Welfare is a precondition for diverse purposes, not itself a common purpose.

THE POSITIVE FUNCTIONS OF STATE POWER

A stylized distinction between state and civil society, between the cruel realm of political compulsion and the happy realm of economic voluntariness, is the center of many right-wing attacks on welfare rights. Freedom is at an end when, ominously and imperialistically, "government spreads into society." The autonomy of civil society, the "prepolitical" nature of extrapolitical life, the utter absence of power relations within the market sphere—these remain potent myths. There is no denying that they were initially promulgated by some classical liberals—think only of Tom Paine. Historically, however, we should probably interpret these exaggerated claims as political programs, not as empirical generalizations. They were exasperated attacks on the (temporarily) most annoying source of social insecurity (i.e., the state), not sociological claims about the capacity of nonpolitical sectors of society to function effectively without government regulation.

The writers I have been discussing were all aware that the state created national markets by breaking down traditional barriers to trade. They also knew that government continued to enforce contract and trespass laws as well as to disrupt spontaneous social monopolies. Without betraying their principles, liberal states built railroads, highways, lighthouses, dams, sewers, and canals—providing facilities essential to the community that individuals would never have been able to fund privately (Hume, 1967, 538–539). As Mill says, there are "a variety of cases, in which important public services are to be performed, while yet there is no individual specially interested in performing them, nor would any adequate remuneration naturally or spontaneously attend their performance" (Mill, 1899, 457).[30] In any case, none of our representative liberals dreamed about a politics-free realm or the pristine autonomy of civil society. Indeed, they all conceived "civil society" as society "civilized" by state action. Despite some rhetorical exaggeration, they did not believe that we could realistically choose an inactive rather than an active government. The only open question was: In what sort of activities should the state engage?

The U.S. Constitution instructs the government to "promote the general Welfare." But what precisely can a liberal state do in pursuit of this aim? One remarkable precedent was Smith's proposal for a publicly financed compulsory system of education, aimed to help the poor (Smith, 1937, 716–740). The market could not be trusted to deliver this precious good. Indeed, Smith justified state intervention in the educational arena as a necessary response to the incompetence of the market or, rather, as a remedy for the humanly disfiguring and crippling consequences of factory work. Specialization transformed workers into miserable citizens, incapable of making informed judgments about political questions (Smith, 1937, 734–735). Mill followed Smith in this line of reasoning. Self-government becomes possible only when the majority has reached a certain level of education (Mill, 1977, 413–421). The right to an education can therefore be inferred directly from the right to participate in collective self-rule: "I hold it therefore the duty of the government to supply the defect [of schools established on a voluntary basis] by giving pecuniary support to elementary schools, such as to render them accessible to all the children of the poor, either freely, or for a payment too inconsiderable to be sensibly felt" (Mill, 1899, 457). State-supported education is a serious annoyance for the pure libertarian because, in this case, government intervention obviously enhances individual autonomy. Publicly provided schooling, as Mill says, is "help toward doing without help" (1899, 456).

But the crucial argument advanced by both Smith and Mill is that educational rights are democracy-reinforcing. Expanding on John Ely's theory of judicial review, Frank Michelman has gone a step further and argued that subsistence, shelter, and health care are all "indispensable means of effective participation" in the political processes outlined by the U.S. Constitution (1979, 677). Admittedly, the idea that implicit (educational and economic) rights are necessary preconditions for the proper utilization of explicit (political and legal) rights is open to serious criticism (Bork, 1979, 695–701). It is not, however, a recent invention but, rather, an idea well known to the eighteenth-century liberals who most influenced the American Founders.

AUTOPATERNALISM AS COLLECTIVE SELF-RELIANCE

Opponents of the welfare state repeatedly denounce its paternalism in the name of citizen self-reliance. But this may well be a false alternative. In the first place, self-reliance must be organized. When an individual walks into court and sues on the basis of a democratically approved statute, he is no less self-reliant than when he establishes a union. All self-reliance, in a complex society, requires social cooperation, indirect techniques, and institutional strategies.[31] As a result, we cannot use the idea of self-reliance to justify a blanket rejection of redistributionist legislation.

Self-reliance does not occur in a legal and political vacuum; it depends upon preconditions that, in some cases, must be provided by the state. Because independence in one respect always implies dependence in another, antipaternalism is a difficult position to espouse consistently. Hobbes, moreover, already provided a partial answer to the accusation of paternalism hurled later at all welfare programs. Peace, as he saw it, is a goal that most citizens share but that no individual is willing to pursue unless he or she can be assured that others will coooperate in achieving it as best they can. Government intervention is justified not merely to protect unwilling victims but also, and primarily, to help citizens do jointly what they all want to do but cannot do separately. In other words, although Hobbes would never have used such language, state-help can be freedom-enhancing as well as freedom-restricting.

Answering the libertarians of his day, Mill explained the autonomy-reinforcing function of state intervention:

> The principle that each is the best judge of his own interest, understood as these objectors understand it, would prove that governments ought not to fulfill any of their acknowledged duties—ought not, in fact, to exist at all. It is greatly the interest of the community, collectively and individually, not to rob or defraud one another; but there is not the less necessity for laws to punish robbery and fraud; because, though it is the interest of each that nobody should rob or cheat, it is not anyone's interest to refrain from robbing and cheating others when all others are permitted to rob and cheat him. Penal laws exist at all, chiefly for this reason, because even a unanimous opinion that a certain line of conduct is for the general interest, does not always make it people's individual interest to adhere to that line of conduct. (1899, 467)

Coercive government intervention can be essential for individuals to overcome collective-action problems and achieve their own goals: "It is in the interest of each to do what is good for all, but only if others will do likewise" (Mill, 1899, 467). By enforcing the norm of fairness (i.e., the self-exemption taboo), the state can enable citizens to do what they genuinely want; that is, it can increase individual self-direction. In other words, justice and freedom, state regulation and liberty, are not nearly so antithetical as right-wing enemies of the welfare state would have us believe.

Even if most Americans wished to help the poor, they might do so only if they believed with some certainty that most of their fellow citizens would pitch in. Transfer programs may be justified on these grounds alone, as even their most adamant opponents admit.[32] But I adduce the free-rider problem solely to make a negative point. All the theorists discussed in this essay have recognized that governmental coercion could help individuals achieve their own goals. As a result, liberalism should *not* be mechanically associated with a hysterical fear of state paternalism or dependence on government. Liberals have always accepted some degree of paternalism, so long as it was autonomy-enabling—somehow a reinforcement of individual freedom as well as an expression of collective self-rule.

CONCLUSION

Most discussions of the normative foundations of the welfare state suppose a fundamental breach with the classical liberal tradition. It is commonly assumed that liberalism was antistatist, hostile to social planning, fond of liberty above equality, unwilling to engage in redistribution, committed to the inviolability of private property, assured of the spontaneous harmony of interests, trustful of the market, rigidly antipaternalistic, hopeful that the public sector would shrink and that the private sector would expand, and so forth. On all accounts, as I have tried to show, this picture of classical liberalism is flawed. As a result, the fundamental continuity between liberal rights and welfare rights is stronger than has yet been realized. Without providing a moral or political justification of the redistributionist state, such considerations considerably weaken the arguments, or at least the bragging rights, of its enemies.

NOTES

1. The latter, *unlike* the Reaganites, repudiate the market for traditionalist reasons.

2. I shall also be discussing Hobbes—a thinker with at least one foot in the liberal tradition.

3. This view is advanced by, among others, Hayek (1960, 176–192).

4. See, for example, Montesquieu (1951, 431).

5. This, despite the one-sided argument of Franz Neumann (1957, 96–148).

6. A concern for the welfare of others, in other words, was built into the liberal definition of legitimate private action. Locke distinguished *proper interests* from improper ones on the grounds that the former were those compatible with the public good: "*Law*, in its true Notion, is not so much the Limitation as *the direction of a free and intelligent Agent* to his proper Interest, and prescribes no farther than is for the general Good of those under that Law" (see Locke, 1965, 347–348 [2, 57]; emphasis in original). Self-interest is subordinate to the just, the right, and the proper, and that means: to the general good. Improper or sinister interests, those violating the norm of justice, must be legally repressed. An ascriptive, hierarchical, demeaning, and oppressive social system, where a few reaped all the benefits and the majority bore all the burdens, might be "peaceful" enough, but it would not qualify as a liberal social order for the simple reason that it would not be just. However orderly, slavery remains a vile and miserable, and therefore unacceptable, estate of man.

7. The analytically unsatisfactory distinction between *droits-libertés* and *droits-créances*, for example, is stressed by Luc Ferry and Alain Renaut (1985, 84–86).

8. The very idea of an "entitlement," writes one conservative opponent of welfare programs for the poor, "challenges the distinction, essential to liberal constitutionalism, between the rights the government exists to protect and the exercise of those rights by private individuals, or between state and society. For an entitlement is a right whose exercise is guaranteed to a certain degree by the government—a right that is therefore exercised to that degree by the government. An equal right to seek a job, for example, becomes an entitlement to a job or rather to the proceeds of a job, which the government performs as it were instead of the worker" (Mansfield, 1985, 13). But liberals have always viewed *security* as a right that the government protects by performing basic police functions instead of allowing citizens to do so.

9. See Note 6.

10. The fundamental superiority of the liberal over the Marxist tradition may lie here: Despite their intense concern with political tyranny, liberals never lost sight of the possibility of nonpolitical or nonstate forms of oppression. Marxists, by contrast, because of their one-sided focus on the owners of the means of production, tended to neglect the equal and autonomous threat to freedom posed by the wielders of the means of destruction. Because threatening concentrations of power were always emerging spontaneously even within the freest society, liberals saw state power as an indispensable counterweight—as an instrument of, rather than simply a threat to, freedom. Their fundamentally double view of the (political and extrapolitical) obstacles to liberty may well have led the most clear-sighted heirs of the liberal tradition, quite consistently, to embrace the welfare state.

11. Nietzsche's "Verachtung gegen Sicherheit" can be found, among other places, in Nietzsche (1973, 786).

12. And he adds: "security no human being can possibly do without"; see also Locke (1955, 27, 45, 47, 48) and Hume (1967, 485, 550).

13. Defending laissez-faire against what he considered a misguided and antiliberal trend toward collectivism, Dicey wrote, in an often-quoted passage: "Few are those who realise the undeniable truth that State help kills self-help. Hence the majority of mankind must almost of necessity look with undue favor upon governmental intervention" (Dicey, 1914, 258). Dicey's choice of words here is striking. "Self-help" originally referred to the private right to avenge perceived injuries without recourse to the judicial apparatus of the state. This was a form of autonomy or self-reliance that seventeenth- and eighteenth-century liberals, too, hoped would disappear. Self-help was indeed killed by state-help, as Dicey suggests, but not accidentally, as a result of some quaint prejudice or optical illusion, and not illiberally, in a fit of drunken statism. Self-help was undermined with open eyes for the security of the overwhelming majority.

14. Similarly, according to Brian Abel-Smith, "the architects of our welfare states . . . did not intend to create a more equal society but to establish a floor of protection at the bottom" (1985, 32).

15. Compare with Mill's statement that "we must beware of admitting a principle of which we should resent as a gross injustice the application to ourselves" (1977, 285).

16. This passage also occurs in Kant (1966, 151–152).

17. In other words, this argument would not justify redistribution to the handicapped. A similar contribution-based conception of distributive justice was advanced somewhat earlier by Voltaire (1961, 25): "Il a fallu des siècles pour rendre justice à l'humanité, pour sentir qu'il était horrible que le grand nombre semât et que le petit nombre recueillît" (It took centuries to bring justice to mankind, to make people realize that it was horrible that the many should sow and the few reap).

18. Writing in defense of the Poor Law of 1834, Mill claims that it solved the most important dilemma of all welfare programs: "how to give the greatest amount of needful help, with the smallest encouragement to undue reliance on it" (1899, 468).

19. His concern for impartiality, of course, does not lead Mill to denounce voluntary charity so long as it is only a supplement to public provision. Well-being is not solely a matter of comparative advantage. What the poor need, primarily, is help, not equality. Distributive justice is still an overriding norm, however, so long as some citizens have more than they need and others are starving.

20. "The greater security of property is one of the main conditions and causes of greater production, which is Progress in its most familiar and vulgarest aspect" (Mill, 1977, 386).

21. Arguably, Locke ascribed a presocial origin to private property in an attempt to outbid the presocial credentials of confiscation-prone divine right rulers. One you-can't-touch-me ideology deserved (and provoked) another. To this extent, the plausibility of Locke's position was essentially wedded to the theological premises of seventeenth-century political debate. It is thus anachronistic and obfuscatory to speak, with Nozick, of a sacred or inviolable or natural right to property in a society where government no longer claims divine sanction.

22. Even when condemning confiscatory redistribution, however, Locke suggested strongly that legitimate redistribution was possible: "The magistrate cannot take away these worldly things from this man or party and give them to that, nor change propriety amongst fellow subjects (no, not even by a law), *for a cause that has no relation to the end of civil government*, I mean for their religion" (Locke, 1955, 49; my emphasis).

23. In his study of "the public interest," J. A. Gunn demonstrated that property rights and self-interest were *republican* principles in the seventeenth century. Who benefited from the ethics of self-sacrifice? Monarchs intent on dynastic aggrandizement, above all others, learned to appreciate the utility of schooling soldiers to forget themselves. To die selflessly, to die for the state, was actually to die for the king's status, his personal prestige. Republicans aimed at wresting power from a war-prone monarch who completely ignored the concerns of his subjects. Thus, they were understandably anxious to rehabilitate

the inviolability of private property and the affiliated principle of self-interest. To affirm property rights and the legitimacy of universal self-interest was to deprive dynastic monarchs of self-oblivious cannon fodder. It also required rulers to justify excessive taxation by explaining the good it would bring to those who were taxed (Gunn, 1969).

24. The classic illustration, in the American case, is the Supreme Court's decision in *Lochner v. New York*, 198 U.S. 45 (1905).

25. Compare with Richelieu's remark: "La désordre fait partie de l'ordre."

26. The liberal doctrine of rights was only fully developed, one might argue, after modern states successfully centralized formerly diffuse social threats or sources of insecurity in one easily identifiable location, thus making it possible to defend against them efficiently.

27. Insecurity produced by private property and the market, be it noted, did not utterly eclipse other forms. Varieties of insecurity did not replace one another but were cumulative. In other words, welfare state liberals can still be concerned with the danger of political oppression and even with a residual threat posed by the mafia and the Red Brigades.

28. For this example, see Larmore (1987, 128).

29. The impossibility of mapping the selfless/selfish scheme onto the good/ bad scheme appears to have been a fundamental insight shared by all liberals. Selflessness can be noble, but it is not always so; history contains many examples of brutal selflessness or (to use Samuel Beer's phrase) "altruism with teeth." Similarly—and this is the idea conventionally associated with Adam Smith— selfish or self-centered behavior is often sinister and immoral, but not always.

30. The same argument, in almost the same words, can be found in Smith (1937, 681).

31. Even to "do it yourself," you must go to a do-it-yourself store and buy a do-it-yourself kit.

32. According to Friedman, "we might all of us be willing to contribute to the relief of poverty, *provided* everyone else did" (1962, 191); see also Posner (1986, 440).

REFERENCES

Abel-Smith, Brian. 1985. "The Major Problems of the Welfare State: Defining the Issues," *The Welfare State and Its Aftermath*, edited by S.N. Eisenstadt and Ora Ahimeir. Totawa, N.J.: Barnes & Noble.

Bacon, Francis. 1986. "Of Seditions and Troubles," *The Essayes or Counsels Civill and Morall*, edited by M. Kiernan. Cambridge, Mass.: Harvard University Press.

Bentham, Jeremy. 1979. "Principles of the Civil Code," *Theory of Legislation*. Bombay: Tripathi.

Bork, Robert. 1979. "The Impossibility of Finding Welfare Rights in the Constitution," *Washington University Law Quarterly*, vol. 3.

Dicey, A.V. 1914. *Lectures on the Relation Between Law and Public Opinion in England During the Nineteenth Century*. London: Macmillan.

Encyclopédie, ou Dictionnaire raisonné des sciences, des arts, et des métiers. 1765. Neuchâtel: Faulche.

Federalist Papers. 1961. Edited by Clinton Rossiter. New York: Mentor.

Ferry, Luc, and Alain Renaut. 1985. *Philosophie Politique 3: des droits de l'homme à l'idée républicaine.* Paris: Presses Universitaire de France.

Friedman, Milton. 1962. *Capitalism and Freedom.* Chicago: University of Chicago Press.

Gunn, J.A.W. 1961. *Politics and the Public Interest in the Seventeenth Century.* London: Routledge & Kegan Paul.

Hayek, Friedrich. 1960. *The Constitution of Liberty.* Chicago: University of Chicago Press.

Hobbes, Thomas. 1965. *Leviathan.* Oxford: Oxford University Press.

Hont, Istvan, and Michael Ignatieff. 1983. "Needs and Justice in the 'Wealth of Nations,'" *Wealth and Virtue: The Shaping of Political Economy in the Scottish Enlightenment,* edited by I. Hont and M. Ignatieff. Cambridge: Cambridge University Press.

Hume, David. 1963. *Essays: Moral, Political, and Literary.* Oxford: Oxford University Press.

――――. 1967. *Treatise of Human Nature.* Oxford: Oxford University Press.

Kant, Immanuel. 1965. *The Metaphysical Elements of Justice.* Indianapolis: Bobbs-Merrill.

――――. 1966. *Metaphysik der Sitten,* edited by Karl Vorländer. Hamburg: Felix Meiner.

Larmore, Charles. 1987. *Patterns of Moral Complexity.* Cambridge: Cambridge University Press.

Locke, John. 1965. *Two Treatises of Government.* New York: Mentor.

――――. 1955. *A Letter Concerning Toleration.* Indianapolis: Bobbs-Merrill.

Mansfield, Jr., Harvey C. 1985. "The American Election: Entitlements Versus Opportunity," *Government and Opposition,* vol. 20, Winter.

Marx, Karl, and Friedrich Engels. 1972. *Werke,* vol. 1. Berlin: Dietz.

Michelman, Frank. 1979. "Welfare Rights in a Constitutional Democracy," *Washington University Law Quarterly,* vol. 3.

Mill, John Stuart. 1969. "Essays on Ethics, Religion and Society." *Collected Works,* vol. 10, edited by J.M. Robson. Toronto: University of Toronto Press.

――――. 1977. "Essays on Politics and Society." *Collected Works,* vol. 18, edited by J.M. Robson. Toronto: University of Toronto Press.

――――. 1899. *Principles of Political Economy,* vol. 2. New York: Colonial Press.

Montesquieu, Baron de. 1949. *The Spirit of the Laws,* translated by Thomas Nugent. New York: Hafner.

――――. 1951. *Oeuvres complètes,* vol. 2. Paris: Pléiade.

Neumann, Franz. 1957. *The Democratic and Authoritarian State.* New York: Free Press.

Nietzsche, Friedrich. 1973. *Werke,* vol. 2, edited by Karl Schlechta. Darmstadt: Wissenschaftichebuchgesellschaft.

Posner, Richard. 1986. *Economic Analysis of Law,* 3rd ed. Boston: Little, Brown.

Richelieu, Armand de. 1961. *Political Testament.* Madison: University of Wisconsin Press.

Smith, Adam. 1937. *An Inquiry into the Nature and Causes of the Wealth of Nations.* New York: Modern Library.

———. 1976. *Theory of Moral Sentiments,* edited by D.D. Raphael and A.L. Macfie. Oxford: Oxford University Press.

Tully, James. 1980. *A Discourse on Property: John Locke and His Adversaries.* Cambridge: Cambridge University Press.

Voltaire. 1961. "Lettres philosophiques," *Mélanges,* edited by Jacques van den Heural. Paris: Pléiade.

5

WELFARE RIGHTS
AS PROPERTY RIGHTS

The political and economic arguments that characterize contemporary welfare states were first heard between 1790 and 1834 in the controversy over the fate of the English Poor Law. It was in this period that the claims of political economy, especially the recommendations of Malthus and Ricardo that the Poor Law be abolished, came into conflict with a philosophic defense of welfare rights. On one side of this debate was Ricardo's assertion that "the principle of gravitation is not more certain than the tendency of such laws to change wealth and power into misery and weakness" (Ricardo, 1977, 3). But throughout this period these claims were opposed by many who believed that, as the *Poor Man's Guardian* argued, "the poor who cannot find employment should be maintained at the expense of the rich till they can. . . . They shall consider themselves to have as perfect a right to that portion of the superfluities of the rich, called the poor's rate, as the rich themselves have to the remainder" (May 23, 1835). Behind the claims of the *Poor Man's Guardian* stood a tradition in which government-funded aid to the poor was justified by neither charity nor utilitarian calculation nor political compromise, but was instead required by justice. The development of that tradition in the seventeenth and eighteenth centuries, the changes it had to undergo before it could end as a defense of the Poor Laws, and an explication of the logic of welfare rights as understood by the theorists of this period is the subject of this chapter.

NATURAL LAW, PROPERTY, AND SUBSISTENCE

In the modern period it is probably unnecessary to start a discussion of property rights that contain a right to subsistence earlier than Hugo Grotius. The model of property rights found in his masterpiece, *De Jure Belli Ac Pacis Libri Tres* (1625), will dominate the discussion of property rights and welfare rights for the next 200 years. Here it will be possible to highlight only a few of his most important points. The first is that his description of the origin of property rights began with God granting the earth to all people for their sustenance. The earth was understood as a common to which all had access. From the earth as common property Grotius demonstrated how use rights and then private property rights could have developed in ways consistent with natural law. The short explanation of this process begins with population growth causing scarcity, discord, and a decline in sociability. Private property was justified because its ability to moderate conflict and increase production saved lives. Whereas use rights seem not to have required the consent of others before they could be exercised, full property rights drew their moral legitimacy from the agreement of others. In one of the most important passages for the understanding of property in the modern period, Grotius wrote:

> Things became subject to private ownership . . . by a kind of agreement, either expressed, as by a division, or implied, as by occupation. In fact, as soon as community ownership was abandoned, and as yet no division had been made, it is to be supposed, that all agreed, that whatever each one had taken possession of should be his property. (1964, 189–190)

Though Grotius had derived private property in ways consistent with natural law, the origin of property in an original common to which all had access influenced the way the earth could be used even after it had become private. Individuals who find themselves without property and unable to obtain aid may legitimately take from others to avoid starvation. This ability of the destitute to take from those who own superfluities is known as the right of necessity. In Grotius' formulation it constituted a return to the original common, at least from the point of view of the starving individual. In necessity, Grotius wrote, "the primitive right of user revives, as if community of ownership remained, since in respect to all human laws—the law of ownership included— supreme necessity seems to have been expected" (1964, 193). One of the legacies of Grotius, then, was a property theory that contained the idea that the earth and its produce must be used to maintain everyone's life, and that the right that individuals have to the earth as a common can never be relinquished. Another way of putting this is to say that no one could be thought to have consented to the introduction of property without attaching to their consent the proviso that in necessity they could without injustice take what their preservation required. Here a subsistence right is part of a property right, rather than a separate right that limits property from without. That is, property rights would not have been recognized as legitimate if they did not carry this limitation.

The last point to notice about the Grotian theory involves the necessary superiority of public over private in a civil association. As a consequence, the rights of the public "are superior to private rights, since they are exercised by the community over its members, and the property of its members, for the sake of the common good" (Grotius, 1964, Bk II, 385).[1] The ability of government to tax and appropriate (with compensation) through eminent domain are, in part, explained by the "greater" right of the public.

Of course, the natural law philosophers who followed Grotius in the seventeenth century had much to argue about. Samuel Pufendorf, for example, in *De Jure Naturae et Gentium Libri Octo* (1680), introduced the important distinction between a negative and a positive community in order to describe more accurately the original common. In a negative community the land is thought of as unowned, while in a positive community it is understood as owned by all (Pufendorf, 1964, 532). It will seem to later theorists that private property is more easily derived from the negative community. He insisted more unambiguously than Grotius that property originated in consent (Pufendorf, 1964, 536–538). Pufendorf also disagreed with Grotius about the right of necessity. Although Pufendorf believed such a right existed, he denied that its invocation meant all property returned to an original common. Instead, he thought of it as simply the ability of the starving person to override the property rights of others. As in this formulation property rights remain intact, it was possible for Pufendorf to insist more strongly on the need for compensation by the starving person once he was economically able (1964, 303–306).

Whatever disagreements there were about the exact formulation of the right of necessity, Hobbes and Locke as well as Pufendorf and Grotius affirmed its existence. Hobbes seems to have thought that the right to self-preservation contained within it a right to subsistence. Thus he included within the rights individuals could not give up when they joined civil society not only the right to defend oneself from assault but also the right to "the use of food, ayre, medicine" (Hobbes, 1968, 269).[2] Moreover, he recommended that those unable to maintain themselves "ought not to be left to the charity of private persons: but to be provided for . . . by the laws of the commonwealth" (1968, 387). Hobbes does not seem to have tied government relief to a welfare right so much as he understood the prudential advantages of providing for the poor through the orderly process of Poor Laws, rather than allowing them to fall into the situation when they could rightfully take from others.

The model used by Grotius based on an original common also provided the framework for Locke's discussion of property.[3] Note that

Locke's description of the common is in the present tense (radical theorists in the 1790s certainly noted as much): "Men, being once born, *have* a right to their Preservation, and consequently to Meat and Drink, and such other things, as Nature affords for their Subsistence. . . . Tis very clear, that God . . . *has* given the Earth to the Children of Men, given it to Mankind in common" (Locke, 1960, 327; my emphasis). Locke, of course, had his own argument for the derivation of property rights from the common, but his emphasis on labor may have been a technical solution to the problem of why occupancy creates rights rather than an important ideological departure. He also saw property rights acquired in the state of nature as resigned to the community at the birth of civil society. He could hardly have been more explicit in his statement that

> (where the Increase of People and Stock, with the Use of Money) had made Land scarce, and so of some Value, the several Communities settled the Bounds of their distinct Territories, and by laws within themselves, regulated the Properties of the private Men of their Society, and so, by Compact and Agreement, settled the Property which Labour and Industry began. (1960, 341)[4]

And like other property theorists of the seventeenth century he saw rights to the original common as requiring the right of necessity.

> But we know God hath not left one Man so to the Mercy of another, that he may starve him if he please: God the Lord and Father of all, has given no one of his children such a Property, in his peculiar Portion of the things of this world, but that he has given his needy Brother a Right to the Surplusage of his Goods. (1960, 205)

Just as Locke's celebrated labor theory had the purpose of deriving property rights without recourse to a contract, it also had the effect of justifying the right of necessity without a contract. Locke's moral justification for both a property right and a subsistence right ultimately rested on the intention of God that the product of His workmanship should live and not starve. Thus, we have found two different foundations for a subsistence right—one based on man's intentions expressed in a contract and the other based on God's intentions. Both will be available for the use of later theorists to defend the idea that the poor have rights.

The acknowledgment of the rights of the poor to subsistence within a framework that defended the current distribution of property characterized the natural law philosophers of the seventeenth century. It was their enterprise to link the institution of private property to the unchanging rules required by natural law. Even the politically radical Locke needed to be able to defend the property rights of his society. After all, part of his charge against the monarchy was that it violated the legitimate rights of landowners. The right of necessity, then, enabled these theorists to defend the division of property to private individuals because it guaranteed at least in theory that those left without land or money were not left to starve. It is difficult to imagine a less threatening interpretation of a right to subsistence than the right of necessity. The poor may have a right to take, but this interpretation does not seem to require that anyone else has an obligation to give. Moreover, necessity required giving the poor neither a job nor land. And in most of its interpretations it required the poor to first ask private citizens and then to ask magistrates before it could be invoked. The requirement to pay compensation for what was taken further brought the exercise of this right under control. It was Hobbes' concern for order and Locke's desire to inculcate virtue in the idle that explained their interest in a Poor Law, not the requirements of justice.[5]

PROPERTY, NECESSITY, AND THE POOR LAW

The use of the natural law tradition to legitimate private property, especially through a conservative interpretation of the right of necessity, continued into the middle of eighteenth-century England. The two best examples of this point of view can be found in Thomas Rutherforth's published lectures on Grotius, which were delivered at Cambridge University in the late 1750s, and in William Blackstone's *Commentaries on the Laws of England*, published in 1764–1767. Though I have argued that the property theories and the right of necessity associated with them were developed in the seventeenth century primarily to defend the legitimacy of the status quo in property relations, it is not surprising that the tradition that grew from them could take turns to the left that the founders could not have foreseen. Both Rutherforth and Blackstone, however, were aware of less conservative interpretations of the natural law discussion of property and tried to struggle against them.

At the center of Rutherforth's discussion was the meaning of the original grant of the earth to mankind and the implications of that grant for the development of private property. For reasons that are impossible to know, Rutherforth did not use Pufendorf's distinction between a positive and negative community, but only the idea of a positive community makes sense of his discussion. For he argued that "all things belonged originally to all mankind" and that individuals in this state had "a common right in a joint stock" (Rutherforth, 1832, 21).

As everyone shared a right to the common, each could take what he or she needed for subsistence. In doing this each was simply taking what he or she was a part owner of. But because each was only a *part* owner, he or she could not take more than could be used. To do so would have been to injure others by depriving them of what they had a right to. Rutherforth argued that the exercise of a primitive use right in a situation of common ownership does not require waiting for the approval of others and that only the idea of common ownership explains why those primitive rights were limited to use (1832, 21).

Rutherforth interpreted Grotius as maintaining that the only way use rights to the common could be transformed into property rights was through consent, either express or tacit: "What a man seizes upon, with a design to make it his own, or to appropriate it to himself, will become fairly his own, or will be made his property; when the rest of mankind, as far as they have an opportunity of observing him, understand what his design is, and show by their behavior, in not molesting him, that they agree to let his design take effect" (Rutherforth, 1832, 25). Rutherforth, not surprisingly, saw Locke's labor and mixing arguments as intellectual competitors to Grotius' theory, inasmuch as they did not require consent for property to develop.

For labor to establish a property right in what has been occupied, which was the way Rutherforth understood Locke's argument, it must be able to "overrule or set aside the right of others." But to "set aside the right of an individual, without his consent, is an injury to him; so setting aside the common claim of mankind, without their consent, is an injury to them" (Rutherforth, 1832, 26–27). Just as it is impermissible to claim that simply working on someone else's property transfers its title to the worker, so it cannot be claimed that laboring on what is owned by all makes it the property of the laborer. Rutherforth also maintained that if it were possible for labor to make private what belonged to all, Locke would not be able to defend the limits he thought should apply to acquisition.[6]

Behind these theoretical disagreements with Locke was another issue. Rutherforth seemed to detect in the labor argument a danger to landlords. Thus, he was at pains to deny Locke's contention that labor is responsible for 99 percent of value: "If neither the timber of his plough, nor the horses that draw it, nor the meat which they eat, nor the manure which he lays upon his land, nor the grain with which he sows it, are his own, what will you rate his labor at?" (Rutherforth, 1832, 30). His anxiety at the possible consequences of the labor argument is made explicit in his example of a tenant who "plows and sows the land" using his own material as well as his labor to raise wheat. "But no one will be led to conclude from hence, that because . . . ninety-nine parts in a hundred are owing to the labour of the occupier, the property, which he has in his own labor, will swallow up the property which the landlord has in the soil; and that the land, because he has cultivated it, will for the future become his own" (Rutherforth, 1832, 31). As we have noted, Rutherforth was right to see these possibilities within Lockean theory.

Grounding property in consent supplies the missing moral element to a labor/occupancy theory. That is, it explains why a mere physical act should create a moral obligation in others. Consent also avoids the problem of finding ways to "domesticate" a theory that emphasizes labor, especially in a period still dominated by absentee landlord/tenant relationships. But consent itself has problems, and these center on whether people would have consented to a distribution in which they or their children could find themselves left out of their nation's wealth altogether. Because Rutherforth thought that people would have "agreed to the introduction of property for the convenience of all, and not for the destruction of any" and are, in any case, barred from alienating the right to "the necessary means of [their] own preservation," the right of necessity always exists. "Thus, where a man must have starved otherwise, it is naturally no theft if he takes vituals which is not his own" (Rutherforth, 1832, 41). The condition whereby a starving person must first ask individuals and the magistrate for assistance and can only exercise the right of necessity if help is not forthcoming is important to Rutherforth. It enabled him to link the English Poor Law to the right of necessity by arguing that since the Poor Law guaranteed aid to the poor, it could never be legitimate in England to invoke this right. "Indeed in our own country, where the civil laws have provided for the poor, there can be no necessity which the civil law will allow to be sufficient ground for taking" (Rutherforth, 1832, 42–43).

Although William Blackstone's *Commentaries on the Laws of England* (1764–1767) is primarily known for its attempt to bring some order to English common law, it included a general discussion of the law of nature as well as a natural law justification of property rights. Blackstone opened his derivation of private property from the principles of natural law with some extraordinary comments.

> There is nothing which so generally strikes the imagination, and engages the affections of mankind, as the right of property; or that sole and despotic dominion which one man claims and exercises over the external things of the world, in total exclusion of the right of any other individual in the universe. And yet there are very few, that will give themselves the trouble to consider the original and foundation of this right. Pleased as we are with the possession, we seem afraid to look back

to the means by which it was acquired, as if fearful of some defect in our title; not caring to reflect that (accurately and strictly speaking) there is no foundation in nature or in natural law, why a set of words upon parchment should convey the dominion of land. . . . These enquiries, it must be owned, would be useless and even troublesome in common life. It is well if the mass of mankind will obey the laws when made, without scrutinizing too nicely into the reasons of making them. (1756–1769)

It is difficult not to see in the first sentence of this paragraph the attitude toward land held by Blackstone and the people he thought would read and use his book. But just as interesting is the fear that an enquiry into natural law might call into question current property rights—no doubt the reason he thought such enquiries would be "troublesome" in "common life" and should not be undertaken by "the mass of mankind."

Of course, Blackstone did not think that natural law properly understood was subversive of current property rights, and it was no doubt to demonstrate this that he engaged in the natural law enterprise. But we need note only a few of his ideas in this discussion. After considering the way occupancy created the first property rights, he explained that occupancy only began the process of establishing full property rights in land and that this process comes to an end only through the laws of early society: "Necessity begat property; and, in order to insure that property, recourse was had to civil society." Or, as he put it another time, "the permanent right of property . . . was no natural, but merely a civil right" (1756–1769). In this last statement Blackstone is explaining that the right to make a will is a creation of civil laws and therefore can be a fit subject for regulation. In fact, it seems clear that property was left off Blackstone's list of natural rights—which are limited to "life and liberty" (1756–1769)—precisely because of the need for the "long and voluminous" regulations that characterized property law in eighteenth-century England. Because property rights had to be regulated, the natural law tradition always saw them as resigned to the political community at its inception. When government is controlled by the largest landowners, as in Blackstone's time, this position does not seem important, but for later theorists it was to become crucial to the defense of collecting the poor rate or redistributing property.

It is also noteworthy that Blackstone was beginning to see dangers in a right of necessity and for that reason denied that it was implicit in the present property system. He disagreed with "Grotius, and Pufendorf, together with many other of the foreign jurists . . . and some even of our own lawyers" (inadvertently showing the strength of this tradition), first, by calling the right of necessity "unwarranted" because it would put property "under a strange insecurity" and, then, by adopting the view we found in Rutherforth that such a right, even if it once existed, was irrelevant in England because of the Poor Law (Blackstone, 1756–1769).

In Rutherforth and Blackstone rather traditional interpretations of the natural law discussion of property ended in a completely complacent acceptance of the status quo. Both were aware of the more critical uses to which this tradition could be put and worked to keep them under control. Rutherforth's stance, especially, is a good example of the conservative interpretation of a welfare right. This right was seen by him as a right to barest subsistence; it did not create in anyone with property an obligation to give to the poor; and yet its very recognition legitimated a private property system of great inequality. The institution of aid through the English Poor Law was justified prudentially (and here Blackstone joined Rutherforth) and further controlled the use of necessity.

FROM PROPERTY RIGHTS TO WELFARE RIGHTS

The development of the idea of a welfare right underwent a dramatic change in the work of Richard Woodward and William Paley, both of whom were Anglican clergyman. They too used the natural law tradition to defend the moral legitimacy of the major institutions of their society. But to a much greater degree than Rutherforth or Blackstone, they saw aid to the poor as important to that legitimacy. Thus, they preached Christian charity to their parishioners and defended the Poor Law against growing attack. Unlike Rutherforth and Blackstone, however, they did not support the Poor Law because of expediency. Instead they explicitly maintained that the rights of the poor gave them a *claim* upon the collective wealth of the country and created an obligation upon those with wealth to support the poor in need. Moreover, this obligation could not be met through private charity alone. Woodward and Paley both used the idea of a morally and legally enforceable debt to describe the relationship of those in need to the wealthy. As they saw this debt as a payment to "inferiors," to use Paley's word, it is probably best to describe their use of welfare rights as paternalist.[7]

Woodward's interest in these issues began after he moved to Dublin in the early 1760s and observed the condition of the Irish poor. He was one of the founders of the House of Industry in Dublin and the author of two widely read essays that advocated the establishment of a poor law in Ireland and supported the continuation of the English Poor Law. Although his *An Argument in Support of the Right of the Poor to a National Provision in the Kingdom of Ireland* (1768) may not be as rigorously argued as we would like, its main points are clear. It is useful, he thought, to think of society as having originated in a contract. In a precontractual period, people should be thought of as having a right to gather their subsistence from an earth owned in common. They would not have entered civil society and resigned their right to use the earth if that made their position worse. Thus, a private property system in which some would be landless would be consistent with natural law only if it could be supposed that those without land would be able to earn a subsistence from their labor. But if an individual was both landless and unemployed, his or her obligation to obey the law of civil society would continue only if that society guaranteed that person's subsistence through a system of aid. No one would have agreed to enter a society in which obedience to the laws against stealing might require his or her starvation. The fact that society was not constructed in this way, that the poor had little say, only added to Woodward's indignation. In a statement that will be cited often later in debates over the Poor Law, Woodward asked rhetorically whether the rich

> are or are not, bound in justice to provide for [the poor] a competent maintenance? If not, by what right did they take upon them to enact certain laws (for the rich compose the legislative body in every civilized country), which compelled that man to become a member of their society; which precluded him from any share in the land where he was born, any use of its spontaneous fruits, or any dominion over the beasts of the field, on pain of imprisonment or death? How can they justify their exclusive property, in the common heritage of mainkind, unless they consent in return to provide for the subsistence of the poor, who were excluded from those common rights by the laws of the rich, to which they were never parties? (1768, 32–33)

Although Woodward's defense of the rights of the poor, his sense that landlords lived off wealth created by the laboring poor, and his awareness that the poor were unrepresented in government may sound extraordinarily critical, they never added up in his mind to an attack on social institutions. In fact, he was at pains to argue more than once "the reasonableness of their [the poor's] subordination in society, and their obligations to obedience" (1768, "Introduction").[8] The fact that he thought aid was best given in a House of Industry because it improved the morals of the poor indicate the primarily paternalist nature of his argument.

But there is in Woodward the crux of a powerful argument in support of the rights of the poor, at least insofar as the contractual model is a useful way to think about the origin of rights. The inclusion of a welfare right in the list of rights that an individual would require before he agreed to obey the law and the insistence that it result in government-funded aid seem more than merely plausible. After all, none of the other rights we would commonly suppose to be included in the social contract would be worthwhile unless the individual had access to the subsistence requirements of an active life. And it seems unlikely that someone out to guard his or her subsistence would be satisfied with the right of necessity—the right to take from others who had no obligation to let them do it. Nor is it correct to think that this view is based on the assumption of a positive community given to all by God, though this is a very important assumption in the period under discussion. In fact, thinking of people as living in a God-less world (or originally in a negative community) brings out even more the importance of individual consent as the only basis for legitimate rules.

By far the most influential natural law discussion of property that was used to defend the right of the poor to aid within a paternalist social view is William Paley's *Principles of Moral and Political Philosophy* (1785). (See also Horne, 1985, 51–52.) Paley suggested to his readers a wide variety of charitable acts. But like Woodward, Paley denied that private charity exhausted moral and civic responsibilities. In a passage that others will cite throughout the debate over the Poor Laws, Paley maintained that

> the poor have a claim founded in the law of nature, which may be thus explained. All things were originally common. No one being able to produce a charter from heaven, had any better title to a particular possession than his next neighbor. There were reasons for mankind's agreeing upon a separation of this common fund; and God for these reasons is presumed to have ratified it. But this separation was made and consented to, upon the expectation and condition, that every one should have left a sufficiency for his subsistence, or the means of procuring it. . . . And therefore, when the partition of property is rigidly maintained against the claims of indigence and distress, it is maintained in opposition to the intention of those who made it, and to His, who is the Supreme Proprietor of every thing, and who has filled the world with plenteousness, for the sustentation and comfort of all whom he sends into it. (1803, 252–253)

The structural similarity of this argument to Woodward's is obvious. Both uphold the justice of private property by suggesting that there are good reasons people living in common would have agreed to it. But they also insist that part of the agreement to allow the common to be divided would have had to be the general recognition that if anyone became too poor, he or she would have a valid claim on the community for the resources necessary for life.

But justifications for any kind of government aid to the poor, particularly for the claim that the poor have a right to such aid, inevitably are met by counterclaims on behalf of the right to property. Paley used the natural law distinction we have already encountered in Blackstone between natural and adventitious (civil or conventional) rights in order to construct a property theory that escaped this charge. Although individuals would have agreed to make property private and God could be supposed to have intended this to occur, the problem remained as to how particular people could come to have property in particular pieces of land. Paley began by dismissing the argument that particular property rights were the result of mankind having tacitly consented to allow those who occupied land to have a property right in that land. The implication seems to be that the poor could not be thought of as agreeing to a distribution of strong property rights that left them without property or the right to aid (Paley, 1803, Vol. I, 123).

Paley is more sympathetic to the position that, as God provided the earth for every person's use, He gave all a right to take what they needed without having to ask others. But this right extends only to the amount of property necessary for a "comfortable provision"; it cannot justify property rights over very large areas. The situation is analogous to that of a banquet given for the freeholders of a district. No one has to ask permission before he sits down and eats; the food and drink were provided for that purpose. However, while the freeholder would have, in effect, a natural right to satisfy his appetite at the banquet without asking others, he was not able to "fill his pockets or his wallet, or to carry away with him a quantity of provision to be hoarded up, or wasted, or given to his dogs, or stewed down into sauces, or converted into articles of superfluous luxury; especially if, by so doing, he pinched the guests at the lower end of the table" (Paley, 1803, Vol. I, 124).

"Mr. Locke's solution" to the problem, basing the natural right to property on labor, also has some merit, according to Paley. But this argument justifies property only "where the value of the labor bears a considerable proportion to the value of the thing; or where the thing derives its chief use and value from labor" (Paley, 1803, Vol. I, 121–122). Labor might confer rights to fish caught, utensils fashioned, and land cleared, plowed, sowed, and harvested, but it cannot provide a foundation for the extensive property rights in land that characterized eighteenth-century England.

The conclusion reached by Paley is that there are no natural rights to property in land. Instead, he argued that "the real foundation of our right is the law of the land" (1803, Vol. I, 124). Whereas proprietors of land cannot claim that their rights to property have been violated when the state that created those rights regulates or taxes the land or the income derived from it, those with little or no land can invoke their natural rights if the laws that created property do not direct it to the uses intended by God. According to Paley, each has a natural right to life that requires that "the productions of the earth should be applied to the sustentation of human life" (1803, Vol. I, 103). He insisted that "all waste and misapplication of these productions [of the earth], is contrary to the divine intention and will; and therefore wrong, for the same reason that any other crime is so" (1803, Vol. I, 103). Some examples of "crimes" listed by him are converting manors into forests for hunting, "letting large tracts lie barren, because the owner cannot cultivate them, nor will part with them to those who can," and destroying food to keep the price up (1803, Vol. I, 104). Paley was also antagonistic to the enclosure of farm land and to absentee owners (1803, Vol. II, 168).

Government regulation of property to aid the poor is sometimes thought to violate property rights. Paley's response was to argue that, as government created property, it could regulate it. It can also be argued that government regulation of property violates the natural right to liberty. But, as Paley pointed out, "to do what we will, is natural liberty: to do what we will, consistently with the interest of the community to which we belong, is civil liberty" (1803, Vol. II, 167).

The general background set by the natural law discussion of property in the seventeenth and eighteenth centuries should now be clear. Private property was derived (either through a contract or a labor argument) from an original common to which all had access. It was agreed to or was consistent with reason (and God's intentions) because it served to sustain life, especially under the conditions of conflict and scarcity. But when anyone's survival was threatened, the right to private property was overridden by the right of necessity. A theory of property could stop at this point, having accomplished its task of legitimating private property. Or, it could continue and for prudential reasons add public relief so that necessity could never be invoked. More important for the history of welfare rights was the possibility of interpreting the terms of the contract that established property in such a way that necessity created a claim on the wealth of a country. Public relief in this last variation was not organized charity, but it was required by justice.

FROM WELFARE RIGHTS TO A WELFARE STATE

In the period from 1790 to 1834, the legacy of the natural law vocabulary concerning property was enormously important to political argument. It was central to the criticisms leveled against Burke throughout the 1790s, it was used to express outrage at the conditions experienced by the poor at the end of the Napoleonic War, and it played an important role between 1829 and 1834 in the ultimately unsuccessful defense of the Old Poor Law against attempts to abolish or revise it. From a more thematic standpoint, we can tie this vocabulary to agrarian radicalism and demands for property redistribution, to early proposals for a welfare state, and to the beginnings of working-class radicalism. In all of these movements, property theory was no longer conservative or paternalist but had become liberal or radical. Because the number of writers who addressed these issues in England in the aftermath of the French Revolution was considerable, we will limit ourselves to considering only a few of those in the welfare state tradition—that is, to those who defended both private property rights and the right to aid.

From M. Wollstonecraft's initial attack on Burke's *Reflections* in her *A Vindication of the Rights of Man* (1790) to J. Thelwall's *The Rights of Nature* (1796), which was written against Burke's *Regicide Peace*, Burke's defense of political inequality was seen as inseparable from his defense of the economic disparities of late eighteenth-century England. As a result the argument for greater political equality was almost always accompanied by a critique of economic inequality. To make these arguments, the natural law discussion of property rights was indispensable. The assumption of an original common to which people had rights that could never be completely given up and the derivation of property from labor (in the Lockean variation) were perfect tools for criticizing large, inherited property holdings.

The most important of Burke's critics was Tom Paine, whose first target was Burke's "An Appeal from the New to the Old Whigs" (1791). Paine contrasted the luxury of the court with the suffering of the poor and argued that "the moral obligation of providing for old age, helpless infancy, and poverty, is far superior to that of supplying the invented wants of courtly extravagance, ambition and intrigue" (Powell, 1985, 199). This theme was continued in *The Rights of Man, Second Part* (1792). The last chapter, in particular, is almost entirely concerned with the conditions of the poor and reads very much as if it were one of the many pamphlets written about the poor in the 1790s. But it stands out from this literature in a few ways. One is that there is no moral indignation at the laziness, improvidence, or sexual standards of the poor. They are treated as hardworking people who are sometimes sick, sometimes disabled, sometimes unemployed, sometimes caring for small children, and sometimes aged. Another difference is that employing children and controlling adults in the workhouse finds no favor with Paine.

His proposals are framed to deal with the situations under which people without savings face considerable hardship because they can no longer work. Of course, he suggests that taxes on the goods people consume should be lowered. But of more interest to us is his occasional use of a welfare right to defend his ideas. Thus, he explicitly argued that his scheme to provide cash payments to those over 50 and to increase those payments to those over 60 was not based on granting "a favor" (Paine, 1961, 479), or "charity" (1961, 480), but was instead a right. "Good policy" and "beneficence," in contrast, were the reasons he gave for the other grants, such as those to new mothers, that made up the rest of his program.

For Paine, the purpose of these payments was not to create economic equality but to alleviate suffering. He was quick to defend private property and to deny that he wanted to level it. But at the same time it is clear that the only property he thought legitimately acquired by natural law was that acquired by industry and labor. This belief enabled him to criticize laws that regulated the wages of workmen as infringing on their property and to propose a progressive tax on land in an effort to motivate people who had inherited large estates to sell some of their land, rather than to let it lie idle and pay taxes on it. He hoped such a tax also would convince the wealthy to divide their estates in their wills. Property so large that it could not have been acquired by the labor of the owner had no special protection from state regulation (Paine, 1961, 488–494). The distinctions implicit here between property acquired by industry and property inherited, as well as between the classes that produce and those that live off inherited property (and government connections), are central to his political philosophy.

Although *The Rights of Man, Second Part* sets out a nascent welfare state with more detail than anyone else at this time had done, it was short on philosophical justifications. But in his years in France during the revolution, Paine was forced by circumstances to find a firmer foundation for his welfare rights. The first suggestion that he would eventually use elements of the natural law discussion of property for this foundation can be found in *The Declaration of Rights,* which he worked on with Condorcet in late 1792. After asserting that the purpose of civil society was to defend natural rights, he listed these rights as liberty, equality, security, property, social protection, and resistance to oppression. The next thirty-two articles of the *Declaration* explained the content of these rights. Thus, liberty included free speech, free press, and the free exercise of religion. Equality entailed that everyone have the same rights and that public employment should be open to all with preference given only for "talents and virtues." Security consisted in the protection of "person, property, and rights." The property rights to be protected were listed in Articles 18 to 24. The first five of these were rights to exclude others. They included the ability to dispose at will of "goods, capital, income, and industry" as well as the right to engage in any trade or profession, the right to participate in a free labor market, the right to representation in taxation, and the right to compensation for public use of individual property. The last two property rights in Paine's list demonstrate that he also understood that property rights were inclusive and required that some part of the nation's wealth be shared by all. In Article 23 he states that education is owed to all members of society, whereas in Article 24 he wrote that "public succors are a sacred debt of society; it is for the law to determine their extent and application" (Paine, 1967, 128–131).

From *The Rights of Man, Second Part* and *The Declaration of Rights* it is clear that Paine thought that individuals in need had a right to assistance and that this right was part of their property right. But it was not until *Agrarian Justice* (1796) that Paine worked out a plausible derivation of inclusive property rights. That is, it was there that he made clear why society owed a debt to individuals that they had a right to collect in the form of education and public assistance. *Agrarian Justice* is sometimes taken to be a dramatic departure from Paine's earlier work—a retreat from his devotion to private property that was forced upon him by the Conspiracy of the Equals of "Gracchus" Babeuf. In fact, it only required Paine to explain more completely a belief in the right to assistance that he seems to have held since *The Rights of Man, Second Part.*

Paine begins his discussion of property with an account of individuals as joint life proprietors in the earth. The air, the animals, and the water join the earth in what he calls natural property, gifts from the creator to all people. To this natural property *"or its equivalent"* all individuals have an equal "birthright" (emphasis added). In the course of civilization individuals improve the land through cultivation. By this labor, some property justly becomes private—or to use Paine's word, "artificial" (Paine, 1967, 324–325). It is because of the legitimacy of artificial property—property that is the invention of man—that Paine opposed Babeuf and all Agrarian Laws (Paine, 1967, 130).

The crux of Paine's argument is that, whereas the value added by cultivation is justly private, the earth itself, because it was given to men and not made by any or all of them, must remain common. Paine argued that when all the earth became owned by a few with no provision made for the rest, the landless were "dispossessed" of their "natural inheritance" (Paine, 1967, 331). He did not suggest that private property should be redistributed, but that individuals do retain a right to receive an "equivalent" for the loss of their share to the common earth (Paine, 1967, 331, 337, 338).

Much of Paine's discussion is imprecise or confusing. For example, he is contradictory on whether the original common is positive or negative. But the outlines are clear enough, and they do provide an explanation of why individuals have a right to assistance and why this right is a property right. The plan Paine proposed in *Agrarian Justice* to satisfy the rights of the landless differs a bit from the proposals of *The Rights of Man, Second Part.* Payments still go to the aged and to the disabled. But instead of the unemployment scheme of *The Rights of Man, Second Part,* Paine advances the idea of cash payments on one's twenty-first birthday to better realize the values of opportunity, independence, and efficiency: "With this aid they could buy a cow, and implements to cultivate a few acres of land; and instead of becoming burdens upon society, which is always the case where children are produced faster than they can be fed, would be put in the way of becoming useful and profitable citizens" (Paine, 1967, 338).

The sources of the funds needed to make payments to the old, disabled, and newly adult follow from the distinctions Paine has made between natural and artificial property. As the cultivator can really claim as his own only the value created by his work, he owes society a "ground-rent" for use of the earth that is owned by all (Paine, 1967, 329). The same principle can also be applied to personal property. "All accumulation . . . of personal property, beyond what a man's own hands produce, is derived to him by living in society; and he owes on every principle of justice, of gratitude, and of civilization, a part of that accumulation back again to society from whence the whole came" (Paine, 1967, 340). His sense that personal wealth is often accumulated more by cheating others—"paying too little for the labor that produced it"— than by labor adds to the justifications for taxing personal property. Paine did not suggest that taxes on land and personal property actually be levied but, rather, was giving reasons why a tax of some sort was justified. His own plan was to levy a 10–22 percent tax on all inheritances, on the assumption that this amount would correspond to the social portion of property (Conway, 1967, 335). As there was no right to inherit, an inheritance tax was the fairest way to collect money. As Paine said, "The bequether gives nothing: the receiver pays nothing" (Paine, 1967, 335).

By far the most important carrier of Paine's critique of corruption and taxation into the volatile period after the end of the Napoleonic Wars was William Cobbett. So enormous was his impact that E. P. Thompson maintains that "it was Cobbett who created radical intellectual culture" in England (1963, 746). In the winter of 1816-1817, his paper, *Cobbett's Weekly Political Register,* had a circulation of between 40,000 and 60,000 each week. Throughout the 1820s his books and pamphlets regularly sold between 50,000 and 200,000 copies. Though his relationship to Paine is complicated, in the period of Cobbett's life and work with which we are concerned, his veneration for Paine is nicely captured in the fact that he brought Paine's bones back to England when he returned in 1819.

The extent to which Cobbett was nostalgic or prophetic, Tory or Democrat, will not concern us here. It is beyond doubt that he failed to assimilate the new language of political economy into his work and that his targets remained roughly similar to those of Paine. His champions were "artisans," "laborers," "shopkeepers," and "coal miners," and his most deeply held values were individualism and independence (*Cobbett's Weekly Political Register*, October 3, 1818). It is not surprising, given the tradition out of which he emerged, his supporters, and his values, that he did not call into question the legitimacy of private property. But it is the purpose off this short discussion of his work from 1817 to 1834 to demonstrate the extent to which he used the natural law discussion of property to attack the large holdings of the rich, argue for the extension of the franchise, and defend the right of the poor to relief. Cobbett is often portrayed as basing his arguments entirely upon his sense of custom and constitutional rights, but so pervasive and powerful was the language of natural rights in discussions of property that its use could not be avoided even by someone self-consciously attempting to defend old England from the dangerous innovations of political economy and industry.

His primary concern with property in the *Weekly Political Register* during the late teens was to identify it with labor so that the respect and privileges given to property in English political life would be extended to those who did not own land. Creating respect for artisans is one of the major themes of the Painite tradition and one of the most important legacies of Locke's identification of property with labor in the *Second Treatise*. Moreover, if labor is "an absolute possession; and ownership complete and unlimited," then it, like all other forms of property, should be able to be taxed only with the owner's consent (*Cobbett's Weekly Political Register*, October 3, 1818). Taxes to pay interest on the debt he detested so much, then, were forms of theft—money taken by the rich from the poor (*Cobbett's Weekly Political Register*, January 9, 1819). Seeing labor as property was also central to defending the right of labor to strike, a situation understood by Cobbett simply as one in which people choose to keep rather than to sell their property at a price they think is too low. "You have labour to sell. You demand a certain price for it. Those who are in the practice of buying your labour think this price is too high. They refuse to purchase at your price, you keep your labour unsold. Well! What is there in all this contrary to the principles either of natural equity, or of law?" (*Cobbett's Weekly Political Register,* December 9, 1818). Cobbett's insistence that the sole foundation of property was labor easily led to a criticism of absentee landlords and ultimately to his recommendation that those who rent and work small farms be made their owners (*Cobbett's Weekly Political Register,* March 10, 1819, May 27, 1819). The present owners should be compensated, though how or by whom remains unclear.

The relationship between the right to relief and the actual operations of the Poor Law dominated Cobbett's concerns throughout the middle and late 1820s as the abolition or revision of the Old Poor Law seemed more likely. In *A History of the Protestant Reformation* (1824–1826) he argued that the Elizabethan Poor Laws were a necessary response to the destruction of the English Catholic Church and its system of poor relief. His nostalgic view of English history is perfectly captured in his statement that before the Reformation, England was "the happiest country that the world has ever seen" (Cobbett, 1829, Vol. I, para. 37). In large part this happiness was a result of the fact that the "titles, and every other species of income of the clergy, were looked upon, and were, in fact and in practice, more the property of the poor than of the monks, nuns, priests, and bishops" (Cobbett, 1829, Vol. II, para. 18). But, as landed property fell into the hands of private individuals and families, the revenue produced by the land was used less to maintain the people than to buy luxuries for the rich. The number of beggars and vagabonds increased dramatically, requiring government action. The Reformation "despoiled the working classes of their patrimony; it tore from them that which nature and reason had assigned them; it robbed them of that relief for the necessitous, which was theirs by right imprescriptable, and which had been confirmed to them by the law of God and the law of the land" (Cobbett, 1829, Vol. I, para. 127). That the government assistance that began with Elizabeth was paid for out of a land tax seemed appropriate to Cobbett, for it was because the poor could no longer work the land that they needed relief.

Though Cobbett is often portrayed as a kind of reactionary, damning the present in the name of a fictional English past, his defense of the Old Poor Law rested at least as much on the idea of a natural right as on an ancient English legal claim. Thus, in Cobbett's most sustained discussion of welfare rights, *The Poor Man's Friend* (1826–1827), he relied heavily on both Grotius and Pufendorf. "Now let us hear what that Grotius and that Pufendorf say; let us hear what these great writers on the laws of nature and nations say," Cobbett announced as he began his refutation of Hale and Blackstone (1977, para. 73). And he proceeded to quote two pages from Grotius and three from Pufendorf on the origin of property and the right of necessity.

In *The Poor Man's Friend*, Cobbett argued that a poor law was neither a prudential measure nor an act of social charity. Rather, it was required by the rights that people would have insisted upon at the origin of society. Cobbett used the idea that private property originated in a contract to maintain that those about to give up their rights to use the common would have insisted that in the event of their dire necessity, property, at least for them, would revert to its common origins. However, the contract that created civil society modified the right of necessity. Regarding this contract, people would have agreed to obey the laws of civil society and to fight in time of war only if they were guaranteed the right to be supported if they became destitute. The first contract established rights to property and the right of necessity, whereas the second established government and changed the right of necessity from a liberty to a claim on the wealth of others that the state would enforce.

> No man will contend, that the main body of the people, in any country upon earth, and, of course, in England, would have consented to abandon the rights of nature; to give up their right to enjoy all things in common; no one will believe, that the main body of the people would ever have given their assent to the establishing of a state of things which would make all the lands, and all the trees, and all the goods and cattle of every sort, private property; which would have shut out a large part of the people from having such property, and which would, at the same time, not have provided the means of preventing those of them, who might fall into indigence, from being actually starved to death! It is impossible to believe this. Men never gave their assent to enter into society on terms like these. (Cobbett, 1977, para. 47)

The consequence of seeing the right of necessity as central to the legitimacy of private property and of seeing state-supported aid as central to the legitimacy of civil society is that the abolition of aid dissolves for the destitute, first, any obligation to obey municipal law (and serve in the armed forces, for example) and, then, any moral obligation to respect others' property. The specter raised by Cobbett was that of morally lawful looting of the rich by the poor if the Poor Law was not maintained.

> Now I beg you to mark well what I say, if civil society get into such a state, that men cannot, by their labour, provide themselves and families with a sufficiency of food and of raiment; if, at the same time, there be no Magistrate, or other person, having authority to take from the rich and to give to the suffering poor, a sufficiency to preserve them against the natural effects of hunger and of cold: if (mark well what I say) civil society get into this state, then the law of nature, as far as regards the

destitute person, returns in its full force. My loaf is no longer exclusively mine: it is yours, as much as it is mine; and you, if you be amongst the destitute persons, are held to have a right to take as much of my loaf as you want to relieve yourself, so that you do not expose me to suffer from want. (1977, para. 34)

The power of Cobbett's analysis can be appreciated only if one realizes that this discussion of the right of necessity is no longer merely theoretical. In the countryside, machines were being destroyed, and barns and houses were being burned.

A common interpretation of the natural right to property sees such a right as entirely exclusive in nature. In Cobbett we find an example of the way that argument can undergo an inversion. In one of his last works, *Legacy to Labourers* (1834), Cobbett makes clear that in his view the only absolute and inalienable right to property is the inclusive right to subsistence. His assertion that landlords do not have the right to do whatever they want with their land is part of his criticism of enclosures and justification for a land tax to support the Poor Law. Their rights to exclude are limited by the rights of others to subsistence. The questions he posed at the beginning of his chapters (or letters as he calls them here) capture his argument.

- Letter IV. Have the landlords dominion in their lands? Or, do they lawfully possess only the use of them?
- Letter V. Can the landlords use their lands so as to drive the natives from them?
- Letter VI. Can the landlords rightfully use the land so as to cause the natives to perish of hunger or cold? (Cobbett, 1834)

Not surprisingly Grotius, Pufendorf, Locke, and Paley (author of "a book of very great authority") are cited extensively. Even though the New Poor Law would not abolish aid, its attempt to make such aid more difficult to receive was incompatible with Cobbett's sense that the rights of the poor required that relief be given in a manner that showed respect.

Cobbett's great hatred for Malthus (and political economy) had many causes, but among them was Malthus' assertion that "there is one right which . . . I am confident [man] neither does nor can possess—a right to subsistence" (1914, 190–191). By the 1830s, however, such a right had found its way even into the work of some political economists. The two best examples of this change are found in the writings of Samuel Read and G. Poulet Scrope. Samuel Read wrote *An Enquiry into the Natural Grounds of Right to Vendible Property or Wealth* (1829) to find a middle path between Malthus and the Ricardian Socialist Thomas Hodgskin. For our purposes that means he opposed Malthus' attack on the rights of the poor but could not justify them by using the idea that all wealth is created by the laborer. Read used the four-stage theory of Adam Smith to argue that the development of private property rights to land from an original negative community were justified. But Read attached to this defense of common land becoming private the proviso that when all the land is occupied, those without land or a job have a right to relief. Property rights and welfare rights are two sides of the same coin: Neither property rights nor a government to protect them would have been agreed to unless they were thought to be to everyone's advantage. Inasmuch as private property increases productivity, it satisfies this requirement. In fact, Read argued that those with no land have as much interest in private ownership as those who do own property. For although many may end up landless, they can prosper through their labor in an advancing economy. Nothing in this argument works, however, for someone with neither land nor a job. Read cited a number of cases in English law in which starving people were acquitted when found taking others' property in order to substantiate his position that starving people were not subject to property law. His conclusion was that property and government are legitimate only if they are understood to include a welfare right. "The right of the poor to support, and the right of the rich to engross and accumulate, are relative and reciprocal privileges, the former being the condition in which the latter is enjoyed" (Read, 1829, 375). He also noted that as rising rents come partly from a general increase in social prosperity rather than from individual effort, that part of rent may be thought to belong to everyone and can be taxed to pay for poor relief without violating the individual rights of landowners.

The most important political economist to defend the Old Poor Law and to believe that the poor had a right to support was G. Poulet Scrope. Scrope wrote a number of articles on the Poor Law for *Quarterly Review* and also considered them in his *Principles of Political Economy* (1833). Throughout all his work he maintained the belief that "the poor have a decided claim, in justice, to a support from the land on which Providence has placed them. . . . Such a provision, therefore, instead of being a matter of charity and benevolence . . . is but the legal concession of a right antecedent even to that of the owners of the soil— a divine right—a right based on the external and immutable principles of intuitive justice" (Scrope, 1832, 66).

As we have seen, welfare rights can be based on the terms of a contract or on a birthright. Although Scrope used both arguments and seemed unaware of the difference between them, he relied most heavily on the idea of a birthright and, to that extent, presented a theory slightly different from that of Read. When Scrope explained what he meant by a "natural right," a "divine right," or a "sacred right" to support, he usually referred to a right to use one's labor on "the common gifts of nature" (1833, 305). The right here is the right to work to earn a subsistence or, if work is not available, a right to the equivalent. Poor Law payments were seen as given in lieu of work. Understanding that work is behind Scrope's argument helps to make clear why he suggested public work projects as the best way to satisfy the welfare rights of the able-bodied who were without employment. Especially in his argument for an extension of the Poor Law to Ireland, he urged that the unemployed be used to build bridges, roads, canals, and ports, and to reclaim waste land. Only if the poor are not employed does a welfare right take the form of cash payments. If the poor are not provided either work or aid, they can invoke the right of necessity and take what they need from the rich without violating moral or municipal laws. It is a happy combination of justice and prudence, then, to respect the rights of the poor, for not to do so creates both injustice and chaos.

Asserting a natural right to relief does not immediately settle arguments about the way relief should be given or about the amount of aid the poor should receive. Yet believing that aid is a right does require that it be given in ways that show respect for the people receiving it. To Scrope this meant that aid could not be given in a workhouse setting and that it must be based on "the natural wants of the pauper, taking into consideration the habitual standard of necessaries among the population" (1834, p. 241). Scrope's most innovative discussion of how to pay for poor relief occurred in his *Principles of Political Economy*. There he constructed what we recognize as a social security insurance system (1833, 316ff.). All employers would be required to put a set amount for each employee in a fund that the unemployed, aged, and disabled would be able to draw upon when needed. By including capitalists as well as landlords in those responsible for funding aid he recognized the new realities of British economic life.

CONCLUSION

In the late eighteenth and early nineteenth centuries, the system of relief known as the Old Poor Law came under attack primarily from those associated with utilitarianism and political economy. Government aid to the poor could be and was defended on grounds of humanitarian concern and political stability. However, because of the way the natural law discussion of property had evolved, poor relief also could be justified by a rights argument. An original common to which all had access, the right of necessity, the derivation of property from a contract, and the limitation of property rights to what had been produced by labor were ample material from which to fashion a welfare right. In fact, the most serious problem faced by the defenders of aid to the poor was not justifying a welfare right, but deciding upon the strength or content of that right. It is not surprising that the idea of a subsistence right as a mere liberty was superseded. People who would be concerned about preserving themselves once all property became private could hardly be satisfied with so weak a guarantee. If rights to speech and religion, for example, were important enough to be claims that others had an obligation to respect and that the state had to protect through police and courts paid for by taxes, preservation could hardly be denied the same status. Of course, as the interpretation of a welfare right moves from subsistence to subsistence historically defined to claims for greater equality, it becomes more controversial. The writers discussed in this chapter gave substance to this right by focusing on children, the unemployed, the sick, and the old, for these are the people for whom preservation is most problematic.

It is not possible to address the intellectual history of property rights in the period from 1603 to 1834 without becoming involved in debates over the nature of liberalism and its relation to the modern welfare state. After all, critics of the welfare state from both the political right and left agree on this history, though one side describes it as the growth of individualism and freedom whereas the other side would add *atomistic*, *selfish*, or *possessive* to all uses of *individualism*. The welfare state's effort to simultaneously protect both property and welfare seems incoherent to both—merely the result of political compromise or control. But if the tradition of analysis discussed in this chapter is accurate, it suggests that property rights and welfare rights were long understood to complement one another rather than to be in an antagonistic relationship. In fact, in this analysis, welfare rights, though defined in different ways, were required by the logic of private property. Here, then, is a history of rights that locates the liberal welfare state in an intellectual enterprise of long standing and a logic of rights that vindicates its dual concerns for property and welfare.

NOTES

I would like to thank Deborah Baumgold and Eldon Eisenach for their thoughtful comments on this chapter and the University of Tulsa for a Summer Research Grant that gave me the time to do the research.

1. See also Grotius (1964, Bk III, 797).
2. See also Hobbes (1968, 212) and Hobbes (1949, 51).

3. See J. Tully (1980) for the best discussion of this relationship.

4. See also Locke (1960, 344): "The possession of land is determined by positive constitutions." For a counterview see Waldron (1984, 98–106).

5. Locke is especially difficult to interpret on these matters. J. Tully seems to me to be much closer to providing an adequate account of Locke's property theory than did Macpherson, yet Tully is wrong, I think, in interpreting the political implications of that theory. Anyone too carried away with the radical Locke would do well to read his proposals for changing the Poor Law. On the one hand, he would fine a parish that allowed "any person to die for want of due relief" (Locke, in Fox-Bourne, 1876, 390); on the other, he would jail some vagrants, seize others and place them in the navy, cut off an ear to punish some (1876, 380), and transport others to the colonies.

6. Rutherforth's rejection of Locke's mixing labor argument is common in the eighteenth century. See, for example, Hutcheson (1747, 132–133) and Smith (1982, 17).

7. For the continuing importance of paternalism see Roberts (1979) and Horne (1985).

8. See also (Woodward, 1775).

REFERENCES

Blackstone, William. 1756–1769. *Commentaries on the Laws of England*, Books I, II, and IV. London: Clarendon Press.

Cobbett, William. 1824–1826. *A History of the Protestant Reformation*, Vols. I and II. London.

———. 1834. *Legacy to Labourers*. London.

———. 1977. *The Poor Man's Friend*. New York: Augustus M. Kelley.

Fox-Bourne, H.R. 1876. *Locke*, Vol. II. New York: Harper & Brothers.

Grotius, Hugo. 1964. *De Jure Belli Ac Pacis Libri Tres*. Washington, D.C.: Carnegie Endowment for International Peace.

Hobbes, Thomas. 1949. *De Cive*. New York: Appleton-Century-Crofts.

———. 1968. *Leviathan*. New York: Penguin.

Horne, T.A. 1985. "William Paley and the Rights of the Poor," *Journal of the History of Philosophy*, Vol. 23, No. 1, January.

Hutcheson, F. 1747. *A Short Introduction to Moral Philosophy*. Glasgow.

Locke, John. 1960. *Two Treatises of Government*. New York: Mentor.

Malthus, Thomas. 1914. *An Essay on the Principle of Population*, 2nd ed. New York: E.P. Dutton.

Paine, Thomas. 1961. *The Rights of Man, Second Part*. New York: Doubleday & Co.

———. 1967. *The Writings of Thomas Paine*, edited by M.D. Conway. New York: AMS Press.

Paley, William. 1803. *Principles of Moral and Political Philosophy*, 14th ed., Vols. I and II. London.

Poor Man's Guardian. 1835. No. 207, May 23.

Powell, D. 1985. *Tom Paine: The Greatest Exile*. New York: St. Martin's Press.

Pufendorf, Samuel. 1964. *De Jure Naturae et Gentium Libro Octo*. Washington, D.C.: Carnegie Endowment for International Peace.

Read, Samuel. 1829. *An Enquiry into the Natural Grounds of Right to Vendible Property or Wealth*. Edinburgh.

Ricardo, David. 1977. *The Principles of Political Economy and Taxation*. New York: E.P. Dutton.

Roberts, D. 1979. *Paternalism in Early Victorian England*. New Brunswick, N.J.: Rutgers University Press.

Rutherforth, Thomas. 1832. *Institutes of Natural Law*. Baltimore: William and Joseph Neal (2nd U.S. edition).

Scrope, G. Poulet. 1832. "On Political Economy," *Quarterly Review*.

———. 1833. *Principles of Political Economy*. London.

———. 1834. "The New Poor Law," *Quarterly Review*.

Smith, A. 1982. *Lectures on Jurisprudence*. Indianapolis, Ind.: Liberty Classics.

Thompson, E.P. 1963. *The Making of the English Working Class*. New York: Random House.

Tully, J. 1980. *A Discourse on Property*. Cambridge: Cambridge University Press.

Waldron, J. 1984. "Locke, Tully, and the Regulation of Property." *Political Studies*, Vol. 32, 98–106.

Woodward, Richard. 1768. *An Argument in Support of the Right of the Poor to a National Provision in the Kingdom of Ireland*.

———. 1775. *An Address to the Public on the Expediency of a Regular Plan for the Maintenance and Government of the Poor*.

RICHARD KROUSE
MICHAEL S. McPHERSON

6

THE LOGIC OF
LIBERAL EQUALITY

*John Stuart Mill and the Origins of the
Political Theory of Welfare State Liberalism*

There has been much debate over the status of John Stuart Mill's socialist aspirations. Curiously, however, there has been significantly less systematic discussion of Mill's vision of a just property-owning economy. Much if not most of the latter has, moreover, focused upon discussion of the significance of Mill's own rather large list of exceptions to his stated, *prima facie* preference for a laissez-faire rule.

Mill is often, in the latter context, taken to epitomize liberal political economy in transition—an eclectic ("shallowly syncretic") figure standing uneasily poised halfway between classical (or laissez-faire) and contemporary (or welfare-state) versions of liberal theory. Present-day representatives of both camps eagerly embrace Mill as an intellectual progenitor. But there is broad consensus on all sides that in affirming the possibility of a just private-property market economy, Mill embraces *some* vision of a reformed or idealized capitalist property regime.

In this chapter, we challenge that consensus. The Millean vision of a just property-owning regime, we argue, is *not* a vision of a reformed or idealized capitalism in any of its standard conceptions. More specifically, and more to the point on the present occasion, we argue that Mill's vision of a just property-owning economy is not an early vision of welfare state capitalism. Mill's theory of justice, we argue, does not provide a justification for welfare state capitalism because it rules out *capitalism* as such (as long as that term implies a division of society into propertied and propertyless classes), while at the same time leading him to oppose all but the most minimal forms of *welfare state* provision. Though Mill does support a minimal welfare state as a matter of second-best or nonideal theory, he firmly opposes the egalitarian redistribution of earned income beyond the minimum essential for the satisfaction of absolutely basic (i.e., subsistence) needs. Yet despite his opposition to the egalitarian redistribution of income, we suggest, Mill's ideal vision of a just political economy—an "egalitarian market economy," as we shall call it, with a widespread dispersion of property rights in the means of production—is far *more* egalitarian than welfare state capitalism in any of its usual conceptions.

Our strategy will be to embed these claims in the context of a broader discussion of Mill's views upon justice in political economy. As our chief concern is with the institutional embodiment, rather than the moral foundations, of Mill's views on social justice, it will suffice to sketch the basics of Mill's moral standpoint briefly. Following the important recent work of Gray (1983) and Berger (1984), we assume that Mill attempts to develop a utilitarian theory of justice and moral rights. For Mill, what distinguishes justice from other moral duties such as beneficence (as we shall see) is that it is owed to assignable persons in virtue of their possession of a correlative moral *right*. A right is an interest that is, or ought to be, recognized by society as a matter of recognized moral rule, and whose protection society is bound to enforce through either law or public opinion. Moral rights, for Mill, are grounded in the essential requirements of human happiness: Certain interests are sufficiently vital to human happiness that we must, as a matter of right, accord them a privileged (though never absolute) immunity from utilitarian trade-off. And we thus have a utilitarian case for adopting certain weighty side-constraints, in the form of rules of justice, on the direct maximization of utility.

What are these vital interests? Two in particular are crucial. First, *security* is a vital interest shared by all human beings, including those who have not yet attained the status of fully rational agency. Second, *autonomy* is a vital interest shared by all human beings who are capable of achieving the status of fully rational agency: The exercise of autonomous choice in thought and action is, for Mill, both in itself a constitutive ingredient of human happiness and a necessary (though not sufficient) condition for experiencing the "higher" human pleasures of intelligence and sociality.

It is possible to discern in Mill three general principles of justice aimed at furthering these two vital interests, which shape Mill's discussions of the matters of interest here. These are (1) a principle of *equal liberty*, which ascribes to persons a moral right to an extensive domain of equal basic liberty; (2) a principle of distribution according to *need*, which ascribes to persons a moral right to the material resources essential for subsistence; and (3) a principle of distribution according to *desert*, which ascribes to persons a moral right to reward in proportion either to productive contribution or to effort.[1]

We shall assess alternative forms of political economy from the point of view of their capacity to promote these three Millean principles of justice. We shall identify five types of economic system explicitly discussed by Mill: (1) laissez-faire capitalism; (2) welfare state capitalism; (3) Mill's ideal version of a private-property market economy, which in important respects foreshadows contemporary notions of "property-owning democracy" or "people's capitalism"; (4) Mill's ideal version of a socialist economy, which roughly anticipates contemporary notions of "market socialism"; and (5) bureaucratic or state socialism. And we shall claim that Millean justice in political economy has two main institutional preconditions: (1) competitive markets, and (2) background conditions that include, *inter alia*, the absence of severe class inequality in the distribution of property rights in productive resources. The first of these requirements, we suggest, eliminates bureaucratic or state socialism as a candidate for a just political economy by Millean standards; the second eliminates capitalism in both its laissez-faire and welfare state variants. Only "property-owning democracy" and "market socialism"—that is, "egalitarian market economies"—satisfy both criteria, and Mill's oft-noted agnosticism regarding the long-run choice between property owning and socialist visions of a just political economy is in fact restricted to the limited choice between these two intermediate alternatives.

Our primary concern in this chapter, however, will be less with the precise character of Mill's vision of an ideal property regime than with his views upon the distinctly nonideal choice between laissez-faire and welfare state capitalism. Mill views laissez-faire capitalism, with its maldistribution of property rights in productive resources, as inherently unjust. *Given* that background of property rights as a constraint, Mill views a minimal welfare state—redistribution to satisfy the claims of basic need—as preferable to an unrestricted regime of laissez-faire. But Mill views that minimal welfare state as itself inherently problematic from the point of view of his liberal principles of justice: He affirms a legal and moral right to welfare but feels compelled to annex conditions to the exercise of this "social" right that annul other basic civil and political rights. The restrictions thus implied upon the scope of welfare provision are strongly reinforced by the limits Mill imposes, for reasons of both justice and policy, on the scope of redistributive taxation of earned income. In opposing the progressive taxation of income, Mill in effect cuts off the main source of revenue that might be employed to finance a more-than-minimal welfare state.

We then proceed to argue that a very substantial distance separates welfare state capitalism—minimal or more-than-minimal—from Mill's broad vision of an egalitarian market economy, in virtue of the sharply differing degrees of class inequality in the distribution of property rights in productive resources that these two different kinds of regime exhibit or would exhibit. More broadly, we claim that these alternative property regimes represent two fundamentally different strategies for promoting justice in political economy: one, exemplified by welfare state capitalism, which accepts substantial inequality in initial property and skill endowments, and then seeks to reduce the consequent disparities in market outcomes through the *ex post* redistribution of income; and another, exemplified by the idea of an egalitarian market economy, which seeks greater equality in the *ex ante* distribution of property and skill endowments, with correspondingly less emphasis upon subsequent redistributional encumbrances. The former emphasizes the egalitarian redistribution of income *within* generations, the latter the egalitarian redistribution of wealth *between* generations. Mill, we suggest, opts decisively for the latter strategy, and his views on the welfare state must be seen in that light.

We have chosen to focus upon Mill for more than purely historical reasons. We believe that Mill's views, though historically dated in important respects, nevertheless provide a valuable source of continuing critical purchase upon the limitations of the welfare state as the preferred institutional vehicle for the realization of liberal values. Even as he affirms a legal and moral right to subsistence, Mill reminds us of a darker and more disciplinary side of the welfare state—a side often lost sight of in views of a straightforward evolution from civil to political to "social" rights of citizenship (e.g., Marshall, 1977)—that is being stressed today by both conservative and radical critics of the welfare state. He likewise underscores some of the moral and fiscal constraints, once again stressed today by both right and left, upon expansion of the welfare state in the direction of an ever-more extensive regime of universal citizen entitlements. Above all, Mill underscores forcefully that the choice between laissez-faire and welfare state capitalism does not exhaust the universe of liberal visions of a just political economy. We conclude with some speculations on the contemporary relevance of Mill's analysis.

THE LIMITS OF LAISSEZ-FAIRE CAPITALISM

It is a fixed point of Mill's judgment that a just political economy will in all cases satisfy two main conditions: (1) competitive markets, combined with (2) state intervention to correct market imperfections (e.g., through the supply of public goods and the correction of negative externalities) and ensure the background conditions essential to distributive justice.

In attempting to determine the proper relationships between market competition and state intervention, Mill begins with a well-known presumption in favor of laissez-faire: "*Laissez-faire*, in short, should be the general practice: every departure from it, unless required by some great good, is a certain evil" (II, 945 [*P.E.*]).[2] Mill favors market allocation, in part, on standard efficiency grounds: He consistently emphasizes that the only alternative to market competition is monopoly, with its sub-optimal allocation of resources, and that the tendency of perfect competition is to level inequalities of remuneration through the elimination of economic rent. Perhaps even more important, however, the market provides an essential institutional basis for morally imperative forms of personal and political liberty. In particular, market allocation supports the important liberty of free choice of occupation because, according to Mill, in the absence of some differences in earnings, as these arise in a competitive labor market, some method for the authoritative allocation of labor would have to be devised. More generally, the spontaneous processes of the market support personal and political liberty by working to prevent the undesirable concentration of power in the hands of the state (III, 937–944 [*P.E.*]). For Mill, these considerations suffice summarily to disqualify—"as too chimerical to be reasoned against"—any vision of centralized or bureaucratic state socialism as a candidate for a just political economy.

But, crucially, Mill's presumptions in favor of laissez-faire require that competitive markets be set within a framework of background institutions designed to uphold distributive justice. Laissez-faire *cannot* be considered in abstraction from the background of initial endowments against which competitive markets operate. Set against the background of an unjust distribution of initial exchange entitlements, Mill agrees with A. K. Sen that the distributive results of perfectly competitive markets will be "perfectly efficient and thoroughly disgusting" (Sen, 1970, p. 22).

More specifically, the unreformed property regime of laissez-faire capitalism is characterized by (1) widespread unfreedom for the vast majority of workers, (2) "great poverty," and (3) "that poverty very little connected with desert" (V, 715 [*C.S.*]). For these reasons Mill advocates a right to basic need satisfaction (i.e., subsistence) and hence prefers a minimal welfare state to an unrestricted regime of laissez-faire capitalism. However, he thinks it necessary for the state to impose quite harsh conditions on those who exercise their right to receive government support, and thus insists that only a very minimal welfare state is morally possible. The capitalist welfare state, far from being an ideal, is for Mill a second-best strategy for ameliorating the worst consequences of unreformed capitalism until more fundamental reforms are achieved.

Mill takes it as a fixed point in our moral judgment that there is a powerful, *prima facie* case for the relief of destitution:

> Apart from any metaphysical considerations respecting the foundations of morals or of the social union, it will be admitted to be right that human beings help one another; and the more so, in proportion to the urgency of the need: and none needs help so urgently as one who is starving. The claim to help, therefore, created by destitution, is one of the strongest which can exist; and there is *prima facie* the amplest reason for making the relief of so extreme an exigency as certain to those who require it as by any arrangements of society it can be made. (III, 960 [*P.E.*])

For Mill, it clearly follows from the moral urgency of this claim that—subject to a series of stringent preconditions to be discussed below—it is "highly desirable that the certainty of subsistence should be held out by law to the destitute able-bodied, rather than that their relief should depend upon voluntary charity" (III, 962 [*P.E.*]). Mill favors this legal right to basic need satisfaction, moreover, without reference to considerations of desert. Unlike private charity, the state "must act by general rules. It cannot undertake to discriminate between the deserving and the undeserving indigent. It owes no more than subsistence to the first, and can give no less to the last" (III, 962 [*P.E.*]). Thus, the welfare provision favored by Mill is not a "gratuity" (i.e., a "public charity" in the sense noted by Goodin in Chapter 2) that can be dispensed entirely at the discretion of the official concerned. Rather, welfare must be provided as a matter of *legal right.*[3]

Given the existence of poverty and destitution, then, Mill favors intervention by the state into the market to ensure "compulsory, collective provision for certain basic needs as a matter of right" (Goodin, 1985, 74). He must, therefore, be counted as an advocate of at least a minimal welfare state.

Mill derives a moral right to subsistence from the vital human interests in security and autonomy. Survival is, of course, the most basic of our security interests, and, again, for needy persons survival often clearly will require not merely forbearance from harmful interference but also a recognized right to resource provision. Moreover, our distinctively human capacities of autonomous judgment and choice can only be exercised by persons who are alive and who, less trivially, have achieved a minimum level of basic need satisfaction, both physiologically and psychologically. "Physical privation" and "moral deprivation," Mill argues, both violate human dignty and autonomy in themselves and can, in a viciously circular way, undermine the energy and initiative essential to escape these very conditions. Though, as we shall see, he is careful to insist that *excessive* assistance can undermine human energy and self-dependence, Mill also acutely recognizes that the complete *absence* of aid can often do the same; properly administered aid, by contrast, can work to facilitate and enhance autonomous human effort, initiative, and so on. "When the condition of anyone is so disastrous that his energies are paralyzed by discouragement," Mill writes, "assistance is a tonic, not a sedative: it braces instead of deadening the active faculties" (III, [P.E.]). Under these circumstances, the poor need more than the spur of their own poverty. They need help, which it is the duty of the state to provide.[4]

LIMITATIONS OF WELFARE CAPITALISM

If the vital human interests in dignity and security constitute not only the basis for the welfare state but also a sufficient reason to reject an unreformed capitalist property system, the welfare state Mill envisions is severely constrained because it necessarily institutionalizes a basic tension between the claims of need, on the one hand, and the claims of equal liberty and desert, on the other. The fundamental rights recognized by the welfare state are contradictory, resulting in an anemic program of welfare provision that systematically degrades the very individuals it is intended to help. For Mill, welfare provision cannot be significantly expanded because this would foster "dependence" on the part of its beneficiaries, and because extensive redistribution would conflict with the property rights of other citizens.

Dependence and Equal Liberty

Although Mill views a right to welfare as necessary to the survival and autonomy, and hence dignity and self-respect, of its recipients, at the same time he feels compelled to annex conditions to the exercise of this right that would in other ways *negate* that dignity and self-respect. For Mill, the right to welfare is a peculiarly self-defeating right—a "social" right that may be exercised only on the condition that one forfeit other crucial civil and political rights. It is, under the conditions in which it must be exercised, at once a necessary condition of human dignity and self-respect and a sufficient condition of their negation.

For Mill, two sets of consequences must be weighed in designing a scheme of public assistance: the consequences of the assistance itself, which are generally beneficial, and the consequences of relying upon the assistance, which are generally injurious. As we have seen, energy

and self-dependence—which are integral to Mill's ideal of human autonomy (see, e.g., XIX, 404–412 [C.R.G.]), and hence crucial to human
dignity and self-respect—can be undermined by *either* the absence *or*
the excess of aid. A scheme of public assistance must therefore be
designed to ensure "the greatest amount of needful help, with the
smallest encouragement to undue reliance upon it" (III, 961 [P.E.]). Rights
to resources, in other words, can have salutary consequences only insofar
as they are self-liquidating (as they are automatically in the case of
education). What is required is "help toward doing without help."

For these reasons, Mill argues, it is crucial that the position of the
welfare recipient be less desirable—"less eligible"—than that of the self-
supporting laborer. The absence of such a "lesser eligibility" requirement
would "strike at the root of all individual energy and self-government"
and, if fully implemented, "would require as its supplement an organized
system for governing and setting to work like cattle those who had
been removed from the influence of the motives that act on human
beings" (III, 961 [P.E.]). Hence, it is crucial that assistance, while being
available to all as a matter of legal and moral right, leave to everyone
the strongest possible incentive to do without it:

> If, consistently with guaranteeing all persons against absolute want, the
> condition of those who are supported by legal charity can be kept
> considerably less desirable than the condition of those who can find
> support for themselves, none but beneficial consequences can arise from a
> law which renders it impossible for any person, except by his own choice,
> to die from insufficiency of food. (III, 961 [P.E.])

It must be emphasized that this "lesser eligibility" principle is required
both from the point of view of the interests of society as a whole and
from the point of view of the long-run interests of the recipients
themselves. From the point of view of society as a whole, "lesser
eligibility" is required to prevent the unlimited drain upon resources
that would occur in its absence, with adverse consequences for both
efficiency (loss of incentives to work) and justice (encroachment upon
legitimate desert claims), as well as to avoid the authoritative allocation
of labor that such a scheme would, at the extreme, arguably entail.
From the point of view of the recipients themselves, it is required to
prevent the permanent forms of welfare dependency fundamentally
incompatible with human energy and self-dependence—and hence autonomy, dignity, and self-respect. Mill conceives that the indignities
temporarily inflicted on welfare recipients are more than offset by the
spur that they provide those persons to restore their independence by
leaving the welfare system.

What, then, are the requirements of this "lesser eligibility" principle? Mill cites the Poor Law of 1834, with its principle of "indoor relief" (Himmelfarb, 1983, 147–176), as having provided the institutional means for its implementation. What seemed clear to Mill was that—at least in a society like his own, where the overwhelming majority of workers were already at or near subsistence—"lesser eligibility" could not simply entail setting the social minimum at a low enough level. For Mill, the exercise of a social right to welfare must, in order to ensure lesser eligibility, involve the forfeiture of civil and political rights enjoyed by other citizens.

Two examples will suffice. The first involves Mill's well-known preoccupation, as a student of Malthus, with the population problem. Given an absolute right to subsistence under circumstances of widespread poverty and deprivation, Mill argues, the indigent will feel no restraint upon their unlimited desire to procreate; it is therefore crucial that society legally limit their right to do so. Those who receive public assistance, either in the form of welfare provision or in the form of a *droit au travail*, must abrogate any right to have children at their own discretion and without limit—a stipulation without which, Mill insists, any such scheme would immediately impose an altogether unacceptable drain upon the resources of society. And though there is for Mill no basic right to unlimited procreation (procreation is an other-regarding activity with a clear impact upon the interests of others), it is clear that such restrictions would involve the abrogation of a civil right enjoyed by nonindigent citizens. This particular forfeiture of equal liberty can stand as a specific example of the broader regime of "restricted indulgence and enforced rigidity of discipline" (II, 360 [*P.E.*]) contemplated by Mill— a regime that would clearly involve the unequal distribution of a wide variety of civil rights enjoyed by other citizens as a matter of basic liberty.

A second example involves the franchise. Mill regards it as "required by first principles, that the receipt of parish relief should be a peremptory disqualification for the franchise. He who cannot by his labor suffice for his own support, has no claim to the privilege of helping himself to the money of others. By becoming dependent on the remaining members of the community for actual subsistence, he abrogates his claim to equal rights in other respects" (XIX, 452 [*C.R.G.*]). It might be thought that Mill here broadly follows writers in the civic republican tradition who affirm economic independence as a necessary condition of political rights, seeing recipients of welfare as lacking the requisite independence (despite a firm legal and moral *right* to such provision). In fact, however, Mill favored extension of the franchise to other economically dependent adults excluded by writers in the civic republican tradition—most notably, of course, women. His argument here seems rather more moralistic: Those who must help themselves to the public purse *deservedly* forfeit their political rights. (Mill fails to note that welfare recipients are not the only category of persons who help themselves to the public purse.)

Now, again, it is clear that Mill never affirmed a basic right to equal political liberty. He insists that the franchise, which involves power over others, is a trust, not a right; and he favors more than one vote for those likely to exercise this trust in the best interests of society as a whole. Nevertheless, Mill is equally clear that the franchise promotes vital human interests: It is (1) essential to the protection of other vital human interests, (2) an important means of moral and intellectual education, and (3) an integral expression of the dignity and self-respect of persons as participants in the common social life (XIX, 404–412, 467–470 [*C.R.G.*]). For Mill, this is an interest that society must, as a matter of recognized moral rule, protect—on the logic of his own definition, that is to say, a *right*.[5] Every sane adult has a *prima facie* right to at least one vote. To forfeit this right, as for Mill the recipients of public assistance must, is to be "degraded" (XIX, 470 [*C.R.G.*]); it is to forfeit one's dignity and self-respect.

What these requirements establish is that, for Mill, any workable scheme of welfare provision must, in order to ensure "lesser eligibility," *stigmatize* its recipients by denying them civil and political rights enjoyed by nonindigent citizens. It it striking that, for Mill, this stigmatization is a conscious *goal* of the welfare system, rather than being, as for many contemporary liberals, an unintended and unwanted by-product of welfare. The moral right to welfare advocated by Mill is, therefore, a deeply ambiguous one. On the one hand, given widespread poverty and destitution, recognition of such a right is crucial to protect the vital interest of persons in survival and autonomy; it is in that sense a recognition of the "equal social worth" of persons, a necessary condition of their dignity and self-respect. On the other hand, in order to ensure the "lesser eligibility" that is for Mill crucial to the success of any scheme of welfare provision, he feels compelled to annex conditions to the exercise of this right that are themselves calculated to violate the dignity and self-respect of the indigent; far from providing the material conditions for the effective exercise of other civil and political rights, this particular "social" right is a sufficient condition of their negation.[6] Thus, for Mill, the capitalist welfare state simultaneously affirms and denies the dignity and self-respect of its clients.

Desert and Redistribution

The second critical limitation of the capitalist welfare state arises from the fact that realizing the right to subsistence requires the redistribution of income through taxation, and this redistribution will inevitably conflict with the legitimate property rights of others. Mill, as we suggested above, views the actual regime of property rights in unreformed capitalism as departing egregiously from the underlying principle of private property: that individuals have a moral right to the fruits of their own labor and abstinence. In unreformed captalism, many will benefit from possessions that they do not deserve—possessions that they inherited or acquired by luck. Nonetheless, even in such a system, any scheme of taxation of substantial scope is bound in some measure to tax deserved rewards, whether the standard is effort or contribution. For this reason, any state welfare provision institutionalizes a tension between Mill's principles of need and desert. Mill is forthright in asserting that the claims of urgent basic need trump those of desert:

> Society mainly consists of those who live by bodily labour; and if society, that is, if the labourers, lend their physical force to protect individuals in the enjoyment of superfluities, they are entitled to do so, and have always done so, with the reservation of a power to tax those superfluities for purposes of public utility; among which purposes the subsistence of the people is the foremost. Since no one is responsible for having been born, no pecuniary sacrifice is too great to be made by those who have more than enough, for the purpose of securing enough to all persons already in existence. (II, 357 [*P.E.*])

One might put Mill's point by saying that the marginal utility of income used to purchase subsistence goods is higher than that used for luxuries, or by saying that providing for our basic needs is more crucial to our basic security/survival and autonomy interests than is rewarding desert.

But as one contemplates expanding the system of welfare provision beyond subsistence, the claims of need become progressively less urgent while the encroachments upon desert become, in Mill's view, rapidly more disturbing. An examination of Mill's views on the income tax shows that his principles of taxation would considerably restrict the capacity of the tax system to finance an extensive scheme of welfare provision.

Although the theoretical underpinnings of Mill's views on taxation are sometimes vague or confused, the thrust of his position is easily stated: With some significant exceptions, most differences in the incomes produced by the market are deserved, and income taxation should be designed so as to disturb only minimally these market outcomes. Mill considered it unjust, on grounds of need, to tax subsistence incomes, and argued that his goal would be best met by a proportional tax on that portion of income that exceeded subsistence. "Each would then pay a fixed proportion, not of his whole means, but of his superfluities" (III, 809 [*P.E.*]). Mill suggested that this scheme followed from his basic principle of "equality of taxation," which he interpreted to mean "equality of sacrifice" (III, 807 [*P.E.*]).

The notion of sacrifice here is ambiguous, but perhaps the most reasonable interpretation is that people at different income levels should bear equal *proportionate* sacrifices (Musgrave, 1959, 98). It can be shown that, if people's utility functions share a common shape and exhibit constant marginal utility of income, Mill's scheme will in fact lead to persons at different income levels giving up equal fractions of the utility they get from their consumption of superfluities. Just as important, from the standpoint of seeing the relation between proportional taxation and the hypothesis that incomes are deserved, is the fact that proportional taxation will leave unchanged the relative utilities of persons receiving different incomes.

Mill sets himself firmly against the progressive taxation of incomes as a general principle, on grounds that it illegitimately encroaches on desert:

> I am as desirous as any one that means should be taken to diminish [inequalities of wealth], but not so as to relieve the prodigal at the expense of the prudent. To tax the larger incomes at a higher percentage than the smaller is to lay a tax on industry and economy; to impose a penalty on people for having worked harder and saved more than their neighbours. It is not the fortunes which are earned, but those which are unearned, that it is for the public good to place under limitation. A just and wise legislation would abstain from holding out motives for dissipating rather than saving the earnings of honest exertion. Its impartiality between competitors would consist in endeavouring that they should all start fair, and not in hanging a weight upon the swift to diminish the distance between them and the slow. Many, indeed, fail with greater efforts than those with which others succeed, not from difference of merits, but difference of opportunities; but if all were done which it would be in the power of a good government to do, by instruction and by legislation, to diminish this inequality of opportunities, the differences of fortune arising from people's own earnings could not justly give umbrage. (III, 810–811 [*P.E.*])

Exemption of subsistence from taxation, of course, introduces a limited amount of progressivity into the tax scheme. Mill thought this progressivity justified because, the claims of basic need being more urgent than those of luxury consumption, to tax them at equal rates would be to impose *unequal* sacrifice. To this extent Mill accepts a notion of diminishing marginal utility of income. But to justify general progressivity in the rates on that ground Mill rejects as "too disputable altogether, and even if true at all, not true to a sufficient extent to be made the foundation of any rule of taxation" (III, 810 [*P.E.*]).

The implied judgments about utility functions here may be fairly shaky, but Mill also offered more general arguments of both justice and efficiency against progressivity. "I do not see how you can, either with justice or policy, tax a person more heavily because he earns more, or because, after having earned more, he saves more. I do not think that you can lay a tax upon energy, or industry, or prudence. It seems to me that even upon questions of justice, apart from policy, there is no stronger or more valid principle than that of not giving any advantage to self-indulgence over industry and economy, even though the effect may be to give some advantage to, or rather, not to interfere with the natural advantage of the rich over the poor" (V, 567 ["The Income and Property Tax"]). Indeed, Mill thought that, ideally, saving should be exempt from income tax, even if this made the system on balance regressive; in any case, he believed that the implementation of this proposal would be impractical.[7] Mill went so far as to call progressivity above the threshold of basic need satisfaction "graduated robbery" (V, 552 ["The Income and Property Tax"]).

Mill would further condemn strongly egalitarian progressive taxation on economic grounds, because excessive taxation in his view undermines incentives to work, save, and invest. A high rate of taxation "is, independently of its injustice, a serious economical evil. It may be carried so far as to discourage industry by insufficiency of reward. Very long before it reaches this point it prevents or greatly checks accumulation, or causes the capital accumulated to be sent for investment to foreign countries" (III, 882 [*P.E.*]).

Mill's predominant view of income taxation thus seeks to minimize its "distorting" influence on market rewards. Insofar as the view is based on considerations of justice, it reflects the judgment that market rewards are by and large deserved. Mill, of course, does recognize that market returns are influenced by the monopoly power of people possessing particularly scarce resources and talents, and in the case of land he argues that taxation should be increased to very high levels. But in general, he waives concerns about monopoly and rent components in contributive rewards. No doubt a major reason for adopting this approach is Mill's judgment that "rent" and "monopoly" returns cannot be identified easily. Mill says that we must view inequalities not simply from "industry, frugality, perseverance" but also from "talents, and to a certain extent even opportunities . . . [as] inseparable from the idea of private property" (II, 225 [*P.E.*]); and he maintains that inequalities resulting from the latter factors, too, must in practice be regarded as *earned:* "As long as the income is in the hands of the person in whose hands it originated, the presumption is, that he earned it" (V, 566 ["The Income and Property Tax"]).

In addition to this pragmatic point, we would conjecture that this approach reflects Mill's judgment that progressive taxation of these excess returns is not an intelligent strategy for attacking their underlying sources. Glaring injustice results from the highly unequal distribution of productive property and from the inequalities of opportunities for education and advancement that are themselves to an important degree a product of property inequality. Only by going to the root of these problems, in a way that taxes and transfers of current incomes do not, can these underlying problems be addressed.

Thus, Mill winds up setting himself quite firmly against widespread progressivity in the taxation of incomes. It would be economically unwise and (to put his point negatively) could not be undertaken without infringing importantly on legitimate claims of desert. Although these commitments do not impose a clear ceiling on the amount of revenue that could be raised, and hence on the scope of welfare provision, they do greatly restrict the flexibility of the state in acquiring resources for extensive welfare provision.

We argued above that, given the background conditions of an otherwise unreformed capitalism as a constraint, the welfare state can, for Mill, satisfy the claims of need only by invading the claims of equal liberty. Similarly, we have now seen how, again given these constraints, the welfare state, for Mill, can satisfy the claims of need only by invading the claims of desert. In both cases the claims of basic need are prior— urgent need claims trump both equal liberty and positive desert claims. But in both cases, the terms of the trade-off quickly impose limits upon the permissible expansion of egalitarian redistribution through welfare state provision. They lead Mill to oppose anything more than a minimal welfare state.

However, these unhappy trade-offs presuppose a highly unequal background distribution of property. Given that distribution, a minimal welfare state is the least imperfect among the available alternatives. But this solution is, for Mill, distinctly second-best. For he believes that, by modifying the background distribution of property, it would be possible to achieve a political economy that, relative to both laissez-faire and welfare state capitalism, would simultaneously advance all three of his ideal principles of justice—liberty, need, and desert. The key to this strategy is sharply to reduce the very substantial sources of *un*deserved privilege that characterize the property regime of unreformed capitalism— and to do it without violating legitimate desert or entitlement claims. To accomplish this, Mill focuses on the mechanisms of intergenerational transmission of wealth. It is to this aspect of Mill's thought that we now turn.

BEYOND THE WELFARE STATE

We have argued that, given the unjust background conditions of an otherwise unreformed capitalism as a constraint, Mill endorses the minimal welfare state as a preferable alternative to an unrestricted regime of laissez-faire. But we have also argued that the welfare state, set against this background of property rights, institutionalizes undesirable tensions within Mill's three principles of justice: It satisfies the claims of basic need satisfaction only by setting them against those of equal liberty and desert. Far from eradicating or ameliorating the root causes of the unfreedom, poverty, and undeserved privilege inherent in the operation of unreformed laissez-faire capitalism—namely, maldistribution of property rights in the means of production—the welfare state advances justice on one dimension (albeit on balance) only by subtracting from it on two others. Welfare state capitalism, as Mill once observed in a different but apposite context, "nibble[s] at the consequences of unjust power, instead of addressing the injustice itself" (III, 953 [P.D.]) It is therefore justifiable only as a matter of second-best or nonideal theory—only, that is, failing a better alternative.

In this section, we shall examine Mill's vision of a just political economy. We shall *not* focus in detail upon an exact specification of the institutional arrangements envisaged by Mill as ideal—avoiding, in particular, a full discussion of Mill's views upon the choice between private-property and social-ownership versions of a just political economy. Though we shall concentrate our attention upon his vision of a just private-property market economy, we shall emphasize the respects in which the broad contours of Mill's vision of an "egalitarian market economy," as we have called it, differentiates that vision (in *both* its private-property and social-ownership forms) from the vision of welfare state capitalism discussed above.

We shall now argue in more detail that these two different kinds of regime—egalitarian market economy and welfare state capitalism—exemplify the two competing approaches to justice in political economy noted at the beginning of this chapter. Welfare state capitalism, on Mill's account, accepts as given a severe maldistribution of property rights in the means of production, or in initial property and skill endowments, and then seeks to achieve justice through the *ex post* (intragenerational) distribution of market outcomes. Egalitarian market economies, by contrast, attempt to achieve a just *ex ante* (intergenerational) distribution of property and skill endowments, with correspondingly less emphasis upon subsequent within-generation redistributional encumbrances. Unlike capitalism in either its laissez-faire or welfare state versions, we shall further argue, egalitarian market economies thus satisfy not merely the first but also the second of Mill's two main institutional preconditions for distributive justice in political economy: (1) competitive markets, and (2) background conditions that include the absence of severe class inequality in the distribution of property rights in productive resources. And we argue finally that, for this reason, egalitarian market economies, if feasible, are clearly optimal from the standpoint of Mill's theory of justice, because they thereby promise the possibility of a simultaneous enhancement in each of its three major requirements.

The first thing to be noted is that Mill is quite explicit in his identification of the strategy of welfare state redistribution as second-best relative to his preferred alternative: The subject of welfare provision would be "of very minor importance . . . [were] the diffusion of property satisfactory" (III, 960 [P.E.]). What, then, constitutes a satisfactory diffusion of property, and how is it to be realized?

At one point in the *Principles of Political Economy*, Mill identifies two basic requirements for resolving the problem of poverty: (1) effective education for the children of the laboring class, and (2) measures that would "extinguish extreme poverty for one whole generation" (II, 374 [P.E.]). Noting that "when the object is to raise the permanent condition of a people, small means do not merely produce small effects, they produce no effect at all" (II, 378 [P.E.]), Mill, in early versions of the *Principles*, identifies two measures for the accomplishment of the second objective named above: (1) colonization, and (2) measures to create a class of small peasant proprietors. The virtue of these two measures, he argues, is that they could accomplish this large objective "without wrong to anyone, without any of the liabilities of mischief attendant on voluntary or legal charity, and not only without weakening, but on the contrary strengthening, every incentive to industry, and every motive to forethought" (II, 376 [P.E.]).

What is interesting about this discussion are not the specific policy recommendations, which Mill himself came to view as historically dated, but the broad framework within which Mill locates them, which he insisted "remain true in principle" (II, 378 [P.E.]) despite the changing details of policy. They suggest that for Mill a successful solution to the problem of poverty must focus not upon welfare state provision, with its attendant "liabilities" and "mischiefs," but rather upon large-scale egalitarian redistribution in the background conditions—the property and skill endowments—that define the environment of market exchange. And yet this goal must be accomplished "without wrong to anyone"—

that is, without the uncompensated confiscation of established entitlements to property.

The ideal vision animating these recommendations can be seen in its purest form in Mill's discussion of the conditions under which a fair choice might be made between the principles of private property and social ownership. Imagine, Mill writes, a body of colonists occupying an uninhabited territory. Property rights in productive resources will be divided fairly among them, so that all are equal at the starting gate. But then "the division, once made, would not be interfered with; individuals would be left to their own exertions and to the ordinary chances, for making an advantageous use of that which was assigned to them" (II, 201–202 [P.E.]).

This, then, is the limiting ideal—we shall call it fair equality of opportunity (Rawls, 1971, 65–90)—in the direction of which Mill wishes to move the property regime of unreformed capitalist society. Mill recognizes "that [the fact that] all should indeed start on perfectly equal terms is inconsistent with any law of private property" (II, 207 [P.E.]); but he insists that a well-designed scheme of law and political regulation could, by mitigating instead of aggravating the inequalities inherent in the natural workings of the principle itself, at least approximate this ideal.

How, consistent with Mill's self-imposed prohibition upon uncompensated confiscation, might this goal be accomplished? First of all, as we have begun to suggest, Mill proposes to limit severely the intergenerational transmission of unequal property and wealth through a scheme for the heavily progressive taxation of gifts and inheritances. The right to bequest, Mill argues, is an integral feature of the idea of private property; but the right of *inheritance* is not. Therefore, Mill proposes to regulate, not what people may give but, rather, what they may *receive* through gift and inheritance. Mill proposes an "accessions tax" that would in effect confiscate gifts and inheritances above a reasonably generous threshold of comfortable independence. His scheme is designed to restrict the intergenerational transmission of unequal property and wealth through a kind of private-to-private redistribution, inasmuch as there would be an obvious disincentive to bequeath more than the threshold amount to any given individual. (Though Mill's scheme involves no formal restrictions upon the right of bequest, it is clear that it would effectively limit that freedom to an important degree.)

Interestingly, Mill purports to justify this proposal through an appeal to the principle of diminishing marginal utility that he elsewhere rejects (above the threshold of basic need satisfaction): "The difference to the happiness of the possessor between a moderate independence and five times as much is insignificant when weighted against the enjoyment that might be given, and the permanent benefits diffused, by some other disposal of the four fifths" (II, 225 [*P.E.*]). The clear difficulty with this argument, however, is that it proves too much: It applies not simply to gifts and inheritances but to other forms of income as well. Thus, to justify the differential (i.e., progressive) taxation of gifts and inheritances, Mill needs a further criterion. He finds this criterion in a straightforward appeal to his concept of desert.

For Mill, gifts and inheritances are like manna from heaven: They are, as noted above, the paradigm instance of the windfall gain, un-ambiguously bearing no relationship to the voluntary labor and absti-nence of those who benefit from them. They are *unearned*. When Mill insists, as he does throughout his writings, that it is "not fortunes that are earned, but those that are unearned, which should be limited for the public good," by unearned he *means* acquired by gift or inheritance. Individuals, he insists, must be permitted, to the maximum degree possible, to keep what they have acquired by their own labor and abstinence within their own lifetimes. But since to succeed to what one has not earned through one's own exertion is a privilege, not a right, there is no injustice in the severely progressive taxation of the inter-generational transfer of these holdings. The doctrine of equality of taxation does not apply (Mill, 1967, 566).

Mill argues that once property rights are attached to persons, indi-viduals are entitled to their holdings, whether or not they deserve them. But on Mill's analysis, these holdings float free, as it were, between generations. Much of the appeal of a scheme of accessions taxation to Mill is that it provides him with a means, consistent with a prohibition upon the uncompensated confiscation of existing holdings, of substantially reducing the undeserved privilege inherent in the property regime of unreformed capitalist society. In his view, it provides a means, consistent with the requirements of conservative justice, of advancing one of his criteria of ideal justice—indeed, as we shall suggest more fully below, simultaneously advancing all three.

It is clear that Mill himself believed his proposals for the progressive, indeed confiscatory, taxation of gifts and inheritances to be *radically* redistributive (Bain, 1882, 89). And it does seem clear that such a scheme, if fully implemented, would have something like the levelling effect ascribed to it by Mill. It is, however, less clear how effective such a scheme, standing by itself, would be, given a highly unequal distribution of property and wealth as a starting point, in fully attaining Mill's stated objectives—either the eradication of extreme poverty for one whole generation or, more strongly, a society with fair equality of opportunity at the starting gate. The clear difficulty is that an accessions rule might stimulate redistribution of wealth within a limited circle of beneficiaries that does not include the worst off: "Wealth circulates as it were around the West of London without ever getting to the East End" (Arneson, 1985).

Related difficulties beset Mill's conception of the institutional means through which widespread ownership of productive property could be achieved in an emerging industrial economy. Mill recognized that "the progress of the productive arts require[s] that many sorts of industrial occupation should be carried on by larger and larger capitals" and, further, that "capitals of the requisite magnitude belonging to single owners do not . . . exist in the needful abundance, and would be still less numerous if the laws favored the diffusion instead of the concentration of property" (III, 895–6, [P.E.]). Therefore, in industry (unlike agriculture), the division of property into small, individually owned bundles (as with peasant proprietorships) was economically unattractive.

Still, Mill thought it "most undesirable that all those improved processes, and those means of efficiency and economy in production, which depend on the possession of large funds, should be monopolies in the hands of a few rich individuals, through the difficulties experienced by persons of moderate or small means in associating their capital" (III, 896 [P.E.]). Mill therefore strongly defended the principle of limited liability as an encouragement to the formation of large pools of shared capital. Although it can hardly be said that Mill fully anticipated the widespread ownership of diversified stock portfolios envisioned in James Meade's "property-owning democracy" (1964), early steps in that direction are clearly present in Mill.

However, as is well known, Mill saw a different path of evolution of associated industrial ownership as more desirable. His preferred arrangement in an industrial context involves the ideal of worker-owned and democratically controlled cooperative firms—an ideal that occupies a central place in Mill's fully developed vision of a just political economy. Yet he envisages the emergence and increasing predominance of these firms through the spontaneous processes of market competition, as a result of the determined self-sacrifice of workers, in ways that remain ultimately unconvincing—Mill's prophecy fails as dismally as Marx's (Ryan, 1984, 176). And similarly, to accomplish universal ownership of diversified stock portfolios through the mechanisms of voluntary dispersal of inheritances and individual savings alone is a doubtful ambition.

As we have said, our goal is not detailed specification of the institutional arrangements envisaged by Mill as ideal. The point here is simply that, in each case, Mill envisages the attainment of his stated objective: (1) without resort to extensive egalitarian redistribution of income by the welfare state, with its attendant "mischiefs" and "liabilities"; and (2) "without violence or spoilation" (II, 376 [P.E.])—that is, without uncompensated abrogation of existing property rights. Whether the goal could in fact be accomplished subject to these constraints must remain an open question—both for Mill and for us.

But these difficulties are fundamentally to one side for our purposes in this chapter. Our main point is that the vision of a just political economy to which Mill aspires—a market economy with an egalitarian distribution of property rights in the means of production—differs fundamentally from the ideal of welfare state capitalism. This is the end that Mill holds in view, whatever the difficulties of the means by which he proposes to attain it.

Our analysis in this section has thus far focused upon Mill's commitment to a more equal distribution of initial *property* endowments as an integral feature of a just political economy. But, as we have already seen in his insistence upon education for the children of the laboring class, Mill applies a similar logic to his discussion of the distribution of *skill* endowments. Mill recognizes that under conditions of unreformed capitalist society, wage income stands in an *inverse* relationship to the disutility of work. This is because of the absence of fair equality of opportunity to invest in human capital: As there is an undersupply of those with the requisite skills, many of the most pleasant jobs are among the most remunerative; and, conversely, as there is an oversupply of those with no skill or training, many of the least pleasant jobs are among the least remunerative. Differences of reward, that is, far exceed what is necessary to equalize their advantages, because the costs of training disqualify the vast majority of laborers from the possibility of competition for a wide range of jobs. (II, 386 [*P.E.*]). Under the conditions of fair equality of opportunity envisaged by Mill, by contrast, we could plausibly expect competition for the more pleasant jobs to increase, with a corresponding decline in the wages that they command, and *vice versa*. Remaining skill differentials would increasingly come to reflect, not unequal opportunity to invest in human capital, but the voluntary *choices* (based upon different rates of time preference, labor/leisure trade-offs, and the like) of persons. At the extreme, the only remaining "endowment-sensitive" differentials would be rents to natural talent— differentials that, when set against a background of genuinely fair equality of opportunity, would not in Mill's view "give umbrage."

We should note that, although Mill might have been able to defend this acceptance of inequalities due to natural talents on pragmatic grounds, in principle treating these inequalities, as well as inequalities emerging within lifetimes through luck, as though they were earned is problematic. Mill's view here is subject to the critique of "starting gate" theories offered by Dworkin (1981): The same logic that applies to property endowments ought to apply to natural endowments and to gains owing to "brute" luck. Indeed, Mill's own treatment of desert acknowledges this point.

Still, in its broadest outline, Mill's vision of a just political economy involves the two main institutional preconditions outlined above: (1) market competition, and (2) the absence of severe class inequality in the distribution of property rights in productive resources. Under conditions of fair equality of opportunity to acquire physical and human capital, Mill envisages a substantially more equal distribution of initial property and skill endowments. And when set against these just background conditions, the market will in turn register a far more equal, and just, distribution of income and wealth than when set against the background of unreformed capitalist property institutions—with correspondingly less need, therefore, for egalitarian redistribution by welfare state institutions.

Mill thus decisively endorses one of the two broad approaches to justice in political economy outlined in our introduction: greater equality in the *ex ante* (intergenerational) distribution of property and skill endowments, as opposed to greater equality through the *ex post* (intragenerational) redistribution of market outcomes. And he endorses this equalization-of-initial-endowments strategy because he believes it to be decisively superior to egalitarian redistribution by the institution of welfare state capitalism from the standpoint of his three principles of justice.

First, with a more equal distribution of property and skill endowments resulting in tight labor markets, with "exit" from exploitative wage bargains a viable option, the widespread lack of equal effective liberty, or wage-slavery, issuing from capitalist property institutions will have been substantially eliminated; the claims of equal liberty will thus have been advanced. Second, for similar reasons, the widespread "physical privation" and "moral degradation" issuing from capitalist property institutions will have been substantially eliminated; the claims of basic need satisfaction will thus have been advanced—this time without encroachment, as with welfare state redistribution, upon equal liberty and desert. Third, through stringent restrictions upon the intergenerational transmission of unequal property and wealth, the widespread undeserved privilege similarly issuing from capitalist property institutions will have been substantially reduced; the claims of desert will thus have been enhanced—but without the uncompensated confiscation that would, in Mill's views, unacceptably encroach upon the requirements of "conservative justice." Therefore, if feasible, the equalization-of-initial-endowments strategy endorsed by Mill seems clearly preferable to the strategy of welfare state redistribution from the point of view of his theory of justice. It promises a non-zero-sum enhancement in each of its three major dimensions.

It should be emphasized, however, that even full realization of the strategy mapped by Mill would not necessarily eliminate the need for certain important forms of welfare state provision. An ultraminimal welfare state in some form would still, arguably, be required to provide for the needs of those who, as it were, fell through the grid of Mill's egalitarian property institutions.[8] A right remains a right even if few, or indeed no, persons need to exercise it at any given moment. It also seems true that under the considerably more equal conditions envisaged by Mill, with a far more prosperous least-advantaged group, it might be possible for any necessary welfare state provision to ensure "lesser eligibility" without having to annex to the exercise of this social right the Draconian conditions seen by Mill as essential in the context of his own society. This in turn raises larger questions regarding the continuing relevance of Mill's arguments. We now turn briefly to those questions by way of conclusion.

SOME CONTEMPORARY IMPLICATIONS

Continuing interest in Mill's analysis of welfare provision stems, in our view, from his clear identification of two alternative strategies for attaining and sustaining a just political economy. What we might label the "welfare state" strategy accepts as given a highly unequal background distribution of property and opportunity, and attempts to redress the resulting injustice through taxes on and transfers of the unequal incomes that result. The "property-redistribution" alternative focuses instead on correcting injustice in the underlying distributions of ownership of physical and human capital principally through attention to the intergenerational transmission of inequality.

We have suggested in other work that a similar contrast in redistributive strategies can be found in the contemporary writings of James Meade and John Rawls (Krouse and McPherson, 1987). The two strategies are, to be sure, not mutually exclusive, even in Mill's thought and surely under contemporary conditions. As we have noted, the right to subsistence that Mill identified would not lapse even if more equal property holdings and opportunities reduced the incidence of claims for help, and therefore a state apparatus to provide welfare would surely continue to be needed. Moreover, the logic of Mill's analysis suggests that differential taxation of "rents" to natural talents and brute luck is justifiable in principle, and that state provision for those with special needs (e.g., those related to ill health) is also legitimate. Both the greater affluence of contemporary developed societies and the increased capacity of modern states to administer such taxes and to distribute such benefits would suggest that welfare state taxation and redistribution would play a significant role in a modern-day version of a Millean just society.

The "welfare state" and "property-redistribution" strategies are complementary in another sense as well. The need, on Mill's analysis, to impose a standard of "lesser eligibility" upon welfare recipients produces, in conditions of otherwise unreformed capitalism, highly distasteful living conditions for the needy. To the degree, however, that the living standards of the least well-off workers can be raised, the impositions of the principle of lesser eligibility can be made less severe. To put it otherwise, one can discourage dependence on welfare either by making recipients less eligible or by making workers more eligible. The "property-redistribution" standard aims at the latter.

Despite these complementarities, the two strategies remain, in Mill's thought, clearly distinct. We have seen in particular that Mill stresses powerful limits on the extent of welfare provision that can be justified in the absence of deeper reforms in the capitalist property structure. Welfare provision, in Mill's view, is morally required, but by itself it can serve only to ameliorate the worst consequences of existing injustices; it is not a possible vehicle for promoting wider reform. Mill's position here is influenced in part by limits on the scope of income taxation that follow from his views on desert and efficiency, but it is much more powerfully shaped by his judgments about the damaging consequences of generous welfare provision.

In formulating these judgments, Mill leaned heavily on the Malthusian argument that families with excess income would always "breed down" to their accustomed standard, so that lasting improvement in their condition would have to be accompanied by basic change in their habits and aspirations. But a welfare system that encouraged dependence would produce exactly the wrong kinds of changes in character: Rather than encouraging industry and self-dependence and orienting needy families toward future improvement, it would encourage irresponsibility, indiscipline, and a lack of forethought. Moreover, given the onerous and ill-paid conditions of labor, any offer of subsistence without strong negative sanctions attached would produce an eager supply of claimants, spreading dependence and subverting the working of labor markets.

Excepting only the explicit Malthusian link between wage rates and population growth, these arguments plainly foreshadow those of many contemporary critics of welfare provision. The psychology of dependence, the discouragement to work effort, the expansion of the welfare rolls, and, notably in recent discussions, the encouragement of irresponsible reproductive behavior—all these are commonly cited as negative consequences of welfare provision. Although most closely associated with such conservative critics as Charles Murray and Lawrence Mead (the critics whom Leon Wieseltier has indeed labeled "neo-Malthusians"), such debilitating effects of the "dole" have also been alleged by leftist critics of the welfare state. It is important to note that evidence supporting the view that expanded welfare provision has been a major cause of such phenomena as rising illegitimacy rates among teenagers, high minority unemployment rates, and so on is quite scarce. As Moynihan (1986) has recently reminded us, our capacity to develop firm knowledge about these matters is quite limited. And certainly the evidence Mill had to rely on was no better.

Still, it would be hard to deny that Mill's account of the damaging psychological effects of dependence continues to carry force, as does his view that welfare policy, while fulfilling the right of the needy to assistance, can also justifiably impose constraints on recipients that discourage dependence and self-damaging or antisocial conduct. As Christopher Jencks has argued in a thoughtful review of Charles Murray's *Losing Ground*, "[A] successful program must not only help those it seeks to help, but must do so in such a way as not to reward folly or vice. . . . [S]ocial policy is about punishment as well as rewards, and . . . a policy that is never willing to countenance suffering, however deserved, will not long endure" (Jencks, 1985, 49). Jencks further notes, in a passage that echoes Mill's views on desert, that the principle of lesser eligibility should be upheld on moral grounds and not simply to influence behavior. Reviewing Murray's example of an abandoned spouse (Phyllis) who does better on welfare than her cousin (Sharon) does working, Jencks observes:

> This will not do. Almost all of us believe it is "better" for people to work than not to work. This means we also believe those who work should end up "better off" than those who do not work. Standing the established moral order on its head by rewarding Phyllis more than Sharon will undermine the legitimacy of the entire AFDC system. Nor is it enough to ensure that Phyllis is just a little worse off than Sharon. If Phyllis does not work, many—including Sharon—will feel that Phyllis should be substantially worse off, so there will be no ambiguity about the fact that Sharon's virtue is being rewarded. . . . Upsetting the moral order in this way may not have had much effect on people's behavior. . . . Even if *nobody* quit work to go on welfare, a system that provided indolent Phyllis with as much money as diligent Sharon would be universally viewed as unjust. To say that such a system does not increase indolence—or doesn't increase it much—is beside the point. . . . We care about justice independent of its effects on behavior. (1985, 47–48)

Now, what is required to enforce the principle of lesser eligibility is historically relative. Mill judged the condition of the typical worker in his day to be so bad that he thought only positive sanctions—the almshouse, denial of the franchise—could do the job. One would hope that in a society as well off as ours, such forbidding measures would no longer be needed. And yet Charles Murray has found it possible to argue for exactly these two measures—"indoor relief" for AFDC mothers and the withdrawal of voting privileges from all welfare recipients—as necessary discouragements to dependence (Murray, 1985). He has also proposed the total termination of welfare for the able-bodied on the same grounds.

Murray offers little argument that such severity is needed, nor (despite his assertions that he has the interests of the poor at heart) does he discuss much how their legitimate claims to assistance should be weighed in assessing his proposals. But even if Murray were right to insist on such harsh restrictions of welfare, that would serve simply to reinforce the need for attention to the other half of Mill's story.

For Mill regarded the need to impose severe limits on welfare provision as part of the case for more thoroughgoing reform of capitalist property relations. If indeed it is true that the alternatives to welfare for today's poor are so bleak that only confinement and disenfranchisement are "less eligible," this is a powerful indictment of the limits on the opportunities they face. It was Mill's view that such injustices could be addressed, consistent with a central role for markets in organizing production and sustaining liberty, either through promoting widespread dispersal in the private ownership of productive property or through the encouragement of widespread worker ownership. We have seen that Mill's development of these alternative conceptions of just property institutions, and especially of strategies for achieving them, was importantly incomplete. He did, however, point in directions that deserve to be followed up.

We submit that contemporary discussions of the role of the welfare state would profit by recovering Mill's interest in the background of property institutions and holdings against which income-redistribution strategies are played out. Mill argued that a more egalitarian background of property holdings would at once lessen the burdens that welfare state redistribution is asked to shoulder and make it easier to meet remaining needs without encouraging widespread dependence. Current discussions of redistribution, at least those that operate within a framework of broadly liberal values are, we suggest, too quick to pose the alternatives of welfare capitalism or unreformed laissez-faire capitalism. The range of alternatives that we would describe as "egalitarian market economies," alternatives that have animated the thought of Mill and Meade and Rawls, deserve a closer look.

NOTES

1. We shall not provide a detailed discussion of the moral foundation of any of these three principles. We shall in particular simply assert without argument that Mill affirms a right to liberty as a component of his theory of justice; and we avoid, as unnecessary to our argument, efforts at precise specification of its appropriate domain. We shall offer somewhat fuller accounts of Mill's principles of need and desert in the course of developing our argument.

2. All references to Mill's writings will be to volume numbers and pages of his *Collected Works* (1965–1977). Major works by Mill will be abbreviated as follows: *Principles of Political Economy* (*P.E.*); *Chapters on Socialism* (*C.S.*); *Consideration on Representative Government* (*C.R.G.*); *Utilitarianism* (*Util.*).

3. Mill's occasional references to public welfare provision as "charity" (as well as his inclusion of welfare provision among the "optional" functions of government in the *Political Economy*) must be viewed either as the product of carelessness or as the result of a decision at these points to defer to common usages.

4. It is worth emphasizing that a right to welfare is not the only right to resource provision that Mill derives from these basic human needs. Another important example of such a right is education. Mill justifies imposing upon parents a legal obligation to ensure that their children receive at least an elementary education. He does so for two reasons: (a) Education is a public good, with beneficial consequences for society as a whole; and (b) children have a *right* to education, as it is essential to the development of their powers of autonomous judgment and choice. To ensure that children of the poor are not denied the resources essential to the fulfillment of this right, Mill favors public financing of elementary education. For Mill, this right to educational provision is unambiguously autonomy-enhancing: "This is not one of the cases in which the tender of help perpetuates the state of things which renders help necessary. Instruction, when it really is such, does not enervate, but strengthens as well as enlarges the active faculties: In whatever manner acquired, its effect on the mind is favorable to the spirit of independence: and when, unless had gratuitously, it would not be had at all, help in this form has the opposite tendency to that which in so many other cases makes it objectionable; it is help towards doing without help" (IIII, 949 [*P.E.*]).

5. Mill's insistence that the vote is a duty, not a right, can best be met by seeing it as a right that we have a duty to exercise in the public good. (See Berger, 1983, 191.)

6. Mill's judgment as to the requirements of "lesser eligibility" depends, of course, upon a series of contestable empirical assumptions—the "population problem," widespread poverty and indigence, a working class at or near subsistence—that may limit its applicability to a society like our own. We take up this question in the fourth section.

7. It should be noted that Mill actually advanced this notion—that the income tax imposes double taxation on savings—in the context of defending lower tax rates on terminable labor and capital incomes than on permanent capital incomes. Mill's argument was that recipients of the former would and should save more, and that those savings should not be taxed. This proposal would in fact probably increase net progressivity.

8. Continuing welfare state provision, in the form of a social insurance principle, might also be justified to provide for a range of *differential* basic needs (e.g., medical care, legal services, aid to the handicapped). We have made this point in more detail in a discussion of Rawls (Krouse and McPherson, 1987).

REFERENCES

Arneson, Richard (1985). Private correspondence with Richard Krouse.

Bain, Alexander (1882). *John Stuart Mill.* London: Longmans, Green, & Co.

Berger, Fred (1984). *Happiness, Justice, and Freedom: The Moral and Political Philosophy of John Stuart Mill.* Berkeley: University of California Press.

Dworkin, Ronald (1981). "What is Equality? Part II: Equality of Resources." *Philosophy and Public Affairs* 10 (Fall): 283–345.

Friedman, Milton (1962). *Capitalism and Freedom.* Chicago: University of Chicago Press.

Goodin, Robert (1985). "Vulnerabilities and Responsibilities: An Ethical Defense of the Welfare State," *The American Political Science Review* 79 (Fall): 775–87.

Gray, John (1983). *Mill on Liberty: A Defense.* London: Routledge and Kegan Paul.

Gutmann, Amy (1987). *Democracy and the Welfare State.* Princeton, N.J.: Princeton University Press.

Himmelfarb, Gertrude (1983). *The Idea of Poverty: England in the Early Industrial Age.* New York: Alfred A. Knopf.

Jencks, Christopher (1985). "How Poor Are the Poor?" *New York Review of Books* 32(8), May 9, 1985.

Krouse, Richard, and McPherson, Michael (1987). "On Rawlsian Justice in Political Economy: Capitalism, Property-Owning Democracy, and the Welfare State." In Gutmann (1987).

Lyons, David (1977). "Human Rights and the General Welfare," *Philosophy and Public Affairs* 6(2).

Marshall, T.H. (1977). "Citizenship and Social Class." In T.H. Marshall, ed., *Class, Citizenship, and Social Development.* Chicago: University of Chicago Press.

Mead, Lawrence M. (1986). *Beyond Entitlement: The Social Obligation of Citizenship.* New York: Free Press.

Meade, James (1964). *Equality, Efficiency, and the Ownership of Property.* London: Allen and Unwin.

Mill, John Stuart (1965). *Collected Works, Vols. II & III: Principles of Political Economy.* Toronto: University of Toronto Press.

———— (1967). *Collected Works, Vols. IV & V: Essays on Economics & Society.* Toronto: University of Toronto Press.

———— (1969). *Collected Works, Vol. X: Essays on Ethics, Religion, and Society.* Toronto: University of Toronto Press.

———— (1977). *Collected Works: Vols. XVIII & XIX: Essays on Politics and Society.* Toronto: University of Toronto Press.

Miller, David (1976). *Social Justice.* Oxford: Oxford University Press.

Moon, Donald (1987). "The Basis of the Democratic Welfare State." In Gutmann (1987).

Moynihan, Daniel P. (1986). *Family and Nation.* New York: Harcourt, Brace and Jovanovich.

Murray, Charles (1984). *Losing Ground: American Social Policy, 1950–1980.* New York: Basic Books.

———— (1985). "Helping the Poor: A Few Modest Proposals," *Commentary* 79(5), May: 27–34.

Musgrave, Richard A. (1959). *The Theory of Public Finance: A Study in Public Economy.* New York: McGraw-Hill.

Narveson, Jan (1967). *Morality and Utility.* Baltimore: Johns Hopkins University Press.

Plant, Raymond, et al. (1980). *Political Philosophy and Social Welfare.* London: Routledge and Kegan Paul.

Rawls, John (1971). *A Theory of Justice.* Cambridge: Mass.: Harvard University Press.

Ryan, Alan (1984). *Property in Political Theory.* Oxford and New York: Basil Blackwell.

Sen, A. K. (1970). *Collective Choice and Social Welfare.* San Francisco: Holden-Day, Inc.

Wellman, Carl (1982). *Welfare Rights.* Totowa, N.J.: Rowman and Allanheld.

Part Three

THE WELFARE STATE

Prospects and Problems

7

ALTRUISM AND
THE WELFARE STATE

Might it be possible to explain the existence of welfare states in terms of the altruistic concern that people generally feel for the welfare of their compatriots? For supporters of the welfare state, such an explanation may well seem an attractive one. For democrats it holds out the possibility that the welfare state will attract popular political support, with people demonstrating their willingness to be taxed to provide welfare for others. For economists, it suggests that the funding of a welfare state may be an example of Pareto-optimal redistribution. If people care about the welfare of others, everyone may be (subjectively) better off in a state of affairs where some resources have been transferred from the well-endowed to the needy. For sociologists, the welfare state, as a public expression of altruism, may help to foster altruism in social relations more generally, leading to a united and caring society.

This somewhat cozy consensus is, however, liable to be disturbed by the rude interruption of libertarians. These unwelcome guests are likely to make a number of critical remarks. To begin with, if people are indeed altruistically concerned about the welfare of their fellow citizens, then it is perfectly possible for them to make private arrangements to express their altruism, through charitable giving. Indeed, such charitable activity is not only a possible alternative to the welfare state but is actually superior to it in two respects. First, genuine altruism has to be voluntary: Forced giving, through the tax system, is no substitute for the real thing. No one likes paying taxes, whereas people generally feel good about donating money to famine relief or the church roof fund. Second, people vary both in the intensity of their altruism and in its direction. A tax-and-welfare system forces everyone in similar financial circumstances to donate the same amount to the same collectively determined ends. A voluntary system is more efficient, because it allows each person to donate the amount he chooses to the cause or causes that he favors. If Pareto-optimality is the criterion, the latter system is unequivocally better.

163

These are familiar arguments, but they form an important benchmark against which to test the altruistic explanation of the welfare state. Let me now say something about the kind of explanation that I have in mind. The *explanandum* is an institution with the following three features: First, it provides benefits (goods and services) to all people in a particular society, regardless of whether they have contributed to the cost of providing them. Second, it provides *specific* benefits that are seen as meeting needs, rather than sums of money that can be used as the recipient pleases. Third, the institution is funded by mandatory taxation, with tax schedules having no deliberate connection with the benefits that various classes of people are expected to receive. In short, the institution is potentially redistributive,[1] specific in its aims, and compulsory. The problem is to see whether the prevalence of a certain form of altruism could explain the existence of such an institution. This in turn raises three subordinate questions. The first is formal: What assumptions must we make about people's motives and beliefs in order to show that they would contract voluntarily into a welfare state with the above features? The second two are empirical: What evidence is there that people do actually have the requisite motives and beliefs? And how far is the historical existence of welfare states to be explained in this way?

I shall have rather little to say about the third question. No one could possibly suppose that the altruism hypothesis provides the full causal explanation for the existence, or detailed shape, of existing welfare states. It competes rather obviously with three "realistic" explanations. One sees the welfare state as an insurance scheme taken out by the rich (or the capitalist class) to buy off the discontented poor. Another sees the institution as a device used by the poor, through majority voting, partially to expropriate the rich. A third sees the welfare state as the creation of a professional class that lives off its proceeds. None of these explanations is patently groundless, and the altruism hypothesis would not necessarily try to displace them. It might, however, fit into a story of the following kind. Whatever the historical origins of the welfare state, it now enjoys a high degree of popular support in Western democracies.[2] This support is remarkably evenly spread across social classes, and it is only weakly related to the benefits that particular individuals expect to derive from welfare services.[3] This consensus forms a significant constraint on political leaders. In particular, programs for trimming the welfare state have to be advanced with great caution, directed at less popular forms of welfare benefit, and withdrawn whenever they meet popular resistance.

This story strikes me as plausible, indeed unexceptionable, and it is sufficient to make the altruism hypothesis potentially interesting to those concerned with causal questions as well as to those whose concern is more explicitly with the justification of the welfare state. It is worth stressing, however, that altruistic sentiments are not the only possible explanation for the observed levels of support. An alternative hypothesis is that people see the welfare state as a scheme of mutual insurance against remote and often unpredictable eventualities (such as illness or poverty in old age); this would make the basis of support enlightened self-interest.[4] Choosing between these hypotheses is not a simple matter. The second will be falsified to the extent that people agree to enter schemes that they can see in advance will be adversely redistributive from their point of view—for instance, if people in good health agree to a scheme whose benefits will accrue primarily to the chronically sick. But it may not be easy to establish that the individuals concerned see things in this way; it may be suggested instead that they are simply very uncertain about their future prospects and play safe by opting for an inclusive scheme, rather than seeking out a less costly form of insurance for the hale and hearty.[5] However, before we can begin to choose between altruism and other competing explanations of popular support for the welfare state, we need to show that the altruism hypothesis is a possible contender in the first place. This brings us back to questions one and two: Upon what assumptions would altruists support a welfare state (rather than opting for private charity)? Is there any reason to believe that these assumptions hold in practice? It seems most sensible to pursue these questions in tandem rather than consecutively. There is little point in producing a logically impeccable derivation of the welfare state if the premises required are wildly implausible: We are not doing political theory for Martians.

PREFERENCE ALTRUISM VERSUS NEEDS ALTRUISM

We need to begin by looking more closely at the meaning of *altruism*. The generic sense of the term is concern for the interests of others: The altruist is someone who is affected by the level of welfare enjoyed by (at least some) others and is moved to act on their behalf. But as we shall see, this definition leaves open a number of possible ways in which the interests of others can enter the practical deliberations of the person in question.

A first contrast has to do with the way in which the "interests" or "welfare" of the others are interpreted. Does the altruist give the *preferences* of other people canonical status, or does he employ some other notion of interests? For instance, is he concerned about meeting the needs of other people as he defines them, even if the people in question would rather be aided in some other way? Collard describes altruism of the latter kind as "meddlesome," a pejorative term that suggests an attempt to interfere with the way that other people run their lives (1978, 122–139).[6] Certainly a meddlesome altruist—or, as I shall describe him, a needs altruist—will want to try to prevent the recipient of his aid from converting it into a form that is subjectively preferred but valued less by the donor. So if a tramp touches me for the price of a hot dinner, I will want to see that the money goes on the meal rather than on a bottle of methyl alcohol.

It may initially seem difficult to make sense of this idea of needs altruism. If we are concerned about other people, shouldn't all that matters be how well off or badly off they feel? Of course, our concern may extend more broadly in time: We may want to give them what makes them feel good in the long run, rather than what they most want at this moment (consider heroin addicts). It still seems that preferences ought to be the final point of reference. Preference altruism follows naturally if one interprets altruism on the lines of a Humean notion of sympathy. The other person's welfare matters to us because his happiness strikes a resonant chord in our frame: We take delight in the other's pleasure, and sorrow in his pain. But although this model obviously fits some cases of giving, it is not the only way in which altruism can be understood.

Another view would see it as a matter of recognizing obligations, with no necessary implication that psychic gratification is involved. We are altruistic because we believe that we ought to be. Obligations, however, normally correlate with specific rights on the part of other people, rather than with their subjectively defined welfare. This is clear enough in the case of promissory and contractual obligations: If I promise Jones to deliver a certain item, I have no obligation to provide him with some other item that he prefers, even if the cost to me remains the same. There seems no reason why this should not also be true of general obligations to provide for others' welfare. We may feel that others' needs impose obligations on us, where "need" means something like "whatever is necessary to allow X to enjoy a decent standard of living in this community." Here "need" is a weakly normative notion, in the sense that its use requires us to identify a set of general capacities and opportunities that people must have to follow plans of life that are specific to them but fall within a certain general range. If people wish to follow a highly idiosyncratic project, requiring an unusual set of resources (for instance, if their idea is to experiment with the widest possible range of hallucinogenic drugs), we will not adjust our notion of need to accommodate them. Concretely, we will not feel obliged to supply them with LSD in place of medical services or decent housing.

The contrast between preference altruism and needs altruism has an obvious bearing on the case for a welfare state. Preference altruists will in general want to provide the objects of their concern with readily convertible resources, enabling them to reach their highest level of (self-defined) welfare—the simplest form of provision being cash redistribution. Thus they will be attracted to negative-income tax schemes and the like. Needs altruists will want to ensure that certain specified needs are met, and will favor provision in kind, with barriers to the conversion of the resources supplied into other forms. In general, then, needs altruism will give us the clearest underpinning for the welfare state, always provided that there is consensus on the range of needs to be met. However, there are special considerations that may lead preference altruists some way in this direction as well. One has already been mentioned: If we suspect that people are liable to make choices that are bad from the point of view of their long-term welfare, preference altruists, too, may favor provision in kind. Suppose, for instance, that we believed that many people would underestimate the risks of serious illness, and therefore would underinsure themselves if provided with cash and left to make their own arrangements for medical insurance; then even a preference altruist would opt for a public health service, at least to cover serious medical problems.

A second consideration has to do with identifying the recipients of aid. Altruists of both varieties will be concerned about efficiency, in the sense that they will want resources to be deployed so as to bring about the greatest possible increase in the welfare (need-fulfillment or want-satisfaction) of the badly off. Giving aid in the form of resources that the recipients can convert to the form they prefer therefore presupposes that the extent of need can be identified prior to the giving.[7] In some instances, medical aid being again the most obvious, this may not be so. Consider the following: Smith is an altruist with $250 to dispose of on ten sick people now ranged before him. The nature and extent of their illnesses is not apparent to him. Doctors charge $50 an hour for their services. Two options present themselves rather clearly. One is to present each invalid with $50, allowing him to buy up to one hour of a doctor's time. The other is to hire a doctor for ten hours and allow the doctor to allocate his time among the ten patients. The merit of the second option is evident: As the doctor investigates, he discovers which patients need extensive treatment and which can be dealt with more summarily. Under the first option, the easily cured will be out of the surgery in a half-hour, with $25 to spend on other items—a morally objectionable outcome for the needs altruist but also (and this is the point being made here) an inefficient result for the preference altruist.

Providing aid in the form of a nonconvertible resource (doctor's time) channels it in the direction in which it can do most good.

Considerations of this kind may thus push the preference altruist, too, toward supporting institutions, such as those of the welfare state, that meet specific needs. Admittedly there are pressures in the other direction (Weale, 1983, ch. 6). To the extent that interests vary—given that people assign differing weights to the satisfaction of their externally defined "needs"—specific transfers will be inefficient. The medical example looks plausible because we assume that almost everyone will give a high priority to physical health. In other cases—say, "decent" housing—it may be that a significant number of people care rather little about having their "needs" met and would prefer to be aided in other ways. Thus, although the argument is not clear-cut, we can say generally that welfare state institutions will be supported most strongly by altruists of the specific or "needs" variety.

Is there any evidence that people's altruistic concern is of this specific sort? It might seem possible to reach such a conclusion from evidence of attitudes toward the welfare state, which reveals that responses vary according to the kind of provision in question.[8] Old-age pensions, education, and the health service are strongly supported, whereas there is less enthusiasm for unemployment benefit, subsidized housing, and child benefit. It might be thought that such differentiations would be made only if people's concern for others were of the "needs" sort. But unfortunately the evidence is not decisive, for preference altruists, too, might have reservations about the less-favored benefits, thinking that in too many cases they were likely to be delivered to people who were not particularly badly off.[9] Child benefit—the least discriminating of these benefits, as in the British case it is available to all parents regardless of income—is also the least favored. Thus, although it seems intuitively likely that for most people altruism does have a needs component, I know of no hard evidence to bear this out.

ALTRUISM AND THE
PROBLEM OF STRATEGIC INTERACTION

I turn now to a second contrast between varieties of altruism, this one cross-cutting the preferences/needs contrast. It presupposes a context in which there are a number of possible donors able to contribute to the welfare of people that they wish to help. Each potential donor, we may assume, has a personal interest in not making a contribution; other things being equal, he would like to keep his resources to spend on himself. On the other hand, if he were the only possible donor, he would give up to a certain amount. In this context, how will people behave?

To add some rigor to the discussion, consider the following simple case. There are two altruistic individuals, A and B, facing a third person, C, who is in need to the extent of 1 unit of resources. A and B are similarly endowed; each, in isolation, would be willing to transfer 1 unit to C (although for neither would this be an absolutely trivial amount). Each can choose to give 0, ½, or 1 unit of resources to C. (Other possibilities are conceivable, but these are clearly the most salient for similarly endowed givers.) There are then nine possible outcomes. Writing A's contribution first and B's second, these are (0,0), (0,½), (0,1), (½,0), (½,½), (½,1), (1,0), (1,½), and (1,1).

Considering just A, there are potentially as many forms of altruism as there are rank orderings of these nine outcomes. Realistically, however, we can narrow the range somewhat. First, we can disregard the three outcomes (½,1), (1,½), (1,1): Whatever else is true of them, A and B must both regard these as wasteful outcomes in which C ends up with more resources than he needs. Second, given our assumptions about A's altruism, he must give top preference to one of the outcomes in which C ends up with one unit of resources: (0,1), (½,½) or (1,0). Even with these restrictions, there are still a fair number of possibilities. I shall confine my attention to four.

The first I shall call the calculating altruist. He is a person who wants to see C helped, but as far as possible by someone else. If he can pass the buck, he will do so. In formal terms (where $>$ means "is preferred to") this means that

a. $(0,1) > (½,½) > (1,0)$
b. $(0,½) > (½,0)$
Depending on the strength of A's altruism, we may have
c. $(1,0) > (0,½)$ or c'. $(0,½) > (1,0)$.

In less formal terms, think of the person who sees someone collapse in a crowded street. She holds back in the hope that someone else will step in, although she would help if she were the only person on hand. This person is a calculating altruist. I describe her as "calculating" because of the way in which her behavior depends on her assessment of how other people will behave. If she expects to be able to get away without contributing, she will.[10]

It may seem implausible to describe such a mean-spirited character as an altruist at all. There is, however, no reason to doubt her concern for the welfare of C. She prefers (1,0) to (½,0) to (0,0). The problem is that it is only the end-state, C's welfare, that counts: Her own part in providing for that welfare is recorded as a loss. Unlike the other characters we shall consider, she has none of what Margolis has called "participation altruism" (Margolis, 1982, ch. 2). She derives no satisfaction from the act of contributing itself.

If A and B are both calculating altruists, and if they have to decide on their contributions independent of one another, then we are immediately in the territory of games theory. Depending on how the outcomes are valued, the game may take the form of a Prisoner's Dilemma or a game of Chicken.[11] As the example has been set up, it is a case of Chicken. A would prefer B to meet C's needs; but if he really believes that B is going to pass by, then he will meet them himself. In other words $(0,1) > (1,0) > (0,0)$. For B, $(1,0) > (0,1) > (0,0)$. As students of Chicken know, there is no stable outcome to the game; each player makes a guess about the other's behavior and acts accordingly.

To illustrate a Prisoner's Dilemma, suppose instead that both A and B have only ½ unit each at their disposal; suppose also that they are both rather weakly altruistic. Both prefer $(½,½)$ to $(0,0)$ but for A $(0,0) > (½,0)$ and $(0,½) > (½,½)$, whereas for B $(0,0) > (0,½)$ and $(½,0) > (½,½)$. Both then have an incentive to contribute 0 whatever they expect the other person to do, and we have the standard Prisoner's Dilemma case in which the equilibrium outcome $(0,0)$ is suboptimal.

In the two-person case, the psychology required to generate a Prisoner's Dilemma seems unlikely to occur very often in practice. It requires that both A and B are willing to contribute ½ unit if this has the joint result that C's need is completely met; on the other hand, neither is willing individually to raise C from 0 to ½ or from ½ to 1. Suppose, for instance, that C needs a pair of gloves. A and B must be willing to collaborate to spend $2 to buy him a pair, but neither by himself will spend $1 either to buy C the first glove or to buy him the second. There is nothing formally wrong here: $1 invested in the collaborative endeavor "buys" more altruistic utility than either individual purchase taken separately (it makes the difference between a completely cold C and a completely warm C). All the same, the conditions are not likely to be met with only two donors involved.[12] But the likelihood of a Prisoner's Dilemma occurring rises sharply as the number of potential donors increases. If there are twenty donors, A may be willing to contribute $1 to a joint purchase of $20 of warm clothing for C but be willing neither to buy the first glove ("He's so cold that one glove will hardly make a difference") nor to buy the last sock ("He's pretty warm now; an extra sock isn't worth $1 to me").

Thus, a population of calculating altruists are liable to find themselves embroiled either in a game of Chicken or in a Prisoner's Dilemma when faced with a group of needy people. The game will be Chicken if each of the altruists would in the last resort be willing to provide for the needs out of his own pocket; Prisoner's Dilemma if he would be willing to provide only for some fraction of the needs as part of a joint endeavor. As the number of potential donors and recipients rises, a Prisoner's Dilemma becomes increasingly likely.

In either case, altruists of this kind ought to be willing to enter an enforceable agreement to donate to the needy. If the game is a Prisoner's Dilemma, each can foresee that a suboptimal outcome (nobody donates) will arise.[13] If the game is Chicken, there is a fair chance either of underprovision (nobody donates) or of inefficient overprovision (more donate than is necessary). The former possibility provides, of course, the standard reply to the libertarian position on altruism: Voluntary donations may fail because, although each potential donor values the outcome of giving, none values it enough to donate of his or her own accord.

There is, however, a short distance to traverse before we arrive at a rationale for a welfare state as a means of extracting calculating altruists from their predicament. A more obvious way out might seem to reside in a collective contract whereby each person agrees to provide X dollars on condition that a specific number of others do likewise. This would appear to solve the game-theoretical problem while retaining the advantage that each person could choose the precise direction in which his or her aid would be given. One might imagine specific charities approaching potential donors to ask for conditional pledges that would be activated only once the requisite number of names had been signed up.[14]

There are two sources of difficulty with this solution. One is practical and has to do with establishing confidence. Each donor, when approached for the second time and asked to hand over his cash, needs to be convinced that the conditional contracts have been signed and that they will be adhered to. It will be difficult (though perhaps not impossible) for a voluntary agency to generate this confidence. The second is more theoretical. For the same reason that calculating altruists will be unwilling to donate independently, they may be unwilling to sign their conditional contracts. They may hope that the charity in question can find enough other donors, so that the desired end is reached without their having to dip into their pockets themselves. Of course, if there were exactly N potential donors willing to give $X, and $NX was the amount required to achieve the desired outcome, they would have no reason to hold back. But this is an unlikely state of affairs, and it is still more unlikely that anyone would *know* that it obtained. So, when approached, the calculating altruist will reason as follows: The chances are either that there exist M($>$N) donors, in which case I will hold out in the hope that some other N can be induced to sign, or there exist M′($<$N) donors, in which case signing up will be pointless (albeit harmless) in any case. Either way there is no good reason for me to sign.

It may seem unreasonable to imagine an *altruist* reasoning in this cold-hearted way; but that would be a more general objection to the postulates that underlie calculating altruism (on which more is said below). The point now is that a population of calculating altruists should welcome a forcible system of transfers to the needy to which no one is exempt from contributing. For each person in the population this is the least costly way of achieving the desired outcome. Each would like to free-ride on the relief scheme if he could; but as that option is impossible without destroying the scheme, it is better to force each person to provide 1/N of the cost. Insofar as the welfare state can be seen as a mechanism of this kind, calculating altruists should welcome (and vote for) its existence.

What if the population is more mixed, containing, say, a proportion of egoists? A forcible transfer scheme is then unlikely to represent a Pareto-improvement (egoists will be made worse off by it unless they all happen to be net recipients) and may or may not maximize the overall satisfaction of preferences (depending on numbers, intensities, etc.). The altruists cannot afford, however, to opt for a scheme that includes only their own number, because by the logic outlined above each will be tempted to exempt himself by simulating egoism. They must, therefore, continue to support an inclusive and compulsory scheme.

On the other hand, if each person has some altruistic feelings, but there are differences in the direction of altruism—that is, we are considering "needs" altruists who disagree to some extent about which needs are worth satisfying—then we might contemplate a scheme by which each person (compulsorily) contributes a certain amount but indicates at the same time how he would like the money spent. Here there are no free-rider problems of the standard sort (no one is allowed to propose that he be the object of aid). There may, though, be difficulties of coordination. Few people are likely to want all the available resources spent in a single direction. More probably they will want money spent on medicine (say) up to a certain point, then on education (say); or else they will have preferences between these items that can be represented by indifference curves of the usual shape.[15] If donors are allowed to indicate only a first preference, there is a risk either that the most popular items will be oversupplied or that, in anticipation of this result, an indeterminate number of people will cast their votes for items further down the list. Even if the contributors are allowed to display a more sophisticated set of preferences, there is still room for people to behave strategically and thus no guarantee that the distribution of resources that results is actually the one that corresponds best to the true preferences of the donors.

Where a welfare state is instituted, the level of contributions (the tax structure) is set by democratic decision, let us suppose, whereas the form of provision is decided by welfare professionals who make an assessment of the relative urgency of needs.[16] This will seem an appealing solution to calculating altruists either (1) if they are preference altruists, unconcerned about which items in particular are provided for the needy; (2) if they are needs altruists in substantial agreement about a rank ordering of needs; or (3) if, despite their differences in this respect, they are alive to the possible inefficiencies of an earmarking system.[17]

The discussion up to this point has been premised on the assumption that calculating altruism is a reasonable way of representing people's altruistic concerns. This assumption may well be challenged. It is certainly implausible as a general explanation of altruistic behvior. As Margolis (1982, 17–25) and Sugden (1982, 341–350) have both pointed out, it would exclude commonly observed phenomena—charities that are supported by a large number of donors, for example—and predict others that seem distinctly unlikely. For instance it predicts that a person about to make a $10 donation to some worthy cause will reduce her contribution virtually to zero if someone else steps in and donates $10 ahead of her. As all the would-be donor cares about is the end result—the charity being $10 richer—she should be happy to free-ride on the other person's gift.[18] Empirically, however, it is clear that people are far less susceptible than this to other people's donations and, indeed, that the interactive effects may tend to operate in the other direction—that is, people may be positively encouraged to contribute by seeing others do likewise (and not only in cases where the good being sought has threshold properties). There are large areas of altruistic behavior that cannot be explained by the hypothesis of calculating altruism.

It should not, however, be dismissed entirely. Some phenomena do seem to fit the model. The example I used to introduce it—bystanders waiting for someone else to go to the rescue of a person who collapses in the street—is only too familiar. The fact also that most people express their political support for the welfare state (i.e., express a willingness to be taxed quite heavily to provide welfare services), while at the same time they are more or less inclined to fiddle their own contributions downwards, suggests a calculating psychology. It is worth noting that in both these cases the costs of contribution are perceived as relatively high. My guess is that people who hold back when someone collapses in front of them do so out of anxiety about how much time and effort will eventually be involved. (Will I end up escorting him to hospital? etc.) Charitable donations, on the other hand, are typically small in relation to income, and their size is completely under control. It may be of importance that the body of experimental evidence that reveals people's willingness to contribute even when they could free-ride on the collective good being provided has been obtained using sums of money that are really quite small (Marwell & Ames, 1979, 1335–1360; Marwell & Ames, 1980, 926–937; Frohlich & Oppenheimer, 1984, 3–24).

The calculating altruist finds himself embroiled in Prisoner's Dilemmas and games of Chicken because, although he values the collective outcome of giving positively, he values his own contribution negatively (as a loss of resources that would otherwise be available for self-gratification). The other forms of altruism I shall consider all attach intrinsic value to the act of giving in some way. They involve what Margolis calls "participation altruism," though I shall make finer distinctions within this broad category.

The first of these subspecies to be considered is reciprocal altruism. The reciprocal altruist is someone who is prepared to contribute to the welfare of the needy, but only on condition that the other members of a designated group also contribute. In the two-person case, A will give to C provided B does also. Whereas for a calculating A the best outcome is (0,1), for a reciprocal A the optimum is (½,½).

Thus: (½,½) > (0,1); and
(½,½) > (0,0) > (½,0) > (1,0).

If B contributes ½, A would prefer to reciprocate by giving ½ himself rather than allow B to increase his contribution to 1. On the other hand, A will not contribute ½ himself, much less 1, if B holds back. Thus (0,0) is a possible outcome if each expects the other not to contribute.

The reciprocal altruist is clearly moved by a notion of fairness. He sees the relief of need as something to which everyone has an equal obligation to contribute. If others do their bit, he will do his without compulsion. On the other hand, he is unwilling to be a "sucker," to lower his own stock of resources only to find that the rest of the group have maintained theirs. Altruism of this sort may again seem mean-spirited, but it is comprehensible and, I believe, practically familiar. Its presence might be accounted for in evolutionary terms, borrowing the idea that reciprocal altruism is a stable phenomenon, whereas loftier sorts of altruists are prone to exploitation by egoists and are therefore liable to disappear in a competitive struggle for survival (Dawkins, 1976, 179–202).

If A and B are both reciprocal altruists, they may find themselves playing an Assurance game. Both prefer (½,½) to (0,0). But each will contribute ½ only on condition that he expects the other to reciprocate. Thus if they have to declare their contributions independently, the outcome depends on their mutual expectation. If they declare in sequence, with A going first, then B will play ½ if A plays ½ and 0 if A plays 0. What will A do? If he *knows* that B is also a reciprocal altruist, then he will play ½ and all is well. If he is uncertain about B's intentions, then his choice will depend on his estimate of the probability of B's contributing (p) and his relative valuation of the two payoffs. He will contribute if $p(½,½) > (1-p)(½,0)$.

Generalizing this result, a population of reciprocal altruists can arrive at an optimum by voluntary means provided they trust one another and can coordinate their behavior. A compulsory welfare state would not be necessary provided that the appropriate level of contribution is established in some way and people are able to verify that others are pulling their weight. It may be difficult to persuade anyone to make the first move because, if each reciprocal altruist demands *universal* contribution, he may be inclined to set p (the chance of everyone else doing their bit) very low indeed. This suggests that compulsion might be needed to start the scheme up; thereafter, provided contributions remain visible, no one has an incentive to pull out.

That conclusion is vulnerable, however, to complications of at least two sorts.[19] One is simply the presence of a small number of egoists or, for that matter, calculating altruists (who will generally behave like egoists in the matter of making individual contributions).[20] If the reciprocal altruist really demands *universal* participation, then even one egoist will sabotage a voluntary scheme. Is that too strong a condition? Empirically it seems to be. Take the example of a whip-round (money collection) for a departing colleague. This seems a plausible case of reciprocal altruism, insofar as most people will adjust their contribution to the "going rate" as established by the first few donors. But such a scheme is not generally undermined by a few recalcitrant individuals. Rather, there seems to be a gradient, differently sloped for different people, relating the number of others who have contributed to their own obligation to contribute ("If it's only going to be me, Bill, and Julia, let's forget the whole thing").

Note, however, that in this sort of case, the stakes involved are relatively small. As we increase them, a demand for strict reciprocity becomes more likely. Consider the following. A department of ten people is instructed to cut its budget by 10 percent by laying off one of its members. The surviving members, altruistically motivated, offer to take a 10 percent cut in salary to save their colleague's job. This proposal does seem vulnerable to the defection of a single participant. Most people will feel the effects of a 10 percent salary cut quite acutely. The sight of a defector continuing to enjoy his usual standard of living may be resented strongly enough to induce further defections. Where substantial costs are involved, it may therefore be necessary to make contributions mandatory even for reciprocal altruists.

A second complication arises if the group in question is composed of people who are altruistic to different degrees. Each is willing to contribute $1/n$ of some amount $X if the others do, but X varies from person to person. Under these circumstances it will prove to be impossible to obtain voluntary contributions in excess of Xi/n, where Xi is the value of X for the least altruistic member.[21] Everyone else is deterred from supplying by the reluctance of this person. A differentiated scheme of contributions would be more efficient. In short, relying on voluntary reciprocal altruism in a heterogeneous population leads to underprovision of need-satisfying goods.[22]

How do these complications bear on the case for the welfare state? They certainly help to show why many reciprocal altruists might favor a system that compels them to contribute toward welfare provision for the needy. They do not of themselves show that such compulsion would be legitimate. For the substance of the argument of the foregoing paragraphs is that a voluntary system might prove highly inefficient for many altruists, in the sense that they would find themselves not contributing in circumstances where, other things being equal, they would be prepared to do so. But what of the position of the egoist or the weakest altruist? If we take it as axiomatic that a scheme of compulsion must have *everyone's* consent (as some libertarians will stoutly maintain), then we still have no case. To take such a stand, however, we must attribute infinite weight to the rights of noncontributors in the face of a principle of fairness that commands majority support. As soon as this assumption is relaxed, the case for a welfare state is easily made.

There may still be some doubts as to whether reciprocal altruism really counts as altruism, even among those who recognize it as a valid account of some parts of our behavior. If altruism is a matter of being concerned about other people's interests, then, although it is understandable enough that we should complain about (and exert moral pressure on) those who could help but don't, how can it be reasonable to make our contribution dependent on the contributions of others? Isn't it perverse of A to withdraw his donation if B fails to donate? Can he really care about C's interests if he does? (Note that this is *not* to be construed as a threshold case—that is, a case in which A's contribution *does no good* unless B also contributes.) Isn't the real altruist the person who begins by giving ½, waits for B to reciprocate (and perhaps tries to persuade him to do so), but in the last resort gives another ½ if B fails to donate (i.e., $(½,½) > (1,0) > (½,0) > (0,0)$)?

These doubts spring, I believe, from the "sympathy" interpretation of altruism mentioned above. Altruism here involves a sense of pleasure felt at another's happiness. This fits some cases, but it is equally possible for altruism to take the form of acknowledged obligation. In the present context the important point is that the obligation is seen as incumbent on the group as a whole. Each person is equally obliged to help other members insofar as these latter are demonstrated to be in need. But no one is obliged to take another's share of the burden upon himself. More strongly—and this is what is required to support reciprocal altruism— no one is obliged to disadvantage himself relative to others in discharging his duties to the collective. (This condition presumably implies a background distribution that is already fair in some sense—so that if A contributes while B does not, A is disadvantaged from the point of view of this benchmark.)

The reciprocal altruist can be contrasted with a third character, the conscientious altruist—or in some discussions the "Kantian" altruist (Collard, 1978, 3–29). The conscientious altruist acts on a maxim that, if followed by everyone in the relevant population, would produce the outcome that he altruistically desires. He does so regardless of how other people are expected, or known, to behave. The conscientious altruist presumably prefers others to act on the maxim as well, but this has no effect on his own behavior. Continuing with our original example, A is a conscientious altruist if $(\frac{1}{2},0) > (0,0)$, $(\frac{1}{2},\frac{1}{2}) > (0,1)$, and $(\frac{1}{2},0) > (1,0)$.

The last condition differentiates the conscientious altruist from a fourth (and last) type, whom I shall call the "superconscientious" altruist. For this person, $(\frac{1}{2},\frac{1}{2}) > (0,1)$ and $(1,0) > (\frac{1}{2},0) > (0,0)$. The superconscientious altruist not only does his own duty but is prepared to do B's as well if B fails to contribute. He still, however, prefers $(\frac{1}{2},\frac{1}{2})$ to $(1,0)$; a person of whom the latter was not true would either be a saint or, more likely, a person whose "altruism" stemmed ultimately not from concern for the interests of C but from status seeking or some such motive.

It should be clear that a homogeneous population of conscientious altruists faces only coordination problems of the informational sort; there are no game-theoretical problems. To reach the desired outcome, all that is necessary is for each person to calculate correctly what proportion of his resources he is to donate. No one's behavior depends on his expectations about others. Superconscientious altruists face only benign behavioral problems of the "after-you" variety (that is, if neither knows what the other's preference ordering is, they may be uncertain whether to donate $\frac{1}{2}$ or 1 and end up by oversupplying C).

It follows that conscientious altruists would have no need of a welfare state, as they would be able to achieve the same result by a system of voluntary transfers. They might find it useful to have a central coordinating authority, but such an authority would simply announce (and not enforce) the level of contributions. Would they positively object to a welfare state? As the case has been described so far, they would have no grounds for doing so, because the welfare state would merely compel them to do what they had good reason to do in any case.[23] Indeed, if the population was not completely homogeneous, they might welcome it as a means of compelling a recalcitrant minority of egoists or calculating altruists—assuming, that is, that they have $(\frac{1}{2},\frac{1}{2}) > (\frac{1}{2},0)$.[24] Note that conscientious altruists are liable to be exploited by calculating altruists— the latter recognizing that the former will contribute whatever they do themselves—and anyone may reasonably take steps to avoid exploitation of this sort ("Why should White sleep happily in his bed knowing that I'm looking after the old and sick?").

This reasoning breaks down, however, if the conscientious altruists are *needs* altruists with differing interpretations of "need." Each will then want to contribute to need as he identifies it, whereas a uniform compulsory system will oblige him to satisfy a schedule of needs predetermined in some way (e.g., by majority decision). However, this very possibility raises some doubts about the cogency of conscientious altruism as a way of representing attitudes to the needy.

The conscientious altruist, you may recall, acts on a maxim that, if followed by everyone, would bring about the outcome that he (altruistically) desires, irrespective of his beliefs about how many others will actually do likewise. How intelligible a view is that? We need to investigate whether individual acts interrelate in such a way that the value of each depends on the response of the remainder. In some cases the interrelation will be relatively insignificant. If I am in a position to save somebody's life—say, by rescuing him from a cliff face—the value of what I do depends rather little on whether other people, similarly situated, would undertake the rescue. On the whole, welfare contributions are not like that. A single contribution, spread across a large number of people in need, will make very little impact. It is even possible to conceive of isolated contributions intersecting in a harmful way.[25] Here, then, the value of the act—and therefore one's decision about the right thing to do—does depend on expectations about other people's behavior. "Doing your bit" makes sense only if enough others are also doing theirs. This is still a different attitude from that of the reciprocal altruist. The latter objects to contributing when others don't, seeing that possibility as unfair or exploitative. The attitude I am now describing is one of wanting to do "the right thing" regardless of others, but understanding that what "the right thing" *is* may depend on how others behave. Nonetheless, the practical effects may be rather similar.

Simple conscientious altruism makes sense where, by acting in a certain way, I can confer a visible good or avoid a visible harm (most examples of conscientious action are probably negative in character— not lying, stealing, cheating, etc.). Deprived of this certainty, people who *would* be conscientious are likely to behave in ways that suggest calculating or reciprocal altruism. This explains, for example, why people respond very differently to the prospect of evading taxation from that of cheating a storekeeper. In a survey, most people (66 percent) said that they might consider evading value-added tax on a plumbing job, and only 35 percent regarded such behavior as wrong or seriously wrong (Jowell & Witherspoon, 1985, 123–126). By contrast, only 18 percent would pocket £5 in change given in error in a store, and 77 percent thought such behavior wrong or seriously wrong. In the latter case, there is a visible harm—the store is made £5 worse off. In the former case, a contribution has been withheld, but there may be uncertainty what its effect would be: Perhaps the government has taken some evasion into account, so my contribution may not be important?[26] Thus we do not have to discount conscientiousness in general in order to believe that it may not provide a secure foundation for a welfare system. The problem is not necessarily that people don't have the right moral capacities but, rather, that the way in which they see their relationship to others (both to other donors and to the needy) doesn't bring those capacities into play.

We might contemplate arrangements that did try to activate conscientious altruism. For instance, it might be proposed that each person should donate to a specific recipient, so that a failure to contribute would have an immediate and visible effect.[27] (This, presumably, is the thinking behind charitable schemes that invite one to "adopt" a family or a community project in the Third World.) The disadvantages of such a proposal are clear. Donations would have to be in cash (no donor could be expected by himself to provide specific aid), and it would be difficult to adjust the sums given to changes in need. We have seen already that even preference altruists might find a cash-donation system less eligible than provision in kind, depending on circumstances. Moreover if a few people default, the effects are more disastrous than under a pooling arrangement. Recall that, *ex hypothesi*, our conscientious altruists are concerned about the overall outcome, and therefore about others contributing, even if their chief concern is that they should do the right thing themselves ($[\frac{1}{2},\frac{1}{2}] > [\frac{1}{2},0]$). Unless assured of everyone's conscientiousness, this is a powerful consideration against a person-to-person arrangement.

An objection of a quite different kind would be that the arrangement envisaged makes the recipient into an object of the donor's charity in a potentially degrading way. This, however, is better dealt with in the context of a general discussion of altruism as a foundation for welfare provision. I shall look at this briefly by way of conclusion. First, let me bring together briefly the impact of the different modes of altruism on the case for a welfare state.

1. Calculating altruists who understand their joint situation will almost certainly wish to institute a compulsory welfare system to extricate themselves from a Prisoner's Dilemma (or a game of Chicken).
2. Reciprocal altruists may wish to institute a welfare state for assurance reasons, and they will certainly wish to do so if they fear exploitation by egoists. A majority of "stronger" reciprocal altruists will wish to impose such a system on a minority of "weaker" altruists.
3. Conscientious altruists will in general need only a coordinating body, but they may also agree to a compulsory system to avoid exploitation by others.

I have suggested that although conscientious action in general is an important and widespread phenomenon, the character of welfare provision is not such as to bring it naturally into play. It seems better to assume that, for the most part, people will behave in this area either as calculating or as reciprocal altruists. In either case, the welfare state has a firm grounding. Although *in theory* a population of reciprocal altruists might manage without it, this result is fragile in a number of respects. It seems likely that voluntary reciprocal altruism could work effectively only in a small and homogeneous group (cf. Sugden, 1984, 783; Taylor, 1982, 52–53).

CONCLUSION

How *good* an explanation of the welfare state does the altruism hypothesis provide? That question can be broken down into two parts: Does the available evidence suggest that support for the welfare state in fact derives from a version of altruism, and, is it desirable that it should? Or, might it be better if a different set of beliefs and attitudes prevailed?

One thought behind the last question is that altruism might be an effective but morally undesirable foundation for a welfare scheme. It would be undesirable because *inter alia* it established the wrong kind of relationship between net contributors to the scheme and net recipients. "Altruism" may suggest a benevolent or charitable attitude toward the needy; this may be contrasted with the view that the needy are entitled to what they receive. On the latter view, the welfare state is a requirement of social justice, not the expression of altruistic concern.

To tackle these questions, let me compare the altruism explanation with two others, the mutual insurance explanation and the social justice explanation. The former holds that people support the welfare state out of enlightened self-interest in circumstances of risk; the latter that people support the welfare state because they hold a principle of social justice that requires distribution on the basis of need. Notice that both these explanations might claim to circumvent the problem of the stigmatized recipient, though in very different ways. On behalf of the former it might be pointed out that no one feels stigmatized when claiming on an insurance policy; and on behalf of the latter, that where a practice of distribution according to need exists, no one is ashamed to receive his fair share.

I have already suggested that the mutual insurance explanation and the altruism explanation may be hard to separate empirically. The evidence for either can often be reinterpreted to support the other. Consider, for instance, the impact of World War II on the development of the welfare state in Britain. Dryzek and Goodin argue that the experience of war increased people's sense of uncertainty about the future and made them more willing to join a risk-sharing scheme. But (as they concede themselves), the same events might also be seen as increasing national solidarity and therefore as enhancing altruistic concern for the plight of fellow-countrymen.[28] More generally, when people are moved to act collectively when confronted by need, it may be difficult to separate a simple altruistic response from a far-sighted appreciation that the same fate might befall them some time in the future.

The two explanations would, however, predict different attitudes toward the funding of welfare schemes. The insurance hypothesis implies equal premiums all round where risks are equal; the altruism hypothesis suggests that the better-off should be contributing to the welfare of the worse-off. Questioned about the existing welfare state, people perceive high-income groups as contributing most to the system, with the high earners themselves holding this view most strongly; when asked about their preferences among fund-raising taxes, most opt for income tax (which is seen as redistributive), with high-income respondents again preferring this more strongly (Beedle & Taylor-Gooby, 1983, 21–27). This suggests that the better-off at least see themselves as altruists, and are willing to continue being such.[29] However, when asked in the same survey which groups got "best value" from the tax-and-benefit system, respondents were more divided, with some perception (especially among low-income groups) that the wealthy did best out of the system. The explanation for this is not obvious, but it may be that there is some awareness of the fact (confirmed in studies such as Le Grand's) that the better-off make more effective use of most of the welfare services provided by the state. If so, then the altruism hypothesis is less clearly supported: The insurance idea is compatible with the view that where benefits drawn differ in a predictable way, so should contributions. Perhaps the safest conclusion to draw is that people are using both of these ideas in their thinking about welfare, not necessarily in the same proportions; some are more inclined to want the system to redistribute in favor of the needy, some to prefer expected benefits and contributions to match one another.

Normatively, of course, the mutual insurance hypothesis is highly vulnerable as an underpinning for the welfare state. If insurance is the aim, then in general it is surely better to allow people to purchase it in a competitive market. Only if uncertainties are so great that no distinctions can be made between people when setting premiums will a universal scheme look plausible. This is surely not the case with all of the services currently provided by the welfare state.

What of the social justice hypothesis? This is also hard to separate from the altruism hypothesis, though for different reasons. The difficulty is that altruism may be construed in a manner that is broad enough to include a concern for social justice. Earlier in the chapter I contrasted two interpretations of altruism, one employing a Humean notion of sympathy, the other involving recognition of a collective obligation to provide for the needy. Does the second interpretation not by definition contain an idea of social justice?

It is, I think, still possible to draw a distinction, along the following lines. Obligatory altruism will involve the idea of a minimum standard of welfare to which everyone must be raised. This standard may be defined in terms of general well-being (by preference altruists) or in terms of an identifiable set of needs (by needs altruists). In either case a concern to raise people to this welfare floor will involve subsidiary distributive principles. However, the altruist will not be concerned about overall questions of distribution; in other words, he will not be worried about the relative standing of people who are clearly above the welfare floor.

It may be said that a conception of justice is necessarily embedded in this view—namely, that everyone in the community is entitled to the standard of living represented by the welfare floor. This is one possible reading, but the case may also be regarded as one of collective benevolence or humanity, with emphasis being placed on the obligations of the donors rather than on the rights of the recipients.[30] Whichever reading is preferred, I want to contrast a view of this kind with a different and stronger idea of justice—namely, one that sees the overall distribution of goods of certain kinds as properly governed by criteria of need. This latter view singles out goods such as medical aid and education, and maintains that relative enjoyment of these goods should depend solely on need.[31] It dispenses with the idea of a welfare floor and looks at a society's general distributive practices.

One clear indication of whether people hold the altruism view or a social justice view of this stronger sort will be their attitude toward people who choose to obtain goods otherwise provided by the welfare state through the market—to private education or private medicine, for instance. In the British case, the evidence suggests that majority opinion (75–80 percent) are in favor of allowing people to opt out of the welfare state and buy their own services privately. At the same time, as noted already, there is a high level of support for the welfare state itself. This combination of attitudes does clearly back the altruism hypothesis at the expense of the social justice hypothesis. People want a welfare floor, but most seem not to mind if people prefer to buy superior medical care or education themselves.

Might it nonetheless be better if opinion were converted to the social justice view? A number of arguments to this effect might be mounted. One is simply that the view is morally correct, and therefore it is desirable for people to believe it and to support its practical implementation. More circuitously, two considerations can be advanced against the altruism hypothesis. First, if the practical effect of basing the welfare state on considerations of altruism is to leave people free to opt out if they choose, the stigmatization problem is liable to reappear, even if altruism takes the form of recognized obligations. What becomes crucial is the number who opt out. So long as it remains the norm to receive welfare benefits from the state, no one is going to feel ashamed or humiliated by taking his or her share. (Under normal circumstances no one now feels these emotions about receiving public medicine or education.)[32] But if the public services become residual, the preserve of a small minority, then use may become a badge of failure, even if public attitudes generally support the idea of welfare as a right. The social justice view, which insists on common provision as a means of ensuring distribution according to need, preempts this possibility.[33]

Second, for the same empirical reasons, a welfare state founded on altruism runs the risk of becoming socially divisive and, therefore, in the long term, of undermining its own foundations. Altruism in general presupposes community, in the sense that a concern for others' welfare implies some way of identifying the others to whom one has special ties, and toward whom one therefore has special feelings and obligations. (This is particularly clear in the case of reciprocal altruism, which analytically presupposes a relevant group to share the obligation to the needy, but is likely to hold for the other varieties too.) If common welfare institutions are established, a mutually reinforcing interaction may occur, where the experience of common consumption of welfare services reinforces the sense of community, which in turn lends additional support to those institutions, and so on. Conversely, if people opt out in increasing numbers, their sense of community may be diminished and their altruism weakened. They may become progressively less willing to be taxed to support socially distant welfare recipients. I am not suggesting that altruistic attitudes might be extinguished entirely, because plainly most people feel some degree of altruistic concern for other human beings considered simply as such (as shown by reactions to famine victims and so forth); but what might increasingly be lost is the special altruism that arises from perception of common ties and a common fate.

For these reasons it may be best to see altruism as a second-best foundation for the welfare state, effective in the absence of a stronger belief in social justice. Indeed, it may well be the case that with the social and political arrangements that currently exist—a fragmented and individualistic society with no strong institutions of citizenship to bring people together—altruistic concern is the most that one can hope for. If so, the altruism hypothesis retains all its practical interest. It is important to discover which welfare arrangements are supported by which altruistic attitudes, and to see how far these attitudes do in fact obtain, even if ideally one would prefer it if people were moved by a more powerful sense of social justice.

NOTES

My thanks are due to the audience at the CSPT conference entitled "Poverty, Charity, and Welfare," Tulane University, February 14–16, 1986, for their responses to this chapter, and are especially due to Bob Goodin, Martin Hollis, and Robert Lane for their comments on earlier drafts.

1. Note that this is not the same as saying that the existing welfare state is an effective agent of egalitarian redistribution. For an assessment of this claim, largely sceptical, see J. Le Grand, *The Strategy of Equality: Redistribution and the Social Services* (London, Allen and Unwin, 1982). Even existing welfare states, however, are redistributive in certain respects—from the healthy to the sick, for instance.

2. There are, of course, variations among countries, both in the form that welfare institutions take and in popular attitudes toward them. My evidence is drawn from the British case, and readers must judge how far it can be generalized.

3. See, for example, Beedle and Taylor-Gooby (1983, 15–39).

4. For this hypothesis, see Drysek and Goodin (1986).

5. That is, they may be anxious that at some later moment they may find that their medical condition forces them to pay higher premiums, or even prevents them from obtaining private insurance at all.

6. From one point of view, of course, all altruistic behavior might be described as "meddlesome," because it alters the circumstances of the recipient. The practical contrast between meddlesome and nonmeddlesome altruism, in Collard's sense, consists only in the preferred form of giving.

7. This point is made in Weale (1979).

8. See Taylor-Gooby (1985) for a convenient survey.

9. Or (and this is a complicating factor), they might be delivered to people who would not be so badly off if they did more to help themselves: Altruism is likely to be qualified in most cases by a principle of desert.

10. The existence of calculating altruism has been confirmed empirically in studies of reactions to emergencies. In particular, it has been shown that people's willingness to respond diminishes as the number of other bystanders increases. See, for example, Darley & Latane (1968, 377–383).

11. The game of Chicken and some of its applications are explored in Taylor & Ward (1982, 350–370).

12. The considerations that would typically make A unwilling to spend $1 on the first glove, say ("What use is a single glove? Hardly any better than no gloves at all") ought generally to make him willing to spend $1 on a second if B buys the first; in other words, the example is likely to rely on a threshold effect of some kind, either to explain A's refusal to move from $(0,0)$ to $(\frac{1}{2},0)$ or to explain his refusal to move from $(0,\frac{1}{2})$ to $(\frac{1}{2},\frac{1}{2})$. But the threshold idea cannot be used to explain both refusals.

13. I omit here discussion of the special circumstances in which voluntary cooperation may occur in a Prisoner's Dilemma. The essential condition is that the game should be repeated an indefinite number of times with the same group of players, in which case it may be rational for each player to adopt a (conditional) cooperative strategy. Investigating whether this condition is likely to apply in the case we are considering (public welfare provision) would take us too far afield. See Taylor (1976) and McLean (1981, 339–351) for discussion.

14. This possibility is canvassed in Nozick (1974, 268), though in relation to a population of reciprocal altruists (for whom the second objection below would not apply).

15. I leave aside here additional problems posed by ill-informed or irrational preferences (e.g., preferences for particular forms of medical research that are unrelated to the real contribution these types of research are likely to make to the saving of life).

16. Clearly it would be possible to mount an empirical critique of the latter supposition, countering it with the observation that welfare professionals are likely to be governed by private interests of various sorts. The critics ought, however, to reflect on whether the same problems might not bedevil voluntary schemes. Have the organizers of charities no private interests?

17. In the third case, one could argue that each person should be allowed to earmark a small proportion of his contribution for specific needs. The argument

here would be that, with relatively small sums involved, no single item will be grossly oversupplied; at the same time, the earmarking would provide the managers of the system with up-to-date information about people's specific concerns. Such a proposal does, I think, deserve serious practical consideration; apart from anything else, it might help to strengthen perceptions of the link between taxation and welfare expenditure.

18. This is a slight oversimplification. The second donation is equivalent to a $10 increment in the first donor's income. With this increment, she might now be prepared to give slightly more than $10 to the charity—say an extra $1. Even this assumes a relatively high marginal propensity to contribute. See Margolis (1982, 20).

19. A third sort of complication, not discussed in the text, is posed for a population whose resources are unequally distributed. In the simple example, A and B are assumed to be equally endowed, and so reciprocity occurs when each contributes $\frac{1}{2}$ unit. With unequal holdings the meaning of each person "doing his bit" may be disputed—witness the familiar debate about which form of taxation (a poll tax, a uniform income tax, a progressive income tax, etc.) best corresponds to our notion of "equal sacrifice."

20. Calculating altruists will consider what chance their own failure to contribute would have on the viability of the scheme as a whole. A single calculating altruist would contribute if he believed that the scheme would collapse otherwise. Two calculating altruists might find themselves playing a game of Chicken if their joint defection would sabotage the scheme.

21. This conclusion rests on the assumption that each contributor demands universal compliance with the level of donation he makes himself. If we weaken that assumption, as in the earlier discussion, things will not look so bad.

22. For this result, see Sugden (1984, 772–787).

23. This conclusion ignores the possibility that the act of giving might be valued only if it is a free choice (i.e., not legally compelled). It is worth noting that Kant himself did not share the latter view, seeing the function of law as one of enforcing duties that moral agents would perform out of a sense of pure duty; there was no suggestion that legal enforcement might preempt the moral motive.

24. This conclusion is entailed by my initial assumption that all altruists must have as first preference one of the states in which C receives 1 unit. It is, of course, possible to conceive of an altruist so narrowly conscientious that $(\frac{1}{2},\frac{1}{2}) = (\frac{1}{2},0)$ ("I've done my duty; let the others take care of their own souls").

25. If people are giving specific items, then a set of transfers may be harmful on balance, particularly if incentive considerations are included (the recipients may be given local incentives that conflict with the incentives that would eventually lead them to globally better outcomes).

26. Of course a similar line of reasoning might be applied to the store ("a big store" in the survey), which makes the difference in response all the more remarkable. Presumably far less than 18 percent would consider defrauding a private individual of £5.

27. See Nozick (1974, 265–266) for this proposal.

28. In an attempt to separate the two hypotheses, Dryzek and Goodin propose as an indicator of the strength of social solidarity in wartime the extent to which luxury goods were rationed; concretely, they use the severity of the sugar ration as their measure, and show that this correlates only weakly with the growth of welfare expenditure. None of this strikes me as very convincing; I have particular difficulty in understanding why sugar should be counted as a luxury for this purpose.

29. The evidence counts this way when we are choosing between altruism and mutual insurance as explanations of the welfare state. It may also, of course, be read as support for the Marxist claim that the welfare state is a device employed by the rich to contain the frustrations of the poor. It is important not to confuse the idea of insurance by each individual against future personal risk with what might be called "class insurance by the rich against working-class insurgence."

30. For this contrast, see Miller (1980).

31. This view relies, in other words, on drawing lines of demarcation between goods, and holding that the appropriate principle of distribution depends on the particular good in question, in the manner suggested by Walzer (1983).

32. "Under normal circumstances" because particular individuals who aspire to private provision may feel a sense of failure if forced to resort to public services. But this would be an entirely private matter, having nothing to do with the public connotations of using the services.

33. A skeptic might reply that people will simply find another way of recording their failure (see, for example, Nozick's remarks about self-esteem in Nozick (1974, 239–243). But although inequalities in consumption generally might have this effect, there is, I think, an important difference between receiving a separate benefit designated as publicly provided and merely having less purchasing power in a market context. The rich and the poor rub shoulders in shops, and although the rich can buy more things, and a greater variety of things, there are not so many that stand completely outside the purchasing range of the poor. Conversely, there are few items that, in themselves, denote the purchaser's poverty.

REFERENCES

Beedle, P., and P. Taylor-Gooby. 1983. "Ambivalence and Altruism: Public Opinion About Taxation and Welfare," *Policy and Politics*, vol. 11.

Collard, D. 1978. *Altruism and Economy: A Study in Non-Selfish Economics.* Oxford: Martin Robertson.

Darley, J.M., and B. Latane. 1968. "Bystander Intervention in Emergencies: Diffusion of Responsibility," *Journal of Personality and Social Psychology*, vol. 8.

Dawkins, R. 1976. *The Selfish Gene.* Oxford: Oxford University Press.

Dryzek, J., and R. Goodin. 1986. "Risk Sharing and Social Justice: The Motivational Foundations of the Post-War Welfare State," *British Journal of Political Science*, vol. 16.

Frohlich, N., and J. Oppenheimer. 1984. "Beyond Economic Man: Altruism, Egalitarianism and Difference Maximizing," *Journal of Conflict Resolution,* vol. 28.

Grand, J. Le. 1982. *The Strategy of Equality: Redistribution and the Social Services.* London: Allen & Unwin.

Jowell, R., and S. Witherspoon, eds. 1985. *British Social Attitudes: The 1985 Report.* Aldershot, England: Gower.

Margolis, H. 1982. *Selfishness, Altruism and Rationality.* Chicago: University of Chicago Press.

Marwell, G., and R. Ames. 1979. "Experiments on the Provision of Public Goods I," *American Journal of Sociology,* vol. 84.

———. 1980. "Experiments on the Provision of Public Goods II," *American Journal of Sociology,* vol. 85.

McLean, I. 1981. "The Social Contract in Leviathan and the Prisoner's Dilemma Supergame," *Political Studies,* vol. 29.

Miller, David. 1980. "Social Justice and the Principle of Need." In M. Freeman and D. Robertson, eds., *The Frontiers of Political Theory.* Brighton: Harvester.

Nozick, R. 1974. *Anarchy, State and Utopia.* Oxford: Blackwell.

Sugden, R. 1982. "On the Economics of Philanthropy," *Economic Journal,* vol. 92.

———. 1984. Reciprocity: The Supply of Public Goods Through Voluntary Contributions," *Economic Journal,* vol. 94.

Taylor, M. 1976. *Anarchy and Co-operation.* London: Wiley.

———. 1982. *Community, Anarchy and Liberty.* Cambridge: Cambridge University Press.

Taylor, M., and H. Ward. 1982. "Chickens, Whales and Lumpy Goods," *Political Studies,* vol. 30.

Taylor-Gooby, P. 1985. *Public Opinion, Ideology and State Welfare.* London: Routledge & Kegan Paul.

Walzer, Michael. 1983. *Spheres of Justice.* Oxford: Martin Robertson.

Weale, A. 1979. *Equality and Social Policy.* London: Routledge & Kegan Paul.

———. 1983. *Political Theory and Social Policy.* London: Macmillan.

8

DEMOCRACY AGAINST THE WELFARE STATE?

Structural Foundations of Neoconservative Political Opportunities

Within any modern state, citizens are structurally related to state authority in three basic ways. Citizens are collectively the sovereign *creators* of state authority, they are potentially *threatened* by state-organized force and coercion, and they are *dependent upon the services and provisions organized by the state.* The notion of citizenship within liberal-democratic welfare states involves all three aspects: citizens are (1) the ultimate source of the collective political will, in the formation of which they are called upon to participate in a variety of institutional ways; (2) the "subjects" against whom this will can be enforced and whose civil rights and liberties impose, by constituting an autonomous sphere of "private" social, cultural, and economic action, limits upon the state's authority; and finally (3) clients who depend upon state-provided services, programs, and collective goods for securing their material, social, and cultural means of survival and well-being in society. It is readily evident that these three components of the concept of citizenship have their ideological roots, respectively, in the political theories of liberalism, democracy, and the welfare state.

These theories—and the corresponding dimensions of the concept of citizenship—can clearly be located on an evolutionary axis that represents the development of the "modern" state. In such a rough historical sequence—as suggested, in a famous essay by T. H. Marshall (1964) among others—first came the "liberal" solution of the problem of state authority as a threat to life, property, and cultural/religious identity. The institutional response to this problem has been the constitutional legal guarantee of freedom and liberty that made certain spheres of existence and activity exempt from state control. This is the *liberal* component of the modern state, the formal limitation of its power, and the exemption of market interaction and other "private" pursuits from

189

state control. It is a set of institutional devices that organizes a protective framework ("rule of law"). This protective arrangement is intended (and often seen) to effectively counterbalance the threatening administrative, fiscal, military, and ideological means of control that the modern state has accumulated.

Second, as the modern state does not have a universally recognized "meta-social" mandate on which its activities can be based, or from which its legitimacy can be derived, it turns to the "people" as its ultimate source of authority. This is the "voice" principle, institutionally embodied in the rules and procedures of *democratic* government and representation. The most important of these are the universal right to vote, competing political parties, general elections, majority rule, and so on.

Finally, the citizens depend upon the state due to the loss *both* of feudal forms of paternalistic "welfare" *and* of individual economic autarchy that the market-controlled nature of industrial capitalism is incapable of fully compensating for. "Insecurity" and the structural incapacity of maintaining the necessary preconditions of the existence of civil society as a whole are no longer purely military problems (to be taken care of by the apparatus of the "warfare state"), but they have also increasingly become a recognized condition of virtually all civilian actors within the civilian life of civil society. They come to depend on a great variety of economic and social policies, the institutional framework of which is today known as the *interventionist welfare state*. Thus the three components of modern state-citizenship relations in the West can be said to be the *rule of law, representative democracy,* and provisions for "civilian security" through the *welfare state*.

The problem I want to introduce by briefly recapitulating these categories and distinctions is familiar from much of the recent literature on the state in general and on the welfare state in specific. It is centered on the question of how stable and viable the architecture of a political system is that is made up of these three institutional components. Two extreme perspectives in dealing with this question can be distinguished. One emphasizes harmony, compatibility, even evolutionary mutual re-inforcement among the three, whereas the opposite perspective emphasizes strains, stresses, contradictions, and incompatibilities. It must remain a theoretical, and ultimately an empirical question as to which of these perspectives is valid, and for what reasons, in what respects, and under what conditions.

The global problem of potential, inherent tensions within this ensemble of three institutional components can conveniently be broken down into three subproblems. These concern the viability of *partial* syntheses— namely, those of (1) the liberal and democratic components, (2) the liberal and welfare state (or, in the somewhat more specific German terminology, *Rechtsstaat* vs. *Sozialstaat*), and (3) the democratic and welfare state components. As far as the first of these three compatibility questions is concerned, which shall remain entirely outside the scope of the present chapter, there exists a large tradition of political theorizing and an equally broad body of literature that is often skeptical and critical in its findings and of which the works of Wolfe (1977), Macpherson (1977), and Levine (1981) are well-known, if heterogeneous, examples. The second compatibility problem, that of the "fit" of liberal and welfare state institutional elements, is a favorite of the (neo)conservative political discourse and will be briefly discussed in a moment. The third set of subproblems is relatively the most neglected one in the theoretical literature, although there is a lot of empirical evidence, accumulated during the 1970s and early 1980s, that gives rise to the concern that the correlation of democratic mass politics and the "welfare stateness" of liberal democracies may be less viable and reliable (in either of its two possible causal interpretations) than most political theorists used to take for granted. It is this subproblem to which most of the present discussion shall address itself.

LIBERALISM AND THE WELFARE STATE

In the early 1980s, much of the dominant discourse of the problems and future developments of the welfare state has focused on the alleged antagonism between the collective civilian security aspect of the state (i.e., the *welfare* state) and the *liberal* aspects of the state (i.e., its guarantee of private property, of contractual market relations, and, hence, of a capitalist economy). This discourse, in which the philosophical and political perspectives of the neoconservative and liberal right prevail, postulates that the welfare state has become too heavy a burden on the economy, the growth potential and competitiveness of which are consequently seen to suffer from the excessive costs and rigidities imposed upon the market by state-organized welfare and social security provisions. On the other side, these theories, predictions, and sometimes also alarmist speculations are countered by arguments and programmatic views by the democratic left, unions, and West-European Social Democratic and Socialist parties and governments. The tableau within which this debate is framed is schematically represented by the following matrix, which categorizes supposed causal links between the liberal principle of a market economy (ME) and the welfare state (WS). The propositions of the neoconservative critique are summarized in cell 4 of the schema.

Controversial as all of the propositions within the four cells of this schema are, they are at least explicit components of a well-established,

FIGURE 8.1
Conceptualizations of the Interaction
Between Market Economy and Welfare State

Causal Link	Supportive	Antagonistic
ME → WS	Expanding private-sector economy generates tax base for "growth dividend" out of which welfare state transfers and services can be financed.	Labor-saving technical change, capital flight, domestic demand gap, etc., undermine prospects for long-term full employment on which WS is premised.
	1 / **3**	**2** / **4**
WS → ME	Provision of skills, health care, peaceful industrial relations, "built-in" demand stabilizers, etc., generates necessary input for ME and support its further expansion.	Excessive tax burden, crowding out effect of state budget deficit, leads to WS as disincentives to invest, employ, and work; and WS causes labor market rigidities and "immoralist" attitudes.

and in many respects, fairly conventional economic, legal, and political debate. The only new (or perhaps very old?) argument within a broad discourse that emphasizes the long-term incompatibility between the welfare state and a liberal market society is perhaps the proposition, put forward by quite a number of recent publications, that the damage that the welfare state inflicts upon the liberal political order is not so much of an immediately *economic* as a *moral* nature. According to proponents of this perspective, the "fiscal crisis" and "economic inefficiency" crisis of the welfare state are mediated through a moral one. Focusing on the highly developed Dutch welfare state, one author, for instance, argues that due to its abstract formal-legal *modus operandi*, the modern welfare state has cut itself loose from the moral resources, common values, and potentialities for solidarity within civil society, thereby rendering these resources seemingly useless and the adherence to solidary commitments worthless, if not positively irrational. This critique of the welfare state condemns its allegedly destructive impact upon the moral fiber of society, and by virtue of *this* effect also upon its economic efficiency and productivity. The author gives the following illustration of what he considers the demoralizing effect and hence the "immoralist" nature of state welfare:

> After a fund-raising event for a charitable goal, members of a voluntary organization are able to present the money personally to the recipients of their benefaction, whereas the recipients of welfare state benefaction remain anonymous members in a bureaucratic system, receive their cheques by mail, while the money of the system has been collected by a gigantic tax system. This welfare package does not require any commitment or initiative, nor can any moral energy be invested in it. Nobody bears any responsibility, nobody is accountable, nobody needs to show loyalty . . . to this abstract system [which, according to this view, is characterized by an] in-built lack of moral principles [and an elective affinity] between the welfare state and the immoralist ethos. (Zijderveld, 1986, 452–453)

Leaving aside the alarmist undertones of this image of the welfare state, there are a number of potentially valid analytical points on which this argument can be based. These include the following:

1. There is a self-augmenting dynamic of demands made upon the welfare state. As more and better-organized groups of clients and claimants are formed, as they voice their demands in competition with each other, and as, in addition to social security and work-related demands, family-related issues are included in the agenda of the welfare state, a self-propelling process of "rising expectations" is set into motion that implies a shift from the prevention of poverty to the universal guarantee of status. As a consequence, the welfare state "does no longer guarantee *minimal* standards of welfare and well-being, but is counted upon as the provider of maximum standards of welfare" (Zijderveld, 1986, 454).

2. The liberal principle of the rule of law and, more generally, the protection and recognition of the private sphere of economic and family life prevent the welfare state from transgressing, except in marginal cases, the limits of formal-legal entitlements and, thus, from distributing benefits according to principles of attributed need and/or demonstrable desert. It also becomes unfeasible to make the receipt of benefits conditional upon any kind of moral obligation to which recipients would have to conform. This situation involves a certain—and easily exaggerated—potential for "'moral hazard' and 'free-riding' that . . . are typical for 'common-pool problems'" (Gretschmann, 1986, 232; Mead, 1986).

3. As social policy makers are forced to take into account the imperatives and potential adverse reactions of the capitalist economy, welfare state programs tend to be "reactive" rather than "active," or "differentiated" rather than "integrated" (Mishra, 1984), except under the most favorable of institutional and economic circumstances (of which the Swedish welfare state is often considered to be the prime example). That is to

say, the liberal nature of the economy prevents social policies from achieving the degree of comprehensive rationality and effective implementation that would make it immune from the corrosive impact of economic change, fiscal crises, and business-cycle fluctuations (Habermas, 1985; Offe, 1984). The very constraints that govern the formation of social policies render them highly vulnerable to changes of economic and fiscal parameters.

To the extent that these observations are valid, they are likely to lead to a cumulative frustration with the welfare state of client and claimant groups (due to point 1), of tax payers and voters (point 2), and eventually of political elites themselves (point 3). Moreover, the conflict between liberal and welfare state principles is emphasized not only by economic liberals but also by humanistic libertarians who have grown increasingly sensitive to the alienating, decapacitating, and depersonalizing effects that the welfare state and its legal-bureaucratic or professional modes of distribution, treatment, and surveillance can have upon communities and individual "life-worlds" (Habermas, 1985; Sachsse, 1986; Illich, 1977).

The (partial) validity of these liberal and libertarian arguments, however, does not enhance the plausibility of the solutions that are typically proposed as a way to overcome the conflict between liberal and welfare state principles. For the assumption that the structural "demoralization" of the welfare state can be overcome by some government-sponsored strategy of "remoralization" is as simplistic as it turns out to be questionable, in terms of both its feasibility and its ethical plausibility. Yet it is exactly this "remoralization" strategy for a post-liberal welfare state that has been proposed, along remarkably similar lines, by Mead (1986) for the United States and by Spieker (1986) for West Germany. Mead criticizes the U.S. welfare state for its "permissiveness," by which he means its failure to impose binding "civic obligations" upon the recipients of its benefits and services. By *civic* obligations—which he contrasts to the more conventional *political* obligations such as paying taxes, abiding by the law, and doing military service—he means such civic duties as accepting (hard and low-paid) work, supporting one's family, respecting the rights of others, and acquiring through formal education the basic skills that are required for literacy and employability (1986, 242). Taken together, these civic virtues make up what Mead calls the competent or "functioning citizen," whose creation he envisages as a function of a new style of social policy that would operate with educational means and outright punishments to shape citizens after this model. "Government must persuade people to blame themselves"; the poor must be obligated to accept "employment as a duty" (1986, 12–13).

The "authoritative"—or authoritarian—paternalism that forms the basis of this proposal is justified by the fact that what is demanded from the welfare clientele is nothing but one set of traditionally American virtues. Thus, "being" American justifies these state-enforced moral requirements of "civic obligation." A similar shift from formal to substantive rationality, from legal entitlement to moral desert, is proposed by Spieker, this time on the basis not of national culture but of Catholic doctrine. According to this author, the welfare state has nurtured a "hedonistic" and "parasitical" conduct of life (1986, 328), against which not only work- and family-related virtues but also an attitude of "friendship toward the state" (1986, 323) must be restored and enforced. Such proposals are symptomatic for both their failures and their latent and quite paradoxical political functions. They "resolve" the tension between the liberal and the welfare components by abolishing both of them, certainly the former. They proclaim a state-sanctioned and state-enforced set of moral standards and virtues, whereas it is evidently beyond the powers of any "modern" state to form a unity of moral will even on the elite level, to say nothing about implementing it by imposing it "authoritatively" on the mass level. Moreover, such proposals do not even bother to recognize the contradiction that what they theoretically (though counterfactually) claim to be a *universal*, generally recognized set of virtues would turn in practice into a specific and highly *selective* disciplinary device directed against clients and recipients of benefits; for none of these authors has ever proposed state punishment for family breakup or failures to comply to the work ethic in *middle-income* social categories. Finally, proponents of plans for a "remoralization" of the welfare state remain symptomatically silent about the obvious problem of what should happen to those who fail as "functioning citizens"—that is, the "undeserving" poor. Although these unsettled questions deprive the "remoralization" approach of much of its intellectual interest, they do not necessarily interfere with its latent political function, which is to undermine whatever norms of trust and solidarity that have remained intact, to label the poor and other welfare recipients as morally unworthy and undeserving, and thus to absolve political elites (and taxpayers in general) from *their* moral obligations toward the recipients of welfare benefits and services by blaming them for failures to live up to their presumed moral obligations.

To some extent, the left-libertarian critique of the welfare state is the inverse image of the neoconservative "remoralization" approach. What the latter calls for as a remedy, the former criticizes as a pervasive component of already-existing state practices. The alienating, depersonalizing, and morally destructive impact of bureaucratic and professional intervention into the life-world of clients is viewed with growing alarm

FIGURE 8.2
Conceptualizations of the Interaction
Between Political Democracy and Welfare State

Causal Link	Supportive	Antagonistic
PD → WS	Strengthening of political power of wage-dependent majority of citizens by universal franchise; collective interest of wage-workers in welfare state; economic power of property outbalanced by electoral "power of numbers"	Welfare backlash; individualism, authoritarian antiwelfare state populism; new particularistic tendencies (tax revolt, institutional racism, etc.)
	1	**2**
	3	**4**
WS → PD	Convergent pattern of party competition; reduction of intensity of political conflict; political integration of entire electorate; "end of ideology"; structural vanishing of political radicalism, which might lead to antidemocratic challenges	Corporatist deformation of PD; marginalization of groups, interests, and cleavages not served by WS; rise of new forms of noninstitutional political conflict

and suspicion; at the same time, no reasonably realistic vision of a communal, solidary, "convivial," and nonalienating alternative to the welfare state has yet emerged very clearly (cf. Sachsse, 1986). All that can be stated is the deep ambiguity of state power, which, according to Habermas, is a "perhaps indispensable, but not truly innocent" instrument for taking care of society's welfare problems (1985, 151).

DEMOCRACY AND THE WELFARE STATE

Let us now turn to the relationship and tensions that exist between the democratic and the welfare components of the modern state of Western capitalist societies. I first wish to explore, in analogous ways, some hypothetical links between these two structural elements (see Figure 8.2).

Concerning these two structural variables, much of the conventional wisdom converges on the intuitively highly plausible assumption that capitalist democracies tend to generate political forces supporting welfare state developments (cell 1) *and* that, unless these forces are defeated by a combination of economic crisis and authoritarian political regime changes, welfare states are seen to generate positive repercussions upon democratic political institutions for the kind of reasons indicated in cell 3. Taken together, these two assumptions seem to capture the essentials of the mainstream of postwar social democratic theory in Europe. The welfare state is, in the words of Richard Titmuss, a set of "manifestations, first, of society's will to survive as an organic whole and, secondly, of the expressed wish of all the people to assist the survival of some people" (1963, 39); and political democracy (PD) is nothing other than the institutional means by which this manifestation and expression of will is made possible. At the same time, political democracy is seen as a powerful means of forcing political elites and ruling-class political representatives to accept welfare state arrangements. "Elite fear of social conflict, and ultimately revolution, was the catalyst in explaining social policy making in interwar Britain" (Gilbert as quoted in Whiteley 1981, 455). Underlying this rather optimistic assumption is (1) a *model of rational collective action through democratic politics* and (2) a model of self-stabilizing and *self-reinforcing institutional dynamics*. In other words, the twin assumption is that rational actors in a democracy will join a pro–welfare state majority and that, once the welfare state institutions are established, they will become increasingly immune to challenges. As it is the central claim of the following theoretical discussion that both of these assumptions are in need of basic revision, and as we need to understand why this is the case, let me elaborate each of them in some more detail.

1. The key figure within the collective rational action assumption is the propertyless male wage laborer who is employed full time and for most of his adult life and whose material subsistence—and that of his family—depends on a sufficient level and a continuous stream of contractual income. He shares these features with a large number of fellow workers who, taken together, constitute the vast majority of the economically active population. Like them, he is exposed to typical risks that are partly inherent in the dynamics of the capitalist mode of production, and of which lack of income or insufficiency of income in cases of disability, illness, old age, and unemployment, but also unmet needs and requirements, are the most significant instances. These wage workers also share some cultural patterns, such as a certain productivist discipline, a sense of solidarity, and the perception of being involved in some fundamental social conflict that divides labor and capital. This overarching sense of solidarity and conflict manifests itself in certain political and economic forms of participation and association, which are seen to be the workers' only available means of promoting their collectively self-evident interests in income maintenance and social security, in adequate working conditions, in continuous full employment and the prevention of poverty, and in the redistribution of income and economic

control, all of which are eventually to be achieved, directly or indirectly, through the interventionist welfare state and its protective and regulatory social and economic legislation and policies. This configuration of conditions and orientations can be described summarily as *labor-centered collectivist statism*.

Moreover, this policy-package of social security plus full employment plus health, education, and housing, plus some poverty-related social assistance is something that could appeal to rational actors *outside* the working class as well, and eventually to all well-intentioned citizens— that is, except for a small minority of the most narrow-minded and selfish ones. This is so for three interrelated reasons suggested by Therborn (1986), all of which have to do with the nature of the welfare state as a provider of public goods. First, any rational voter, according to this line of argument, is supposed to support (and be prepared to make disposable income sacrifices for) the welfare state as it helps to *avoid* collective *"evils,"* ranging from street crime to the spread of contagious diseases to economic recession to disruptive political conflict. Second, support of the welfare state can be seen as an *investment* in a positive public good, such as the development of human resources, labor productivity, and so on. Finally, and in accordance with prevailing standards of the political culture and community norms, support for the welfare state can be perceived as the fulfillment of universalistic or altruistic *social obligations* and, hence, of normative preconditions of legitimacy and justice. With all these class-related, interest-related, and normative considerations to rely on—so it is supposed—why should such support fail to be forthcoming in a democratic polity?

2. The corollary assumption is one of institutional self-reproduction, inertia, and irreversibility that would by and large immunize welfare states, once they are established and entrenched, from challenges and basic revisions. This assumption, which appears rather heroic today, can still be based on the following set of arguments. Within an established welfare state, none of the competing political parties can attempt, for reasons of their interest in winning votes, to abandon the welfare state accord, and this is more the case as the range of *individual* goods (such as income) provided by the welfare state broadens and the proportion of the population that benefits from these goods increases. Furthermore, large-scale and complex programs (such as the various branches of social security of Western European welfare states) tend to commit political elites to their continuation, especially if major corporate collective actors are involved in social policy formation and implementation—an arrangement that would serve as a "muffling effect of social policy" (Øyen, 1986) and discourage protest. Finally, centripetal elite politics and the constraining power of existing programs, budgets, and legislation not

only interact with each other but also condition favorable developments of public opinion and mass ideological orientations (cf. Coughlin, 1980). In other words, along the line of this "institutional inertia" argument, the welfare state can be expected to breed its own sources of political support, partly via the broadening self-interest of individuals and groups who receive such benefits as inflation-proof pensions, and partly via the mechanism of ideological accommodation. What emerges from this brief elaboration of the "institutional inertia" assumption is a reassuring picture of interlocking virtuous circles that, taken together, amount to a giant negative-feedback mechanism of the welfare state in operation. Note that all of the component arguments, concerning both the "rational collective action" and the "institutional inertia" assumptions, are based on the presumption of rational action on the part of individuals, classes, parties, unions, elites, voters, and clients of the welfare state.

However, this overall picture—which normally, and not unfairly, is associated with social democratic political theory—is hopelessly antiquated if we look at Western European welfare states and their foreseeable futures in the mid-1980s. In none of these states has any constitutional change taken place that could be said to have come even close to the abolition of democratic procedures and institutions. And yet both the situation itself as well as its perception and interpretation on elite and mass levels have changed in dramatic and unanticipated ways. This new divergence between democratic politics and social policies is so pervasive and consistent that it cannot be accounted for in terms of transient deviations from a stable long-term trajectory. It must be understood, or so the core thesis of this chapter suggests, as a reflection of structural changes and new situations in which rational political actors (both individual and collective) find themselves. The mutually supportive relationship of mass democracy and welfare stateness (as depicted in cells 1 and 3 of Figure 8.2) no longer amounts to a convincing hypothesis. On the contrary, there are many indications, as well as meaningful theoretical assumptions and conjectures, that lead us to expect that democratic mass politics will *not* work in the direction of a reliable defense (to say nothing about the further expansion) of the welfare state.

The dependent variable that thus needs to be explained is the stagnation and partial decomposition of welfare states in Western European democracies since the mid-1970s. There can be little controversy about the phenomenon itself, although the overall picture—including national variations—is hard to capture by a few indicators, especially as economic conditions, institutional structures, and cultural traditions in these countries produce a great deal of variation. Such empirical variations are not pursued further here. I suggest the following list of indicators, which produce a fairly uniform picture of what has been happening since the mid-1970s.

1. There has been a continuous and sometimes rather dramatic series of electoral losses and defeats of social democratic and socialist parties—that is, of the traditional hegemonic forces of pro–welfare state political interests and alliances. In fact, as of 1986 social democratic–led governments have been pushed back to the northern and southern margins of Europe—in sharp contrast to the situation in the late 1970s and early 1980s. On the level of public opinion as measured by longitudinal and comparative analyses of survey data, it has been observed that "in general, the direction of the change has been to the favor of anti-welfare state views." (Pöntinen and Uusitalo, 1986, 26; Ringen, 1986). Differences of scholarly interpretation do not concern the direction of this change, but the extent to which it already has occurred, with only a few authors having found reasons to believe that the population "in general [is] either satisfied with provision or supports more expenditures" (Taylor-Gooby, 1983, 175; cf. Alber, 1986).

2. There has been an equally marked and often abrupt discontinuity in the development of the *absolute* level of welfare state expenditures, leading either to stagnation or to slow decline of budgets, in contrast to a continuous rise of expenditures during virtually the entire period since World War II. One careful study of these fiscal and expenditure developments finds that "cuts are on the political agenda in a way which would have been unthinkable a generation ago" (Whiteley, 1981, 460). Even a country that has so far been relatively unaffected by changes in growth rates and governments—namely, West Germany—shows a sharp decline in the proportion of social policy legislation that implies increases in benefits or coverage. Whereas a full 81 percent belonged in that expansive category during 1950–1974 and only 8 percent of the new legislation involved cuts, the federal legislative output for 1975–1983 consisted of 56 percent of new laws implying cuts (although only 27 percent of the laws of this period led to increases) (Alber, 1986, 31).

3. There has been an even more dramatic decline of welfare state transfers and services relative to the level of need that is itself caused by unemployment and demographic as well as sectoral economic changes. As a consequence, for instance, a growing rate of unemployment coincides with stagnating unemployment insurance budgets—a coincidence that leads either to a deterioration of benefit entitlements and/or to increased exclusiveness of entitlements of the unemployed.

4. The growing gap between (what used to be recognized as) need and actually provided services and benefits has not led to large-scale and/or militant conflict in defense of the welfare state and its continued

expansion. On the contrary, patterns of political conflict have shifted, among others, in three directions. One is the mainly unpromising phenomenon of militant, sectoral, local and regional strikes, and some-times riots, such as occurred in the British mining and printing industries and in poverty-stricken communities. Another is the sometimes dramatic electoral defection of the core working class to liberal-conservative political forces, implying a strong sign of political support for anti–welfare state cuts and legislation even among those who belong to the classes and social categories in whose name the ideals and ideologies of state-provided welfare have traditionally been advocated. Finally, a further shift in the type and issue-content of political conflict has revolved around problems (such as the rights of citizens, environmental questions, feminist and peace issues) that are absent from the welfare state's agenda and are now being carried out by nonclass social movements (cf. Offe, 1985).

5. Parallel to these changes of policy and politics, there are strong indications that—on the level of elite opinion and ideology of the political left—the *egalitarian-collectivist* component of its theoretical heritage is receding in significance, whereas *libertarian, anti-étatist* and *communitarian* ideals and projects have become increasingly dominant. It is exactly at the moment of severe challenges and defeats that major forces within the political left seem to abandon what for most of this century has been the left's central project—namely, a collectivist-étatist version of industrialism. This shift of the left's own ideological orientation is well captured by Przeworski and Wallerstein:

> The predicament [of the left] is political: historical experience indicates that governments cannot be trusted with precisely those alternatives that would make a difference, those that require large doses of state intervention. The dilemma of the Left is that the only way to improve material conditions of workers and poor people under capitalism is through rather massive state intervention, and the state does not seem to be a reliable mechanism of intervention. The patient is sick, the drugs are available, but the doctor is a hack. (1986, 13)

On a more analytical level, Habermas has raised the problem that the welfare state, after having reconciled to some (limited) extent the tension that exists between the capitalist economy and the democratic polity, is now confronting a dual problem as a consequence of which it is deprived of the mobilizing potential of its utopian vision: On the one side, it is met with distrust by core working-class and upwardly mobile social categories that defect from collectivist ideals, and on the other by those who, though recognizing the welfare state's accomplishment of some measure of social justice, become also aware of its built-in contradiction between state power and life-world, or between the welfare state's method and its goal (Habermas, 1985, 149–152). Taken together, these two sources of growing frustration and disappointment would force the defenders of the welfare state to reformulate their political vision in quite fundamental ways.

RETHINKING THE METHOD OF THE MACRO-SOCIOLOGY OF THE WELFARE STATE

Largely in line with the hypotheses contained in the left-hand columns of Figures 8.1 and 8.2, recent comparative historical research has confirmed that the rise of the welfare state has been correlated with such variables as economic growth, democratic political mass participation, bureaucratic centralization, and the rise of collectivist tendencies in dominant ideologies and public opinion (cf. Wilensky, 1975; Alber, 1982). Underlying much of this research is a macro-methodology that relates economic, political, and cultural aggregate indicators to policy outputs and their historical accumulation. What is missing in this analytical design is the role of individual actors and their style of rational responses. Structures do not *directly* translate into outcomes and developments; they do so by virtue of the responses, interpretations, memories and expectations, beliefs, and preferences of actors who *mediate* the link between structure and outcome. The recent resurgence of methodological individualist approaches in the social sciences has helped a great deal to remind us of this missing link within much of the macro-sociological research tradition.

Not only do beliefs and preferences intervene and mediate between structures and dynamic outcomes but, in addition, the *knowledge* that exists about the relationship between structures and outcomes can influence the individual agents' strategic selection of beliefs and preferences. This is what macro-sociological correlation analysis often fails to appreciate. Sociological knowledge not only *presupposes* certain patterns of "rational" individual responses to economic, institutional, and other structural conditions; such responses are also, conversely, shaped and changed by actors equipped with available knowledge and cognitive expectations. I wish to use this model of a circular loop—social knowledge as based upon "typical" patterns of action and social action as based upon available knowledge (including uncertainty and ignorance)—in order to explore the weakening of the sociopolitical base of the welfare state that is suggested by the five generalizations enumerated earlier.

Let us take as an example the hypothesis, depicted in cell 4 of Figure 8.1, that relates the welfare state to the fates of the market economy in negative, or antagonistic, ways. The type of behavioral patterns that would mediate such a causal relationship are easily deduced from a theory of self-interested economic actors. The respective behavioral propositions, which are well known from much recent neoconservative and market-liberal theorizing, research, and ideological proclamations, are basically threefold. First, the institutions of the welfare state tend to impose an "excessive" tax burden upon investors, who therefore will refrain from investment, or seek investment opportunities abroad, or even disinvest. Second, the institutions of the welfare state provide benefits to "potential" workers who therefore will be less pressured to adapt to the labor market (or, for that matter, to the economic responsibilities of family life) because they expect that their needs will be taken care of through social welfare and state-provided services. Third, this dual disincentive effect of the "excessive" expansion of the welfare state is not accidental but, rather, is systematically promoted by a category of people who are often summarily referred to as the "new class"—namely, government bureaucrats, professionals, planners, academics, liberal makers of public opinion, and the like.

Now, the response of most social scientists when confronted with such propositions has been to treat them as (or to transform them into) *testable hypotheses* and to determine their *truth* according to the standard procedures of empirical research. For example, an often-invoked variant of the second proposition is the claim that unemployment insurance benefits are "too high" and tend to generate perverse steering effects. This is said to be so (1) because these benefits allow employable workers to survive on benefits rather than adapt to the market or (2) because they allow unemployable workers or workers who are actually unwilling to accept employment to obtain benefits by simply, if fraudulently, registering as unemployed. After this specification has been made, the proposition is then tested by more or less sophisticated statistical methods, analyzing data across time, across states and countries, or across various categories of the unemployed. In this particular case, such studies result in a reasonably consistent refutation of the proposition. The finding tends to be that the objects to which this proposition refers simply do not behave the way the proposition predicts. But it is important to realize that this procedure is just one of three very different ways by which the validity/invalidity of politically relevant propositions can be established or criticized.

It is a normal, if sometimes saddening, experience of social scientists who are engaged in such empirical "testing" of politically relevant propositions that these often show a remarkable capacity to survive the negative outcome of the test, and that they continue to make political impact in spite of their empirically demonstrated falseness. Consequently, we must conclude, there are sources of validity *other* than empirical proof and conformity to the data. These sources appear to be sufficiently powerful to immunize people against (negative) empirical evidence. How can this immunity be accounted for? Take the proposition that welfare state spending functions as a disincentive to investment. If an adherent to this proposition is confronted with the well-known data showing that there is a *positive* correlation between rates of economic growth and percentages of welfare expenditures in GNP in all OECD countries over the past thirty years, he or she may still defend the proposition by claiming that the particular country in question is a special geographic case, or that the given economic and political conjuncture is a special case in time, so that the empirical generalization can be dismissed as inconclusive. Also, and in a somewhat more sophisticated manner, it might also be claimed that the proposition may not be true in and by itself, but that it is nevertheless made true by the fact that a relevant number of strategic actors are perceived or even known to *believe* in its truth—a fact whereby the original falseness of the proposition will become true by virtue of the mechanism of a self-fulfilling prejudice. In this way, the behavioral consequence of false beliefs creates the basis for accurate beliefs.

Furthermore, and on a sociologically more serious level of argumentation, it might be claimed that such "prejudices" not only exist but that they also are rooted in certain changes of structural conditions in response to which actors might adopt these propositions for *individually rational reasons.* In accordance with this type of argument, certain interpretive patterns (such as those represented by our three propositions in cell 4 of Figure 8.1) are conditioned by, and rational reflections of, structural changes that are taking place within the environment of action (the "opportunity structure") of relevant actors. For example, it could be claimed that the disincentive-to-work effect is something that people are rationally led to assume of each other as a behavioral tendency under conditions of, say, a generally perceived weakening of the family as an institution, or of a weakening of the protestant work ethic, or of an increased working-class segmentation. Similarly, the behavioral responses of investors to marginal increases in welfare spending may be derived from their situational context, such as changes in the competitive strength of a particular industry, anticipated political changes and so on.[1] What we see here is a second potential source of the social validity of beliefs. The first source is the one that social scientists rely upon when measuring correlations between variables and test the behavioral assumptions that make up the causal link between these variables. It appears to be a naive and self-congratulatory assumption of social scientists that, due to the authority of "scientific truth," such findings are likely to form the one and only rational basis for beliefs concerning social reality. Quite to the contrary, there are always rational reasons to adopt cognitive premises in addition to those prescribed by social science. This is particularly the case if the scope of generalizability of the truth-claim of the social science is seen to be questionable and limited. Proposition X may have been true so far, but will it continue to be so? Behavioral assumptions have been confirmed by study Y, but do these assumptions apply to the people I have to interact with, too? A hypothesis that has been refuted in one substantive area (e.g., unemployment insurance) may still be valid in the context of another substantive problem area (such as family allowances). Who knows? Such perceptions of fluidity, unpredictability, and rapid change may well give rise to strategically adopted cognitive premises of action, and such strategic belief formation is in fact structurally induced and suggested by conditions that are perceived as volatile and highly uncertain. The trust in scientifically grounded truth depends upon the trust in the coherence and continuity of the world—and thus the breakdown of the latter affects the former. It also gives rise, at the same time, to an interest-related, or strategic-interactive, criterion for the adoption of beliefs. Examples include the rule that one should always expect the worst, or mistrust other people, or commit oneself to opportunism, or disbelieve scientific as well as normative representations of the world, or adopt beliefs that minimize the costs of disappointment.

It should be clear from these examples that the social validity of such propositions stands, as it were, on *two* legs, one being the testable correspondence of the proposition with facts and events in the outside world and the other being the way in which actors are constituted and rationally motivated to accept the proposition as a cognitive premise and as a guide to a particular mode of action, so as to consider it creditable and to adopt it as a belief—often with the consequence that the proposition is *then* validated as an empirical truth, due to the operation of a self-fulfilling interpretation loop.

There is, of course, a third type of validity of beliefs that is diametrically opposed to the second one. Its basis is neither empirically demonstrated *truth* nor strategically selected interpretation guided by *interest*, but *trust* in the validity of such norms as reciprocity, solidarity, or justice. With respect to this type, belief formation follows normative conceptions of the respective segment of reality—conceptions that, as long as they prevail, are counterfactual and infallible and therefore immune from empirical refutation and/or strategic selection. The structural condition that can give rise to such normative foundations of validity-attribution are probably the opposite from those underlying our second type: the firmly established collective identities, homogeneity, immobility, and continuity that Rousseau described as the precondition of a viable "volonté générale" (or Durkheim described as the condition of "mechanical solidarity").

Depending on which of these three criteria of "social validity" of such propositions we concentrate on, the task of the social scientist in testing, confirming, or criticizing such claims differs considerably. For instance (and this is most important in the present context), how do we deal with politically consequential beliefs of the second type, which are "real in their consequences" but, at least initially, unsupported by empirical fact? Their social validity results, as we have seen, not from their cognitive adequacy but from their interest-dependent individual attractiveness as a political project under conditions of high uncertainty and, thus, from strategic considerations. In such cases, both the reference to facts (i.e., type-1 beliefs) and to norms (i.e., type-3 beliefs) fails. Strategically selected and adopted beliefs, being based on interest, defy critical assessments of their irrationality, which are based on either truth or norms.

As a way out of this dilemma, it seems to me that we must return to the level of empirical analysis—this time, however, not of the *facts* to which the propositions in questions refer but of the *actors* and their individually rational reasons for accepting these propositions as valid. From this perspective, the correspondence that would become the focus of critical attention is not the correspondence between facts and propositions. Neither would it be the correspondence between values and political projects. Rather, it would be the correspondence between certain types of social actors and the parameters of choice given within their situation of action, on the one side, and their rational motivation to adopt certain interpretive patterns about the world, on the other. It is this latter type of sociological approach to the analysis of the welfare state—an approach that could perhaps be described as a combination of structural, phenomenological, and rational-choice approaches—whose contours I want to explore further.

Returning to our two matrices and the propositions that are schematically represented by them, the question is no longer "Who is right?" but, rather, "Which types of structural changes, perceptions, and specific uncertainties make it rational for various categories of actors to adopt, and to act on the basis of, either of the conflicting interpretive perspectives?"

RATIONALITY, TRUST, AND WELFARE

The case of the liberal conservative democratic attack on the welfare state is easily reconstructed in terms of rational-choice theory. As we know from Mancur Olson's theory of collective action, there is no natural reason for a public good to be produced even if it could be shown to be in the interest of each individual member of a (large) collectivity. For rather than contributing to the production of the public good, the more desirable option to the rational individual is to let everyone else pay for the good while the individual takes a "free-ride" on the efforts of others without contributing himself. As long as the benefits from the goods cannot be limited to those who have actually contributed to its production, free-riding is a rational strategy from the point of view of the individual utility maximizer. This is so for three reasons: first, because one's own contribution to the good would be so small as to make no real difference (in a "large" group) for the continued production of the good; second, because the good is in fact available as a "public" good (i.e., free of charge to its individual consumers); and, third, because individual actors, with or without having read Olson, may have reasons, according to their perception of the propensities and inclinations of other actors, for suspecting that the latter will fail to cooperate or continue to cooperate in the relevant future, which would make one a "sucker" if one were to contribute to the provision of the good. As a combined consequence, and as everyone waits for the others to contribute to the good, the good, although collectively beneficial, will not be produced in the first place.

This well-known paradox serves as the backdrop for the analysis of cases in which collective goods *are* actually produced. In such cases, the question must be asked: What makes the members of the group act so "irrationally" (according to the individual calculus specified above) as to actually act *in accordance* with their collective interest? The answer that Olson—who is quite careful to avoid the use of any sociological category such as "norms" or "values"—has to provide comes in either of two versions. Either the people do not, in fact, act "irrationally" because they are rationally attracted to contributing to the collective good due to the existence of some "selective incentives" that are made available only to those who do contribute (in which case the collective good becomes a mere *by-product* of individual benefit-seeking); or such seemingly irrational behavior occurs because someone *forces* individuals to cooperate, in which case they do not win an individual benefit from contributing but, rather, avoid the punishment that would result from noncooperation. With these two specifications, the main argument appears to remain valid: Whenever someone contributes to the production of the collective good, that person does not act irrationally if it can be shown that he or she does so on the basis of a rational motivation through either the gain from selective incentives or the avoidance of punishment; in all other cases, rational cooperation is not to be expected.

This type of argument, however, works only as long as the punishment for noncontributors (to concentrate on this case alone, as it has a real world parallel in mandatory social security schemes) is imposed in a strictly *authoritarian* way—that is, without the option being open to the individual in question to avoid the alternative of either contributing or being punished for not contributing. The *democratic* citizen, in contrast, would in fact *have* the option to impose his or her will upon the government in order to prevent it from imposing *its* will upon the citizen (i.e., in the form of compulsory contribution under the threat of punishment).

Seen from this perspective, the problem of democracy is that it moves—in theory as well as in practice—beyond an account in terms of simple coercion. It does so "by introducing a framework wherein *legitimacy* may be tested" (Taylor-Gooby, 1983, 166; my emphasis). Democracy puts citizens in a position in which they are able to coerce the coercer, and it becomes quite likely that they will use their democratic rights in this way if they have to believe that a sufficiently large number of other citizens will join this strategy to force state authorities to *refrain* from forcing citizens to contribute—unless they consider the state's authority legitimate. Among such reasons can be the following: (1) Many people believe that many *other* people believe that the incidence of costs and benefits of a given program or legislation are redistributive in nature; therefore, it appears to be in their rational self-interest to adopt this belief themselves, even in spite of individually available factual counterevidence, and to join those acting on the false belief that their action will be profitable. (2) Such democratic evasion from collective-goods contribution may also be attractive for the reason that it is channeled through voting—that is, through an institutional mechanism that renders individual behavior invisible (secret ballot) and noninteractive (simultaneous voting, which renders infeasible the emergence of an assurance game). The paradox thus appears to be this: Unless citizens consider the state's authority legitimate, they can obstruct mandatory cooperation through the democratic ballot. As far as state provision for welfare is concerned, its legitimacy is dependent not only upon the citizens' perception of the nature of the rulers or the government but also upon the perception of fellow citizens and the anticipation of their action. Thus, if only a legitimate authority within a solidary society (i.e., one consenting on the legitimacy of the authority) can enable the state to enforce cooperation, why is such authority necessary in the first place? Why can't it be fully replaced by voluntary collective-goods production?

In other words, explaining collective-goods production by reference to state authority and mandatory contributions is not really an explanation but, rather, the first step into an infinite regress that can be halted only by some axiom concerning the pre-given and unquestionable existence of state authority as the ultimate coercive power. Short of such an axiom, state authority that enforces collective-goods production must be considered a collective good in itself, thus suffering from the same analytical problem that it supposedly solves. As Talcott Parsons demonstrated in a famous argument against Thomas Hobbes, no deductive link exists between the ideal selfishness of the inhabitants of the state of nature and the origin of state authority; Hobbes' suggestion that there is such a link "is really to violate his [utilitarian] postulate [and] to posit a momentary identity of interest" (Parsons, 1968, 238).

Consequently, the problem of selfish noncooperation cannot be explained away by the existence of state authority, because the latter owes its origin—and continued existence—to dispositions on the part of citizens toward cooperative action. If universal and pure selfishness makes the state necessary, it also makes the state impossible because no state can emerge from a condition of such selfishness. And neither can a state maintain itself in the context of pure selfishness, least of all a democratic state.

To be sure, the individual in a democratic polity would not be able to escape the binding force of authority as long as she or he remains the *only* one who wishes to stop the government from imposing a punishment on noncontributors. But, given a democratic polity, there is no reason to expect that she or he would *remain* the only one, given the fact that (by virtue of the bare minimum definition of democracy as a system under which dissent is not punishable) there would be a zero-cost attached to noncooperation by voting. For instance, citizens would vote into government office a party that promises to do away with virtually all forced cooperation in the production of collective goods. In the absence of a sense of legitimacy not only of the government itself but of the intertemporal and intergroup distributive impacts of social policies as well, what we would expect to see is a dynamic of actual defection, anticipated defection, anticipated anticipation, and so on, leading to a self-propelling or "autocatalytic" chain of causal effects.

This exercise in Olsonian logic of collective action seems to demonstrate that there is at least one case in which the logic does not work: that in which the "collective good" of *abolishing* the compulsory cooperation in the production of collective goods (or, for that matter, the "indirect" production of collective goods through the selective incentive effect) is to be had at a zero-price, which is actually the case in a democracy. But because zero-cost dissent is a real possibility, it would affect all production of collective goods (for large collectivities), which, according to Olson, can only be explained as resulting from the selective-incentive or compulsory-contribution effects. Consequently, we would be back to square one in our attempt to understand why, among rational actors, collective-goods production occurs at all *in a democracy.*

Unless we want to stick—against the Parsonian argument—to the now questionable assumption that pure self-interest *can* lead to the constitution of an absolute authority that henceforth is immune from citizens' choosing their opting-out option, we will have to take another road. The only alternative seems to be to hypothesize that actors produce collective goods not because of the rational capacity to maximize utility and to avoid punishment but because of their normative disposition to do so, or because of the relationship of trust, reciprocity, sympathy, and fairness that they have experienced as existing between themselves and their fellow-contributors. For what else than such legitimizing notions, motivations, and identities could lead them, in a democracy, to continue to cooperate, even though they *could* withdraw at zero-cost, thereby debasing the authority that compels them to act as rational contributors?

These theoretical considerations are less remote from the problem at hand than it might appear. The problem is to theoretically test the hypothesis in cell 2 of our Figure 8.2. For the above arguments lead us to conclude that (1) if a polity is a democracy and (2) if the state is also (and continues to be for any length of time) a welfare state, then this coexistence of structural features of the polity in question cannot be accounted for in terms of class interests (as in cell 1) but must be explained in terms of legitimizing values, attitudes, and practices that inhibit and prevent actors from behaving in ways that would effectively subvert collective-goods production while remaining attractive from the standpoint of pure rational individual utility maximizers. In other words, if a democratic state is a welfare state, this is the case not *because* of democracy but *in spite of* democracy. It must be due to solidarities and modes of normative integration that underpin the continued production of collective goods and guarantee this production, notwithstanding the fact that democracy provides a greater and less expensive opportunity and even temptation to "opt out" and to obstruct this production than any other form of government.

To be sure, even the most ideal-typical selfish citizen would not necessarily be disposed to obstruct *all* collective-goods production by the use of the democratic ballot. Mandatory liability insurance, for instance, might be an exception to this rule, because it generates a collective good for the insured. This type of insurance, however, will be supported by the rational, selfish actor only as long as the operation of the insurance is perceived to be distributionally neutral. That is, the condition of rational consent to *mandatory* insurance is that provisions are taken which guarantee that no one can profit by exploiting the rest of the community of the insured. But this can be taken for granted only if access to the insurance is restricted to persons who regard each other as "our kind of people" or "the likes of us," whereas "cheaters" (who would be defined either as those who get away with less than their proportional contribution, or as those who extract more than their "fair share" of benefits) must be restrained or excluded. This problem is illustrated by the constant pressure on private liability, health, and life insurance companies to organize, by the differentiation of their rates and benefits, "homogeneous risk communities" so that no segment of the membership of the insured feels threatened by the systematic opportunity of other segments to exploit the collectivity of the insured.

Slightly more complicated cases in which rational utility maximizers will still be prepared to cooperate in the production of collective goods are those in which a redistributional game *is* being played, but where the actor does have reasons to believe that, in spite of such redistribution effects, he or she will derive either (1) indirect benefits or (2) special advantages from his or her continued cooperation. They will derive *indirect benefits* if the redistribution involved helps to satisfy certain moral imperatives that each considers as binding for him- or herself (e.g., charity), or if such redistribution helps to serve his or her own interest. Concerning the latter point, it is known that within business and employers' associations, the smaller firms often derive more than a proportional share of benefits while paying a less-than-proportional share in membership dues, thus making them clear net winners from cooperation. However, the reason that large firms find such subsidization of the small in their indirect interest, too, is to be found in the fact that otherwise the small firms might exit from the association, thus depriving all members, including the large ones, of the collective good of being able to speak in the name of the *entire* industry. It is thus exactly because of the redistribution component that everyone—and not just the winners—is better off. In such cases, even redistributive arrangements may be seen as being in everyone's interest—if only up to the point at which the small-business sector within the association starts to make "exploitative" and hence "unacceptable" demands upon the collectivity. Again, the continued production of collective goods appears to be premised upon some shared notion of sameness of nonrival commonality of interest.

The other case is that of *special advantages* provided for cooperation from the outside: Although the weak gain more than the strong, even the strong receive more than they would be able to under any alternative arrangement that would become available to them through noncoop-eration. This is (or perhaps one should say this used to be) the case with many old-age pension social insurance arrangements, in which expected benefits for middle- and high-income participants are higher than can be anticipated from private insurance or individual savings alternatives, due to income-graduation, wage indexation, and favorable entry conditions for higher income brackets. Such special advantages, which we could think of as a compensatory *external* subsidization of the *internal* subsidizers, were often used, in the 1950s and 1960s, as a political "bribe" that was quite consciously designed to keep the better-off within the pro–welfare state alliance, and to dissuade them from considering noncooperative exit-options.[2]

But for this mechanism to work, it already presupposes, on the part of the better-off in the cooperative game, a considerable measure of trust that the promise of comparative advantage will actually be honored by any further government—a trust that in the field of old-age pension insurance is rendered notoriously shaky by current and foreseeable demographic and labor market trends. Again, there is a limiting case in which trust in either the willingness or ability of future governments to honor the deal is weakened and/or in which the price that the better-off demand for their staying within the alliance begins to be perceived as "excessive."

An interesting further case in which collective-goods production (or abstention from the democratic option of opting out) is to be expected is weakness of will. I'll consent to being forced to contribute to some collective good (such as social security) if I think of myself as a person who (e.g., for reasons of near-poverty) is incapable of doing what my long-term interest would require me to do—namely, to save for consumption in old age. Similarly, I'll consent to mandatory insurance if the redistributive effect (e.g., in favor of those who live longer and at the expense of those who experience a below-average life span after retirement) is something that I approve of as a norm of solidarity, without, however, being sufficiently certain of my actual willingness and ability to live up to that principle in concrete cases. In both cases, the collective arrangement is accepted as a "self-paternalist" precommitment that is meant to protect me from the consequences of my own irrational inclinations to disregard either my own future well-being or that of my fellow citizens to whom I feel committed. A further rational motivation to join the collective arrangement may result from the consideration that its common-pool nature makes it more cost-efficient: The more people participate, the less expensive (or qualitatively more specialized and adequate, as in public health services) the unit of output becomes.

But note that all these conditions are highly sensitive to empirical counterevidence and strategic fabrication of evidence under conditions of uncertainty. Under some conditions and perceptions, my willingness to cooperate may no longer make sense; this situation, in turn, can cause domino effects in the perceptions and attitude changes of others. For instance, if I conceive of myself as someone who is conscientiously prepared to provide for his own future need; or if I think that others are either not deserving a share of my income, or deserve only what I shall be willing to give on an *ad hoc* and *ad personam* basis; or if I feel that the expected economies of scale in collective services do not materialize, or are weighed by monopolistic exploitation by the supplying organizations, or must be paid for in terms of poor quality and excessive standardization—all this will damage my rational motivation for cooperating and, therefore, will damage the collectivist arrangement as a whole. It is only my trust that my precommitment will not work out to my disadvantage, that others are worthy of participating in the common pool of resources, and that the latter will not be exploited by provider agencies that leads me to accept this "self-paternalist" arrangement.

In all these cases of cooperative production of public goods, the critical sociological variable is some notion of commonality of interest and fate, of "sameness," or a sufficiently binding conception of a durable collective identity, which is the ultimate resource that keeps cooperation intact beyond its initial phase. Operationally speaking, the notion of sameness, or of collective identity, is the threshold at which actors not only pursue rational calculations of individual and instantaneous costs and utilities but also act on the basis of trust. Such trust also has a social dimension (trust in other people) and a temporal dimension (trust in the continued validity and bindingness of norms and institutions). At this threshold, individual actors shift, as it were, from an economic paradigm of choice and contingency into a sociological paradigm of normative bindingness and order. It is not only the durable production of public goods that is, as I shall argue, impossible without some underlying conception of sameness and collective identity; it is even impossible to define precisely the notion of a public good (such as is supposedly provided by the welfare state) without making at least implicit reference to the idea of a collective identity.

The economists' definition of a public good is based on the criterion of nonexclusiveness: If the good exists at all, it serves all, not just those who have paid for it. This is exactly why no one would rationally and voluntarily be prepared to pay. This is also why payment must be enforced (or tied to selective incentives) in order to produce the public good. But the "publicness" of the good is not a quality of the good itself but a reflection of the interpretive perspective under which people *view* the good. Take defense as a prototypical textbook example of a public good. Even here, "inclusiveness" is not something that is inherent in a defense apparatus but, rather, exists in the perspective under which it is regarded by agents in society. Its "publicness" is entirely dependent upon that society's trust in the nonexploitative or nonredistributive nature of the good and its functions. In order for a "good" to be a "public good," there must be a collectivity, the members of which refer to themselves as "we." In the absence of such a collectivity (which in the case of defense is normally conceptualized as a nation or a bloc of nations), there would not be a referent to whom the good is a public good. The defense arrangement would be seen not as a benefit for "all of us" but as the outcome of a redistributional or exploitative game that takes place between tax-payers and defense-contractors, military personnel and civilians, defense and civilian sectors of the budget, internationalist and national political orientations, pacifists and militarists, and so on. It is only the self-conception of a collectivity as a nation that puts an end to this type of reasoning in terms of individual and group pay-offs, and replaces it by a discourse of collective benefits. This example should alert us to the fact that the "nationhood" of a collectivity cannot be taken for granted, as little as the existence of other collective self-conceptions can; and that without such notions of "sameness" and collective identity, public goods cannot be produced (or, if produced, cannot commonly be perceived as "public" and as "goods")—least of all in a democracy, where there is, by definition, no ultimate authority that would be able to order such production by the fiat of its sovereign power.

If in the course of social change existing notions of sameness come under strain and stress, the seemingly self-evident public good undergoes a *Gestalt*-switch and turns into the object and outcome of a distributive game. Before this switch occurs, a social policy—say, the introduction of unemployment insurance—will be generally discussed and perceived in terms of the creation of a just society, the guarantee of peaceful industrial relations, or the maintenance of aggregate demand. But *after* the switch, the very same policy will be viewed in categories of equivalence, exploitation, and redistribution—for example, in terms of inappropriate burdens being imposed on the industrious and active parts of the workforce, and of undeserved benefits being granted to the unemployed. Note that in this model example, the interpretive framework within which events are perceived has changed, *not* the policy measure itself. Other examples of such an evident switch from a solidaristic framework (strong and extended notions of "sameness") to a framework of equivalence calculations include education and health policies. In education, the shift is typically from an emphasis on every person's right to the fullest development of one's potential, or from human capital considerations (which are ultimately seen to serve the interest of the national economy) to an emphasis on violations of fiscal fairness or the autonomy of parents, on competitive distortions in the job market or on undue opportunities granted to teachers to promote their collective status interests. In all these cases, the underlying process is one in which dominant "parameters of sameness" are narrowed down: from the universalist notion of human rights of all human beings, to the interest of the nation, to the interest of certain categories of tax payers, professional groups, and cultural communities, and finally to the interests of the individual. In all such cases, the decisive change occurs not on the level of objective events and facts but on the level of interpretive frameworks and the strategic adoption of beliefs and expectations. The calculative attitude toward individual and short-term costs and benefits is therefore nothing that is inherent in human nature or in eternal standards of rational action; on the contrary, it is the product of disintegration and decomposition of cultural and structural conditions that constrain and inhibit such utilitarian orientations.

How can such a narrowing of parameters of sameness, or the fragmentation of collective identities, sympathies, and solidarities, be accounted for? Three approaches have been suggested. First, one can explain such shifts in terms of a moral or normative political theory, pointing out that broad humanitarian conceptions of human rights and human needs must be given priority over selfish or otherwise "narrow" interest orientations. To this school of thought would also belong the philosophical idea of an evolutionary sequence of styles of moral orientation, be it linear along an axis of universalism (Habermas, 1985), or be it cyclical according to a model of "shifting involvements" (Hirschman, 1982). Second, the shift can be causally explained in terms of changing political elites, alliances, coalitions, conjunctures, and ideologies, as a consequence of which elites' strategies are seen to undermine and disorganize "large" collectivities and to entice and encourage citizens and voters to adopt a socially narrow and shortsighted perspective in defining their own political preferences. Thus, recent analyses of the "right turn" in the United States (Ferguson and Rogers, 1986) and of the syndrome of "authoritarian populism" in Great Britain (Hall and Jacques, 1983; Jessop et al., 1984) have interpreted these phenomena as the outcome of a design of reactionary political elites to invoke selfish individualist attitudes, to provide these attitudes with a moral pretext, and thus to divide solidaristic alliances, and even the nation as a whole, along the nonclass divide of respectable versus morally questionable and undeserving citizens and social categories. Socialist authors have recently shown an understandable, though in my view one-sided, tendency to rely on this "elitist" interpretation exclusively. Thus, Krieger writes that the attack on the principles of the welfare state is only part of a broader project to reshape political community. . . . Particularistic and even explicitly divisive appeals replace the integrative universalist norms of the welfare state. . . . Policies . . . are part of a strategy to reinforce particularism . . . [and] to divide citizens in highly valuative categories of "us" and "them.". . . "They" are blacks, the unemployed, the clients of the welfare state, the strikers. (1987, 186–187)

The problem with this approach is that it seems to assume that political elites are actually capable of shaping and changing mass attitudes, opinions, and perceptions, rather than merely providing excuses and justifications for reorientations that are conditioned by nonpolitical causes. As little as a pro–welfare state climate of opinion can be created by political elites, an anti–welfare state orientation can be imposed through policies alone. This point is well expressed by Taylor-Gooby when he writes, referring to Habermas:

The problem is that the social mechanisms that produce allegiance are not under the control of policy, because they originate in a different level of society. . . . The basic problem is that the political system cannot itself guarantee to produce the values required to assure loyalty to its policies. Values derive from culture which is independent of the state. (1983, 168)

Without denying the legitimacy and potential usefulness of either of these approaches, let me suggest a third, more sociological and at the same time more structural approach. It starts from the assumption that collective identities and parameters of "sameness" are not chosen by individuals for morally good (or bad) reasons, nor that the scope of sameness is imposed upon social actors by either the laws of moral evolution or the manipulative efforts of political elites and ideologists. What we must look for, instead, are *structural* changes within modern societies that condition, suggest, and steer the prevailing interpretive patterns of "sameness." Within this sociological perspective, it is assumed that the patterns of, for example, the division of labor, of cultural differentiation, of political organization and representation are underlying determinants of what kind and scope of collectivity people refer to when using the word *we*.

DESTRUCTURATION OF COLLECTIVITIES

It has often been observed that the most advanced and stable welfare states exist in those European societies that are highly homogeneous. Take Sweden as the prototypical case: It has an economy that is small and highly export-dependent; a polity that is characterized both by long-term social democratic governance and hegemony and by a virtually unparalleled associational density of highly centralized interest associations; a society and culture that, compared to other Western European countries, is not only highly egalitarian (as a consequence of past redistributive welfare state policies) but also uniquely homogeneous as far as the striking absence of ethnic, regional, linguistic, religious, or other major cultural cleavages is concerned. A further characteristic is Sweden's nonparticipation in supranational military (NATO) and economic (EEC) organizations—a trait that this country shares with Austria and (partly) with Norway (i.e., with two of the other most advanced welfare states). All these features would suggest that in Swedish society the prevailing conception of "sameness" is very broad and inclusive, and that there exist powerful structural and cultural factors that effectively prevent the majority of Swedes from shifting to a view of their welfare state that would emphasize exploitation, unfair redistributional effects, free-riding, and similar utilitarian or "rational-choice" perspectives. But even in this rather exceptional case of Sweden, new divisions, antisolidaristic strategies, symptoms of lack of trust in the welfare state's administration, and particularistic tendencies have surfaced in the early 1980s that seem to put into question major achievements of public policy and neocorporatist interest-intermediation between large and centralized associational blocks (Lash, 1985; Pöntinen and Uusitalo, 1986, 20ff.).

When T. H. Marshall (1964) theorized the inherent tendency of parliamentary democracies to transform themselves into strong welfare states (cf. cell 1 of Figure 8.2), he took for granted (in his time this could rightly have been assumed to be unproblematic) the existence of large, self-conscious, and well-organized collectivities and class organizations of labor that would use the ballot for strategies of social reform and expansive social policies. Since the mid-1970s, however, we have witnessed a fairly rapid decomposition or destructuration of such collectivities. There are many indicators suggesting that political preferences and orientations of increasing segments of the electorate are a reflection of this process of fragmentation, pluralization, and ultimately individualization of socioeconomic conditions and interest-dispositions. Issue-orientation versus party-orientation in voting; the increasing significance of plant-level over sectoral regulation of industrial conflict, and of sectoral over centralized national regulation; social, economic, and cultural cleavages that crosscut the dividing lines between classes and class-organizations—all are frequently observed symptoms of society-wide destructuration processes.

The disorganization of broad, relatively stable and encompassing commonalities of economic interest, associational affiliation, or cultural values and life-styles is in my view the key to an adequate understanding of the general weakening of solidaristic commitments. If it no longer "makes sense" to refer to a broad and sharply delineated category of fellow citizens as "our kind of people," the only remaining interpretive referent of action is the individual who refers to herself or himself in rational-calculative terms. This reorientation may be accelerated by political campaigns of the populist right, which, as it were, "cross-codes" people according to criteria of moral worthiness and unworthiness. Or it may be retarded by appeals to universalist moral standards that should not be sacrificed. But these appear to be variables of secondary importance, whereas primary significance rests with new forms of structural and cultural plurality leading to the virtual evaporation of classes and other self-conscious collectivities of political will, economic interest, and cultural values whose existence must be considered, as I have argued before, a necessary condition for solidary and collectivist attitudes and ideologies. The imagery of a fluid and mobile "patchwork" is often used to describe a newly emerging structure of society and pattern of conflict—conflicts that are no less severe or irreconcilable than those represented in class-conflict modes, but which differ from them in that the new pattern is made up of a plurality of relatively small groups and categories that are rapidly shifting in size, influence, and internal coherence with no dominant axis of conflict being generally recognized.

My thesis is that the welfare state as we know it—as a major accomplishment of postwar Western European societies—is rapidly losing its political support for these reasons of structural change, and that this development can be fully explained neither by economic and fiscal crisis arguments nor by political arguments emphasizing the rise of neoconservative elites and ideologies; nor can it be undone by moral appeals to the justice and legitimacy of existing welfare state arrangements. What this structural disintegration process leaves behind is an interpretive pattern that is deeply distrustful of social policies as "public goods" and that tends, instead, to unravel such policies in terms of gains and losses, exploitation, free-riding, redistribution, and so on—that is, in individualist "economic man" categories, the behavioral consequences of which are best captured and predicted by rational-choice theory.[3]

To be sure, the destructuration process and its ideological and eventually political repercussions are not uniform across countries, social classes, income categories, gender groups, or groups defined by party affiliation; nor do they affect individual components of the welfare state, its programs, and its institutions to the same extent. But some generalizations are in place in spite of these differences. One highly consequential destructuration occurs in the longitudinal dimension: The future is seen not to be a continuation of the past as far as economic growth, fiscal policy, and employment are concerned, and this anticipation undermines the plausibility of the traditional social democratic "solution of painless redistribution by funding welfare from expansion" (Taylor-Gooby 1983, 171). Another generalization concerns an increasing differentiation with respect to the popularity that various components of the welfare state enjoy. Some programs and institutions—such as old-age pensions and the health sector—find a greater acceptance than others (such as unemployment insurance, family allowance, youth programs, and social assistance)—the intuitively plausible reason being that it is much easier to conceive of a broad and inclusive alliance of potential beneficiaries in the first case (since "all of us" expect to be old and sick in the future) than in the second, where clients are much more easily marginalized and stigmatized. But given the fact that the most serious of the fiscal problems of the welfare state emerge in its old-age pension and health programs, the relatively greater support for these programs is also qualified by the individually rational temptation to "opt out" and shift to private forms of provision. "There has developed during the last two decades a whole series of substitutes for publicly provided social safety nets, such as private life insurance [and] firm pensions . . . which are even cheaper as they often pool 'good risks'" (Gretschmann, 1986, 233). One might even suspect that, under these conditions, it becomes strategically rational for some middle-class elements to express (insincere) support for the continued public provision of some minimal health and old-age pension, because that would make the conditions for private provision all the more favorable—just as they express strong and effective support for public transportation because they wish to use their private cars on pleasantly uncongested streets.

Let me just mention some of what in my view must be considered the underlying causes for the destructuration of self-conscious interest communities in advanced industrial societies and, hence, of the cultural and normative underpinnings of the welfare state.

1. Within the labor force of these highly industrialized democratic societies, there are increasing disparities of life-chances among the totality of wage-workers. These disparities depend on variables such as industrial sector, ethnicity, region, gender, and skill level. In view of such disparities, the organizational, political, and cultural resources by which some measure of commonality of interest could be established and politically enforced become increasingly debased and powerless.

2. The prevailing patterns of economic, industrial, and technical change generate the well-known disjunction between changes in economic output and changes in employment. As a consequence of this pattern of "jobless growth," the percentage of people who find themselves in the condition

of open unemployment, hidden unemployment, or labor market marginalization, or who are rendered unemployable or discouraged from labor market participation, is rising. These categories of people, who are most desperately dependent on the welfare state's provision of transfers and services, are, however, politically most vulnerable. This is so because there is little reason, either for the propertied middle classes and capitalists or for the core working class, to adopt the material interests of this "surplus class" as their own. Such reason does not exist for the core working class because there is little empirical reason to fear that the "surplus class" could function as an effective "reserve army"—that is, by depressing wages and undermining employment security in highly fragmented and stratified labor markets. Similarly, there is little reason for the middle class and for employers to fear that the existence of a growing "surplus class" could lead to disruptive forms of social unrest and conflict, the prevention of which could be "worth" a major investment in welfare policies—or even the full maintenance of those that exist.

3. Encompassing alliances of a pro–welfare state orientation thrive in the "good times" of economic growth and full employment (i.e., positive-sum games) and tend to decompose under zero-sum conditions. The potential for "public-regarding" and solidaristic political commitments appears to be exhausted in many countries, both after the experience of real wage losses in the late 1970s and early 1980s and in anticipation of moderate growth rates and persistently high levels of unemployment and insecure employment, which are often justifiably seen to be exacerbated by the existing levels and modes of extracting the fiscal resources of social security through payroll taxes. In that sense, the economic crisis of the welfare state generates individualistic political attitudes and orientations and thus translates, without much need for liberal-conservative mass mobilization and political organization, into a political crisis of the welfare state.

There seems to exist an asymmetry between the sociopolitical processes that result in the expansion of welfare states and those that lead to cuts and the eventual decay of social welfare policies. In the upward direction, what is needed are broad electoral and interest group alliances that converge on the institutionalization of collectivist arrangements. These arrangements will then persevere, due to the inertia and entrenched interests of what has been set up. In order to survive, all that is needed is the absence of strong oppositional political forces. In contrast to the expansion, the decline is normally not initiated by reactionary mass movements and political forces. It normally originates from anonymous economic imperatives, such as budgetary pressures and fiscal as well as labor market imbalances, that suggest cuts in social expenditures. In the presence of such economic difficulties, the tendency toward cumulative cuts could be halted only if a strong and unified political alliance were in place to defend existing arrangements. But it is exactly the formation of such an alliance that is rendered unlikely by the fragmentation, pluralization, and individualization of interests. As a consequence, uncertainty in the social dimension (concerning which political forces and social categories could be relied upon as trustworthy partners in a defensive alliance) is reinforced by uncertainty in the temporal dimension (concerning the problem of how much current sacrifice is likely to be compensated for by how much future gain in growth, employment, and security). In Western Europe at least, cuts in welfare expenditures do not typically occur as the political consequences of "tax revolts"; they simply "suggest themselves" as a consequence of changes in macro-economic indicators, and they can be implemented without much political cost in view of the weakness of resistance. Although the rise of the welfare state requires mass mobilization and large political coalitions as a sufficient condition, its demise is mediated through economic imperatives as well as through the silent and unconspicuous defection of voters, groups, and corporate actors whose heterogeneous structure, perceptions, and responses stand in the way of the formation of an effective defensive alliance. To put it somewhat simplistically, it takes politics to build a welfare state but merely economic changes to destroy both major parts of it and potential sources of resistance to such resistance.

4. Not only the goals of welfare state policies (which consist in the prevention of poverty, the guarantee of social security, and the provision of public health, education, housing, and other services) meet with decreasing political support. It is also the *means* by which the goals have been traditionally implemented—namely, through bureaucratic and professional intervention—that seem to have lost much of their acceptance and are increasingly seen in the corrosive light of a distributional and exploitative game. That is, these means are no longer universally considered a rational instrument for the implementation of "public goods" but are increasingly seen as a rational and highly effective strategy of a self-serving "new class" to cement its positions of power and privilege, and at the same time as an ineffective or even counterproductive ("dependency-creating" and "decapacitating") way of responding to the needs of clients and recipients.

5. A particularly important factor that helps to understand anticollectivist and anti–welfare state reorientations of public opinion in Western democracies is the quantitative growth of the middle class, particularly the "new" or "salaried" middle class. As far as the *upper* strata of this broad social category are concerned, the welfare state has distributive

effects that are clearly in their favor, a fact that can partly be explained through the logic of political "bribes" referred to above. Thus one author concludes that

> the members of the salaried middle class seem to be the main beneficiaries of the welfare state. In pension, health, housing, and education it seemed that the better off you are the more you gained from the system. In terms of service, tax allowances and occupational welfare, the managers, administrators, professionals, scientists, [and] technologists working for large organizations benefited considerably more than manual and routine white collar workers. (Gould, 1982, 417)

However, such special advantages and upward redistributive effects have failed to buy the political support of those who benefit not only from services and income-graduated transfers but also from the secure and continuously expanding employment the welfare state had to offer them. The greater this income and the more numerous the privileges, the greater becomes the upper middle class's inclination to look for *private* alternatives to welfare state services, the most important of which are old-age pension and health services. The higher the status and income that the welfare state provides one, the *lesser* becomes the rational motivation to have one's privileges tied to (foreseeably precarious) collectivist arrangements and, accordingly, the greater the inclination to look for—and to support in elections those parties that propose designs for—private market alternatives. The dilemma of the welfare state is clear enough: Any emphasis on egalitarian "flat rate" policies would alienate those better off, whose income would be used to subsidize the transfers to the less well-to-do. But the opposite policy—that of strong income differentiation and status maintenance—would also not help to keep the recipients of higher incomes within the alliance, for this policy reinforces and creates privileges that their beneficiaries are understandably unwilling to share with the rest of the welfare state's clientele.

As far as the *lower* middle class is concerned, including some segments of the skilled core working class, its allegiance to the welfare state is notoriously questionable. Members of this "middle mass" have formed in various countries the political base of tax revolts and the "welfare backlash." Wilensky, who has conducted large-scale comparative studies of these phenomena, concludes that "as rich countries become richer, the middle mass as a political force becomes more fluid, torn loose from traditional political identities, and more strategic, larger and more potent as a swing vote" (1975, 116). He sees a "developing political rage of the middle class" (1975, 118). This tendency, as described by Wilensky, would reverse an old and strong, positive, statistical correlation between welfare collectivism and economic growth and lead to a situation in which, as more people live in prosperity, they are *less* inclined to endorse such arrangements. It seems that dissolving "traditional political identities" are not openly replaced by pure individualism, but that such a shift to individualism is provided with a justification by the formation of identities of a moralizing and/or particularistic kind. What is least popular with the "middle mass" are programs that benefit those supposedly *morally* inferior categories (such as unemployed youth and single parents) and ascriptively defined minorities (such as ethnic or national ones).

A final observation concerning the widespread political defection of the middle class from collectivist welfare arrangements refers to the fact that since the mid-1970s, many of the political energies of these social categories have been invested, as it were, in issues, campaigns, and conflicts of a nonclass, nonredistributive nature, ranging from civil rights to feminist to ecological to peace causes and movements. The reverse side of this shift in political style and emphasis of middle-class political activism is, of course, a deemphasis on conflicts having to do with social security, distributional justice, and solidarity.

6. The disappearance of a plausible and mobilizing political program or project within the European left, which would instill an idea of a mission or vision of sociopolitical transformation in the mass constituency of socialist, social democratic, and labor parties, is a further important factor in the process of destructuration of collective identities based on social class (or the nation at war or under the threat of war) and distributive interest. The failure of hegemonic projects—be it of etatist planning or of economic democracy—has left the traditional protagonists of the welfare state in the highly defensive position of "maintaining what we have" (*"Besitzstandswahrung"*), which in turn allows parts of their constituency to begin to think about evasive strategies in case this defensive position fails—a case that is predicted with considerable resonance by conservative and market liberal elites.

Three observations and perceptions that are widely shared tend to deprive the welfare state of the moral appeal of a just and "progressive" sociopolitical project. One concerns the evident incapacity of governments—including social democratic ones—to apply causal and preventive therapies to those socioeconomic problems that the welfare state must then solve in an *ex post* and compensatory manner by throwing ever-rising amounts of money at them. For example, a generous level of unemployment compensation for those out of work is affordable only if an active and preventive full-employment policy keeps the number of those who are entitled to such benefits relatively small—in much the same way in which, as Schumpeter observed long ago, the construction of faster automobiles depends not so much on the invention of more powerful engines as on more effective brakes. Similarly, the idea of universal health insurance coverage of all employees and their families loses much of its moral plausibility if no one is able either to implement large-scale and effective preventive health programs or to control the "cost explosion" in health (i.e., the price-setting behavior of pharmaceutical manufacturers, doctors, and hospitals). If, as a consequence, the proportion of income that is deducted for mandatory health insurance reaches record levels (currently at 13 percent in West Germany), without any objectively measureable improvement in the general health status of the population, the *Gestalt*-switch referred to earlier sets in with particular force: What used to be thought of as a solidary arrangement guaranteeing the protection of the health of all irrespective of income is now seen as a giant redistributive game with widely dispersed and high costs for clients, and concentrated and even higher benefits for suppliers of services.

Second, the moral appeal of the welfare state resides in the perceived justice of its distributive effects. However, as these distributive effects come to be seen as intertemporal (i.e., self-paternalist) and not intergroup (i.e., redistributive), the appeal and legitimacy of the welfare state project as a secularized and modern version of Christian ideals of charity must necessarily suffer severe damage, particularly as the gap between the living conditions of those depending on social security systems and those depending on welfare, social assistance, and other means-tested and family-related programs becomes wider.

Third, pessimistic perceptions and interpretations both of the *effectiveness* of the welfare state (i.e., its capacity to intervene causally into the need- and cost-inflating socioeconomic processes) and the *legitimacy* of the welfare state (i.e. its capacity to implement moral standards of redistributive justice) develop a self-reinforcing and self-propelling dynamic. This is so for the simple "sinking-boat" strategic reason that if one sees oneself as belonging to an alliance that is doomed to lose, one better quit it earlier than others. Doing this, however, will convince others that defecting is the only remaining option for them, too. In view of the giant fiscal problems that must be anticipated for the welfare state in connection with probable demographic, labor market, health, and family developments, such interactive chains of individual rational responses are quite likely to occur; in addition, the traditional pro–welfare state alliance of social democratic parties and unions is ideologically and hegemonically ill-equipped to prevent this dynamic in most Western European countries.

As a combined effect of these structural changes, we may anticipate the rise of behavioral orientations of voters and citizens that give support to anti–welfare state policies—not primarily because of bad intentions or irrational drives or because of a sudden shift to neoconservative or market-liberal values and attitudes, but because of beliefs and preferences that are rationally formed in response to perceived social realities as well as to actual experiences with the practice of existing welfare states.

What all of this amounts to is the prediction that the neoconservative denunciations of the welfare state are likely to fall on fertile ground, thereby setting in motion a political mechanism of self-fulfilling predictions and interpretations. This does not mean, however, that the neoconservative analysis and the empirical arguments on which it claims to base its validity are "true" in any objectively testable sense, nor that they are "right" according to substantive criteria of political legitimacy and social justice. They are, for all the reasons specified above, simply highly effective and self-confirming as a political formula with which electoral majorities can be formed, and with which existing, large, solidaristic communities of interest can be further disorganized. As a formula, it can be challenged only by a democratic left that moves beyond its traditional defensive positions and adopts new concepts, goals, and strategies whose outlines today remain largely uncertain.

NOTES

This chapter is the revised, expanded, and integrated version of papers presented to conferences at the New School for Social Research, Tulane University and Aarhus University. The author wishes to acknowledge the helpful criticisms, suggestions, and comments he has received from John Dunn, Klaus Gretschmann, Martin Hollis, Bob Jessop, John Keane, and Timothy Tilton.

1. The model case for this strategic and reflective behavior can be observed in voting. It is certainly wrong to assume today in Western democracies that most voters are motivated in their voting behavior by their attraction to particular parties or candidates alone. When we vote, we normally do so not only for a party but also for or against a certain election *outcome*. This we are able to do because of the ample availability of pre-election survey results, which allow us to take the expected behavior of all other voters into account when forming our beliefs and preferences.

2. This problem would not be altered substantially if the possibility of democratic *rule*-making (of laws and constitutions) were taken into account as a further and rather obvious complication. Such rules can in fact perform the function of (self-)binding devices, which make democratic decisions *temporarily* immune from revision and obstruction. But as such binding rules (be they *de lege* or *de facto*) are never absolutely and indefinitely binding, and as it appears highly questionable from the point of view of rational actors even to attempt to extend the bindingness of rules into the indefinite future, it is not the "opting-

out" argument itself, but only the rapidity with which the consequences can unfold, that is affected by such rules.

3. The growing acceptance of rational-choice theory also appears to have resulted from this "structural" reason. Its fundamental methodological assumptions are in essence antistructural, antifunctionalist, and antinormativist and are thus in a way antisociological (relying on psychological and economic paradigms instead). But it is exactly this new paradigm and the dramatic shift in the intellectual climate in much of the social sciences that lends itself to a sociology of knowledge interpretation: It corresponds to a centerless, atomized, and destructured condition of social life. As I lack the space here to elaborate this interpretation further, let me just suggest that I find the interpretation fruitful for understanding the growth not only of rational-choice theory but also that of its twin phenomenon—namely, the rise to prominence of "postmodernist" approaches based on the work of Foucault and Lyotard.

REFERENCES

Alber, J. (1986). "Der Wohlfahrtsstaat in der Wirtschaftskrise. Eine Bilanz der Sozialpolitik in der Bundesrepublik. Eine Bilanz der Sozialpolitik in der Bundesrepublik seit den frühen 70er Jahren," *Politische Vierteljahresschrift* 27, No. 1, 28–60.

—————— (1982). *Vom Armenhaus zum Wohlfahrtsstaat. Analysen zur Entwicklung der Sozialversicherung in Westeuropa*, Frankfurt: Campus.

Alt, J. (1979). *The Politics of Economic Decline*, Cambridge: Cambridge University Press.

Coughlin, R. M. (1980). *Ideology, Public Opinion, and Welfare Policy*, Berkeley: Institute of International Studies.

Esping-Andersen, G. (1985). *Politics against Markets: The Social Democratic Road to Power*, Princeton: Princeton University Press.

Ferguson, T., and Rogers, J. (1986). *Right Turn: The Decline of the Democrats and the Future of American Politics*, New York: Hill and Wang.

Free, L. A., and Cantril, H. (1968). *The Political Beliefs of Americans: A Study of Public Opinion*, New York: Simon & Schuster.

Gould, Arthur (1982). "The Salaried Middle Class and the Welfare State in Sweden and Japan," *Policy and Politics* 10.

Gretschmann, K. (1986). "Social Security in Transition—Some Reflections from a Fiscal Sociology Perspective," *International Sociology* 1, No. 3, 223–242.

Habermas, J. (1985). "Die Krise des Wohlfahrtsstaates und die Erschöpfung utopischer Energien." In Habermas, ed., *Die neue Unübersichtlichkeit*, Frankfurt: Suhrkamp, 141–163.

Hall, S., and Jacques, M., eds. (1983). *The Politics of Thatcherism,* London: Lawrence and Wishart.

Hirschman, A. O. (1982). *Shifting Involvements, Private Interests and Public Action*, Princeton: Princeton University Press.

Illich, I., et al. (1977). *Disabling Professions*, London: M. Boyars.

Jessop, B., Bonnett, K., Bromley, S., and Ling, T. (1984). "Authoritarian Populism, Two Nations, and Thatcherism," *New Left Review*, No. 147, 32–60.

Krieger, J. (1987). "Social Policy in the Age of Reagan and Thatcher," *Socialist Register*, London: Merlin Press.

Lash, S. (1985). "The End of Neo-Corporatism? The Breakdown of Centralised Bargaining in Sweden," *British Journal of Industrial Relations* 23, No. 2, 179–203.

Levine, A. (1981). *Liberal Democracy: A Critique of Its Theory*, New York: Columbia University Press.

Macpherson, C. B. (1977). *The Life and Times of Liberal Democracy*, Oxford: Oxford University Press.

Marshall, T. H. (1964). "Citizenship and Social Class." In Marshall, ed., *Class, Citizenship and Social Development*, Chicago: University of Chicago Press, 71–134 (first published in 1949).

Mead, L. M. (1986). *Beyond Entitlement: The Social Obligations of Citizenship*, New York and London: Macmillan.

Mishra, R. (1984). *The Welfare State in Crisis*, Brighton: Harvester Press.

Offe, C. (1984). *Contradictions of the Welfare State* (edited by John Keane), London: Hutchinson.

———— (1985). "New Social Movements: Challenging the Boundaries of Institutional Politics," *Social Research* 52, No. 4, 817–868.

Øyen, E. (1986). "The Muffling Effects of Social Policy: A Comparison of Social Security Systems and Their Conflict Potential in Australia, The United States and Norway," *International Sociology* 1, No. 3, 217–282.

Parson, T. (1968). *The Structure of Social Action*, New York: Free Press (first edition, 1937).

Pöntinen, S., and Uusitalo, H. (1986). "The Legitimacy of the Welfare State: Social Security Opinions in Finland 1975–1985," *Suormen Gallup Oy Report*, No. 15 (Helsinki).

Przeworski, A., and Wallerstein, M. (1986). "Why Is There No Left Economic Alternative?" Unpublished manuscript, University of Chicago.

Ringen, S. (1986). *Does the Welfare State Work?* Oxford: Oxford University Press.

Sachsse, C. (1986). "Verrechtlichung und Sozialisation: Über Grenzen des Wohlfahrtsstaates," *Leviathan* 14, No. 4, 528–545.

Spieker, M. (1986). *Legitimitätsprobleme des Sozialstaates*, Bern: Haupt.

Taylor-Gooby, P. (1983). "Legitimation Deficit, Public Opinion and the Welfare State," *Sociology* 17, No. 2, 165–184.

———— (1985a). *Public Opinion, Ideology and State Welfare*, London: Routledge & Kegan Paul.

———— (1985b). "The Politics of Welfare: Public Attitudes and Behavior." In R. Klein and M. O'Higgins, eds., *The Future of Welfare*, Oxford: Basil Blackwell, 79–91.

Therborn, G. (1986). "Challenges to the Welfare State," Unpublished paper, Institute for Political Science, Catholic University, Nijmegen, Netherlands.

Titmuss, R. M. (1963). *Essays on the Welfare State*, 2nd ed. London: Allen & Unwin.

_____ (1971). *The Gift Relationship*, London: George Allen & Unwin.

Whiteley, P. (1981). "Public Opinion and the Demand for Social Welfare in Britain," *Journal of Social Policy* 10, No. 4, 453–475.

Wilensky, H. L. (1975). *The Welfare State and Equality: Structural and Ideological Roots of Public Expenditures*, Berkeley: University of California Press.

Wolfe, A. (1977). *The Limits of Legitimacy: Political Contradictions of Contemporary Capitalism*, London: Macmillan.

Zijderveld, A. C. (1986). "The Ethos of the Welfare State," *International Sociology* 1, No. 4, 443–457.

ABOUT THE CONTRIBUTORS

Robert E. Goodin is reader in government at the University of Essex (United Kingdom). He is an associate editor of the journal *Ethics* and is the author of *Political Theory and Public Policy, Protecting the Vulnerable*, and, with Julian Le Grand and others, *Not Only the Poor: The Middle Classes and the Welfare State*.

Stephen Holmes is associate professor of political science at the University of Chicago. He is the author of *Benjamin Constant and the Making of Modern Liberalism* and a number of articles on modern political theory.

Thomas A. Horne is associate professor of political science at the University of Tulsa. He is the author of *The Social Thought of Bernard Mandeville* as well as a number of articles on modern and early modern political theory. He is currently finishing a book on the intellectual history of property rights from the early seventeenth century to the middle of the nineteenth century.

Richard Krouse was associate professor of political science at Williams College. He authored a number of articles on John Stuart Mill, on conceptions of property and economic justice, and on liberalism and democracy.

Michael S. McPherson is professor of economics at Williams College and a research fellow at the Brookings Institution. He is coeditor of the journal *Economics and Philosophy* and has written extensively on problems of economics and organization and on the theory of justice. He is currently writing a book on the financing of higher education.

David Miller is official Fellow in social and political theory, Nuffield College, Oxford. He is the author of *Social Justice, Philosophy and Ideology in Hume's Political Thought*, and *Anarchism* and coeditor of *The Nature of Political Theory* and *The Encyclopedia of Political Thought*.

J. Donald Moon is professor of government at Wesleyan University. He is a coeditor of *Dissent and Affirmation* and the author of a chapter in the *Handbook of Political Science* titled "The Logic of Political Inquiry" as well as a number of articles on the philosophy of social science and on the welfare state.

Claus Offe is professor of political science and sociology at the University of Bielefeld. He is author of *Industry and Inequality, Social Class and Public Policy, Contradictions of the Welfare State, Disorganized Capitalism*, and numerous other books and articles.

Raymond Plant is professor of philosophy at the University of Southampton. He is author of *Hegel, Political Philosophy and the Welfare State*, and numerous articles on problems of the welfare state.

INDEX